THE STATE I[

FREEDOM PRESS CENTENARY SERIES
Volume 6. SELECTIONS FROM FREEDOM 1965-1986

FREEDOM PRESS CENTENARY VOLUMES

To mark the Centenary in 1986 of FREEDOM PRESS and of our journal *Freedom*, a special 88-page issue of *Freedom* was published with the title FREEDOM/A HUNDRED YEARS/ October 1886 to October 1986

In addition a series of six volumes, with supplements in some cases, is nearing completion.

Vol. 1 Selections from *Freedom* 1886-1936
   Supplement: Act For Yourselves! by P. Kropotkin, 20 articles published 1886-1907 and now reprinted for the first time.

Vol. 2 Spain 1936-1939: Social Revolution and Counter-Revolution. Selections from *Spain and the World*
   Supplement: The May Days: Barcelona 1937

Vol. 3 World War – Cold War: Selections from *War Commentary* and *Freedom* 1939-1950.
   Supplements: Neither East Nor West, selected writings by Marie Louise Berneri 1939-1948.
   British Imperialism and the Palestine Crisis: Selections from *Freedom* 1937-1949.
   The Left and World War II: Selections from *War Commentary* 1939-1943.
   Neither Nationalisation Nor Privatisation: an anarchist approach. Selections from *Freedom* 1945-1950.

Vol. 4 Selections from *Freedom* 1951-1964.

Vol. 5 A Decade of Anarchy: Selections from the monthly journal *Anarchy* 1961-1970.

Vol. 6 The State is Your Enemy: Selections from *Freedom* 1965-1986.

All the titles will be available singly in paperback as they are published. Hardback sets will be available. Full particulars from FREEDOM PRESS.

THE STATE IS YOUR ENEMY

Selections from
the anarchist journal *Freedom* 1965-1986

FREEDOM PRESS
London
1991

Published by
FREEDOM PRESS
84b Whitechapel High Street
London E1 7QX
1991
© FREEDOM PRESS
ISBN 0 900384 57 3

Front cover: *Legacy of Empire* by Philip Sansom,
from *Freedom* 27th May 1978

Printed in Great Britain by Aldgate Press, London E1

CONTENTS

Editor's Introduction

Today the political Left has reached an impasse. A quarter of a century ago there was a swing to the Labour Party amongst fashionably progressive opinion in Britain, so that when it won the General Election in October 1964 under the leadership of Harold Wilson, after what he called 'thirteen years of Tory misrule', some of its supporters in the Campaign for Nuclear Disarmament thought that it might not only introduce socially progressive measures but even 'Ban the Bomb'.

At the same time the Tonkin Gulf Incident had led the United States Government under Lyndon Baines Johnson to intervene in a civil war in Vietnam supporting the Government of the South against the Vietcong guerrillas, who were aided by the Government of the North backed by China, under the pretext of defending democracy against communism. The result was the growth of a new anti-war movement, but one heavily influenced by Marxists of various brands, including those of the 'New Left' who had transferred their allegiance from Comrade Stalin to Chairman Mao.

Today American and British troops are in the Middle East to fight for Western oil interests and we are asked to believe once again that a war over economic interests is in the 'defence of a small nation'. Whatever the outcome, there will soon be another General Election in Britain in which for the first time for over a decade the Labour Party is being seriously considered as a possible winner, but there will be fewer illusions about its claims to represent socialism than there were twenty-seven years ago. For if there has been a qualitative change in our society, it is that the vast expansion of higher education and a higher standard of living have created a population better informed, broader-minded and with less social class distinction and yet an increasing proportion of which is prepared to express a dissatisfaction with the quality of life. People no longer believe that any of the political Parties will bring about change in society, and apathy is the result.

This book is published in the belief that we do have a choice, of a kind not offered to us by any of the political alternatives. For the individual in the Western World who has the capacity to imagine a better world than our present one and the urge to change things for the better, the choice is between a dazzling career doing worthless work and being careful not to do anything that might risk one's chances in the career structure, together with the abnegation of personal responsibility by the casting of one's vote for one or other

8

of a bunch of career politicians; or alternatively, identifying oneself with the oppressed of the earth, which inevitably means that resistance to the power structure of society is necessary and sacrifices have to be made.

For we here define the State in the words of the anarchist Errico Malatesta exactly one hundred years ago as:

the sum total of the political, legislative, judiciary, military and financial institutions through which the management of their own affairs, the control over their personal behaviour, the responsibility for their personal safety are taken away from the people and entrusted to others who, by usurpation or delegation, are vested with powers to make the laws for everything and everybody, and oblige the people to observe them, if need by, by the use of collective force.

In this sense the word State means government, or to put it another way, it is the impersonal, abstract expression of that state of affairs personified by government: and therefore the terms abolition of the State, society without the State, describe exactly the concept which anarchists seek to express, of the destruction of all political order based on authority, and the creation of a society of free and equal members based on a harmony of interests and the voluntary participation of everybody in carrying out social responsibilities.

Today the system is stronger than ever. As long as Nation States and economic competition survive so will international strife persist. If people want peace and freedom, they must destroy the present power structure of society, and to do that they must cease to delegate their responsibilities to political leaders.

I have grouped the articles in this book under convenient headings, the first half being an analysis of the British political scene and the second half looking at international affairs, but the sections cannot be taken in isolation; indeed the most casual reader will easily perceive an added dimension in that a pattern emerges of the system based on the international arms trade and the battle for resources under which we live.

The events of Paris in May 1968 are featured, and show that the libertarians among the young students were far advanced in their attitudes compared with the industrial workers whom the Marxists regard as the progressive class 'under the right leadership' (though did they unconsciously reflect the belief of Marx and Engels that the bourgeoisie would produce its own grave-diggers?). That even the rebellion of youth was heavily influenced by Marxist thinking was shown in the remark of Daniel Cohn-Bendit that 'I am, if you like, a Marxist in the way Bakunin was', as if those two thinkers

9

had not represented diametrically opposed approaches to social revolution a hundred years earlier. So little were the ideas of the anarchists understood that it was thought that anarchism meant a more violent type of protest, and thus some of the demonstrators outside the American Embassy in London in March 1968 could imagine that it was possible to be an anarchist and support Ho Chi Minh. It may be some measure of progress that the articles from this period seem just a little dated today in that their writers felt constrained to address a Marxist-dominated protest movement. But if the young protesters may have been naive, what of their mentors in the universities who for a generation had been busily promoting Marxism as the alternative to the Labour Party social-democratic tradition: E.P. Thompson, Eric Hobsbawm, the neo-Marxists like Marcuse, and the gurus like Régis Debray who climbed onto the bandwagon of 1968? With the collapse of Communism in the Soviet Union and Eastern Europe and the revelations about the Communist regimes they have all had to rethink.

Martin Jacques, Editor of *Marxism Today*, had this to say:

What we are witnessing now, with the opening of the Berlin Wall, is nothing less than the reunification of Europe and, with the closing of the cold war, the beginnings of the reunification of the world. What we are also seeing is the beginnings of the reunification of the socialist movement, which has been divided ever since 1914 into its rival socialist and communist traditions.

The international communist movement is now surely at an end. That does not mean that independent communist parties will not survive, but they will no longer enjoy the same kind of common purpose and they will no longer exist as separate organisms from the social-democratic tradition. (Speech to congress of the Communist Party of Great Britain, 25th November 1989)

In other words, the communist bloc is moving towards a mixed economy somewhat to the left of the British Labour Party.

As for the Labour Party, after thirteen years of Tory Government, Neil Kinnock hopes to come to power by discarding all the socialist elements remaining in his party; his Shadow Foreign Minister Gerald Kaufman 'blames Mrs Thatcher's successive election wins on those 'cultists' in the Labour Party, led by Tony Benn, who frightened away the electorate' (*The Observer* 3rd February 1991).

An ex-Cabinet Minister in the last Labour Government until he fell foul of Harold Wilson in 1976, Benn has established the Socialist Movement, an attempt at a left-wing revival, which last November held a conference in Manchester Town Hall on 'Freedom, Democracy and Socialism' for 'people from all backgrounds who are determined the world must change'. Behind a rag-bag of 'aims, hopes and aspirations' about the environment and the rights of minority groups, Benn's Socialist Movement comprises the following aims: scrap nuclear defences (but keep conventional ones), 'common ownership of banks, land and major companies' (renationalisation under state control), restoration of full trade union rights – but why the need for trade unions in a socialist society (surely Mr Benn as a former advocate of 'workers' control' would have the workers in control of the 'banks, land and major companies') unless it is to be run by a class of people whose interests conflict with those who work in them? Arms expenditure reduction (but there will still be expenditure on arms) and 'support for national liberation movements' which can only mean that arms will be sold to whichever side in a war the new socialist government decides it is politic to support. But the Socialist Movement also stands for 'unconditional British withdrawal from Ireland', so which national liberation movement will it support there?

Tony Benn's Socialist Movement appeals to the romanticism of those who still think that the system can be changed if only the right people are put into Parliament. But no one could be adopted as a parliamentary candidate without undergoing a long induction in the game of party politics, and anyone with a reputation as a radical will remain on the back benches. A few weeks ago, Clare Short MP, described by the Press as 'a left-wing firebrand', resigned from the Labour front bench after refusing not to criticise her party's support of the Government over the Gulf War – and Short was *not* criticising the United Nations action, but only voiced *concern* with its conduct (i.e. bombing likely to result in greater civilian casualties) – while Joan Ruddock MP, former Chair of the Campaign for Nuclear Disarmament, who had published an 'Appeal for Peace' agreed to mute her criticisms and now faces the possibility of deselection by her own Constituency Party – as does Peter Shore, former Labour Cabinet Minister, because of his *strong support* for the Government's action in the Gulf War.

And we are told that Neil Kinnock has had to support the Government line in support of the Allies fighting Saddam Hussein so as not to lose points in the opinion polls, while a survey carried out by National Opinion Polls for the *Sunday Times* (17th February 1991) concluded that:

Television pictures, filmed under official Iraqi guidance, of burned bodies being carried out of a reinforced Baghdad shelter have, according to the survey, had little effect. More than eight in ten people said the increase in Iraqi civilian casualties had made no difference to their support for the allied effort. Nor is there any public pressure for a change in bombing tactics. Some 71% said they did not think the allies should stop bombing military targets in or near Iraqi cities, even if civilians were killed and injured.

People who say such things are out of touch with reality, but as Peter Kropotkin in his book *Mutual Aid* noted, in our reading the heroism of the miner who rescues his comrades is taken for granted, while the heroism that is promoted is that of the soldier on the battlefield. In this book is a short section headed 'Disasters' which shows how, when faced with catastrophes, natural or man-made, the principal of mutual aid among ordinary people comes to the fore and shows up the fundamental uselessness of Governments.
March 1991   CHARLES CRUTE

Note

698 issues of *Freedom* were published between January 1965 and October 1986 when to commemorate the centenary of Freedom Press a special 88-page issue was published which is available as a Freedom Press title.

In 1965 the paper was appearing in a four-page newspaper format 40 times a year, alternating with the monthly journal *Anarchy* edited by Colin Ward. After 1970, when *Anarchy* had ceased publication, full weekly publication was resumed, but the paper went fortnightly, doubling in size, in mid-1975 and from 1984 appeared as a monthly magazine.

In 1987 Freedom Press launched a quarterly journal, *The Raven*, and *Freedom* resumed fortnightly publication as a newspaper in 1990.

Philip Sansom contributed cartoons over two signatures; 'philip' when the idea was his own, and 'SKITZ' when he was illustrating someone else's idea.

THE LABOUR PARTY IN POWER

Productivity for What?

Just as the Prime Minister, Mr Wilson, has been touring the capitals of political influence selling not a 'socialist foreign policy', if such a thing is conceivable, but the idea that a Labour governed Britain is a more rational, stable ally in the realm of international power politics, his lieutenant, Mr Brown, has been busy persuading employers' organisations and trade unions to cooperate with the State in putting into practice, not socialism, but a planned drive for efficiency and productivity.

In themselves, efficiency and high economic production are excellent objects. and many of the restrictive practices that have been used as objects of derision by the capitalist press are equally condemned by anarchists for the different reason that they divide workers against each other when they should be united against the boss. However, the policies which Mr Brown and his Department of Economic Affairs are trying to bring into being are fundamentally anti-socialist. It is for that reason that we attack them in the columns of FREEDOM and challenge the so-called left-wing MPs and their supporters in the broader socialist movement to do the same.

First of all, if a thing isn't worth doing it isn't worth doing well, and if increased efficiency results in more military aeroplanes and rockets being produced, or more effort being expended on projects designed to win national prestige rather than to satisfy the needs of ordinary people, then no one is any better off as a result. One of the important problems that working people should be facing is what their work is being used to produce, not just how efficiently they are producing anything. The Brown approach, that it doesn't matter what is being produced so long as there is a lot of it and it gets sold, is both dangerous to our welfare in general, and dangerous insofar as it diverts the attention of workers and trade union organisations from these real social problems into chasing the false objectives of capitalist production records.

Secondly, the plans make no progress towards ending the exploitation of man by man which is inevitable in an authoritarian society. (Anarchists differ from Marxists in seeing that it is inevitable in any society where power is held by a minority, or 'Government', whether social democratic or communist in outlook, as well as in capitalist States.) Nor do they take any step towards increased control of the production process by the workers. The accounts of the declaration of the intention to seek an incomes policy do speak of 'two sides' in industry, 'management', and 'the unions'. We prefer to think of the two sides as being 'capitalism', despite the fact that it often prefers to present itself in the role of manager rather than profiteer, and 'labour' which is unfortunately so badly misrepresented by most union leaders. It is true that over the last half century, the advance in technology has resulted in an increase in the material standard of living of almost everyone in societies like the United States and Western Europe, even though it has left behind the submerged seventh, or fifth to which Brian Abel-Smith and Michael Harrington have been drawing attention. However, the position of the workers relative to the profiteers has not improved, and it almost seems as if the economic reward a man gets for his labour is inversely proportional to its social value. All this comes about simply as a consequence of the fact that the control of society lies with coteries of directors, executives and financiers, with the top ranks of the Civil Service and with professional politicians, and not with the people who do useful work, by hand or brain.

In discussing questions relating to economic policy on the large scale, it is much more difficult to present a clear anarchist alternative than it is for questions like sex, freedom from censorship and so on; but it is necessary for the very reason that it is difficult, that economics and the power that goes with it lies at the basis of everything else in society. It may be true that at present nothing can be hoped for except minor reforms, but even if this is so, we should see that the reforms are in the right direction, that more effort goes into useful production and less into waste and the war industry, and that workers win a greater degree of control over what they do and how they do it. If there is a crisis of production, a sterling problem, and a need to export more, the working class should not be allowing its representatives to sit in Whitehall signing agreements to cooperate with the bosses and the state in getting rid of these problems, but should be exploiting the opportunities presented by these crises to get every ounce of advantage over the bosses in terms of wages, conditions and taking as much of the control of production over as is possible.

There is only one worthwhile restrictive practice in the long run, and that is to restrict the capitalists, politicians and other parasites from living on the workers' backs.

9th January 1965   P.H.

The Economic Circus

Ever since the accession of the Labour Government last autumn, the newspapers have regaled us with horrifying stories of the imminent collapse of the economy, which was supposed to be a consequence of the international financial world's lack of trust in the 'socialist' Government. Simultaneously, Wilson, Brown and their colleagues have been blaming every difficulty that might lead to loss of popularity with the voters on the machinations of the 'gnomes of Zurich' who are supposed to be plotting their downfall out of fear and hatred of socialism.

Both of these lines are, of course, the currency of political mass journalism, on the basis of which our supposedly educated democracy forms its judgements. Firstly, the economy is not controlled to any important extent by the elected Government, but largely by directors of companies like ICI, professional Civil Servants and manipulators of money in the City and, in view of that, the present Government's policy is not, and cannot be, different in any substantial way from that of the previous one. Secondly, however much we dislike the activities of the gnomes of Zurich, they obviously have considerable knowledge and ability in making financial judgements, and they would not have risen to the top of their profession if they had seen a red revolution on the horizon every time a social democratic Government was elected to office.

However, after eight months of hearing from Conservative politicians and the press that the import surcharge, the high Bank Rate, and the weakness of sterling, due directly to the Labour Government, have been leading the country to disaster, the news during last weekend was that business men who had been enjoying a boom for all this time were beginning to wonder whether it could last much longer!

The Role of the Press
The result of all this must surely convince anyone, or confirm those
who knew it already, that the press is not out to create a well-
informed climate of opinion in which democracy can flourish, but
to confuse the issues in people's minds for the benefit of the political
interests which it serves. This was the gist of George Brown's
weekend contribution, in which he attacked the conspiracy against
the Government. However, instead of calling on the people to set
up a newspaper which would not be under the control of capitalist
finance, which would be the logical answer to the problem he
raised, he ended his speech with a dramatic call to disbelieve any
criticism of the Labour Government that appeared in print, stop
going on strike, and to refuse to buy goods for which the housewife
knows she is being overcharged. In other words while the Tory
press wants everyone to believe that their economic difficulties are
due to the Labour Government's policies, which they find uncom-
fortable, Brown wants everyone to believe that they are due to
the particular thorns that are getting in his flesh.

All this propaganda takes it for granted that the most important
contribution to the world's wealth is being made by the people
who, either in London, New York or Zurich, manipulate the Stock
Exchanges and deal in currency and finance, or by politicians whose
laws may affect what they do to a minor degree, and this notion
is obviously reflected in the salaries that these people receive,
compared with those of ordinary workers! If there were any truth
at all in the idea that politicians and financiers have a necessary
part to play in a rational economic system, then they have made
a hell of a mess of the present one.

The Failure of Capitalism
The anarchist case is based on the fact that financiers and politicians
are not only unnecessary, but that their activities distort the economic system and deprive the working people of the comfort, security
and freedom, which could surely be available to everyone in this
industrialised scientific and technological era which everyone
praises so highly.

Sixty years ago, when the world's capacities for production of
material goods was less highly developed, the Labour Party itself
set out to convince the workers of this truth, and we suggest that
the reason why it failed was not that the idea itself was wrong, but
that the political path that the socialists chose led those who had
found their personal emancipation in governmental power to con-

fuse and deceive the workers, because having found a comfortable niche in capitalist society they were no longer eager to change it.

The real needs of the world's population do not fluctuate from day to day, except for emergencies for which adequate provision would be made in a rational society, but should either remain fairly constant or show a gradual rise as people learn to demand more from life. Consequently, if production were planned to meet these needs, which we emphasise could be met without any difficulty or sacrifice on anyone's part, there would be no need for crises, no worry about booms and slumps and no problem of the weakness of sterling. The crises of production that do occur are solely due to production being geared to profit and competition and, in the international capitalist world, a nationalised company is just as much concerned with profit (and uninterested in providing goods and services where they are needed) as a private firm.

It is natural, within the context of capitalist economics, that financiers and shareholders do not ask what is needed by the world, in which case there would be far more food produced and fewer status-giving luxuries, more easily-built houses and fewer luxury flats, but what is likely to sell. Since several of them get the idea at the same time, someone is bound to be left with a factory equipped to produce goods that cannot be sold, and the easiest excuse is to blame it on lack of competitiveness in the export market, high labour costs, or anything to deflect attention away from the fact that capitalism is an extremely wasteful and inefficient system. If it were only the shareholders who suffered when they came out last in the draw, as it would be if textbooks on economics were to be believed, we would shed no tears, but the tragedy is that ordinary people are always the losers in the competition between financiers. When there is a crisis in the motor car or aeroplane industry, the cars and obsolete planes lie out in the dumps while the workers get the sack, and millions of other people are living in the slums of our big cities which would have been eliminated years ago if the skill of these workers had been employed on solving this problem.

What Can be Done?
What we would like to get across to the workers of Britain and the world is that the pseudo-problems caused by fluctuations in dollar reserves and sterling strength are not basic to the real problems of producing enough for a good standard of living. They are purely ripples on the surface which may favour or hurt an individual capitalist, and in the latter case bring out a wordy denunciation of

the current Government. They will certainly hit groups of consumers and wage earners and affect their voting allegiance, but are in themselves only the constantly recurring symptoms of the fundamental sickness of capitalism.

The abolition of the system based on production for profit is not mentioned as a possible solution by any of the major political Parties (or any other Party within sight of power), and can in fact only be carried out by workers acting together in their own interests independently of politicians.

That obviously lies a long way in the future, but for the present let us make our contribution by following George Brown's advice and disbelieving what we read in the press, but go a little further and disbelieve anything that politicians tell us, and build up movements suitable for dealing with the realities and not the superficialities of social and economic life in our society.

19th June 1965   P.H.

Socialism Must be a Movement of the People

It is typical of the supposedly socialist intellectuals of England that the *New Statesman*, in its issue of 2nd July should appoint itself to hold an inquest on 'The State of the Left'. The leading contributor to this parade of despair was Malcolm Muggeridge who traced the series of shattered hopes through which his generation had lived, the rise of the Labour Party from a band of idealistic pioneers to the Government we have today, and the Bolshevik corruption of the Russian Revolution. His captivating style makes these disappointments seem like the consequence of a tragic fate outside the control of mere mortals, until one begins to ask what were the socialists of Britain and, in particular, the *New Statesman* brand doing during that period, and were there really no alternatives?

During the inter-war years, the realistic moderates of that movement were behind the Labour Party, hoping to vote it into power and at the same time give it a socialist policy, and pouring scorn on the revolutionary minorities who didn't believe that the election to office of the Labour Party would make the slightest impression on the power structure of British society. In the thirties, despite the purges, despite (or perhaps because of) the Communist counter-revolutionary policy in Spain, the social-democratic Left looked on Russia as the socialist fatherland. The anarchist movement was publishing factual accounts of the terrorism of the Cheka and the rise of the Communist Party bureaucracy in Russia from the 20's onwards, and the rest of the socialist movement didn't want to know. During the War the *New Statesman* told us to rally round and support capitalism because the capitalist States of the Allies were engaged in a war against fascism, and then socialism would fall into our laps after the War. After the War it told us to join hands with America against the former socialist fatherland! All, of course, in a spirit of critical support, but support nevertheless, and at a time when minority movements, including the anarchist press, were pointing out that socialism would never be achieved as a result of compromise, political fiddling or following power-hungry leaders. We may therefore be forgiven for taking the air of inevitable doom purveyed by Muggeridge and the *New Statesman* with a pinch of salt, and putting the blame squarely on the shoulders of those very people whose policies sold out socialism to the hacks and careerists of the Communist and Labour Parties.

The words of 'The Red Flag', sung at every Labour Party Conference, contain the assertion that the people's salvation can only come by their own hands, and not through the goodness of any messiah. But the tragedy of the Labour movement has been that it has constantly fallen victim to the easy belief that some dynamic Party would take over the reins of government and put everything right, or that if things weren't so good in England, socialism had been achieved in some other country not very far away. What has failed during the last half century has not been socialism but the idea that it can be achieved through government. It would be more to the point if the *New Statesman* held an inquiry into 'The State of Government' and decided not to support that corrupt institution in the future, but to educate people to co-operate among themselves and do without it!

These reflections are relevant at the present time, when the Commonwealth Prime Ministers' Conference has had its annual meeting, when interest has been stimulated in foreign affairs by the international power struggle taking place at the expense of the people of Vietnam, with China and Russia jockeying for influence throughout Africa and as far as names are concerned, everyone is a socialist now.

Everyone will agree that there is a certain determinism in history, in that a society cannot change overnight from one system to another one chosen at will. But one of the bad influences of the materialist approach to history is that the perversions of socialism that have appeared in 'liberated' countries have been welcomed by many sincere people who should know better, as being inevitable and even desirable.

Thus the socialist movement wastes its time taking up positions in support of one or other of China or Russia, of providing excuses to bourgeois opinion for the newly emerged dictators of Africa and the bloodthirsty demagogues of the Arab States. At the same time socialist opinion, being committed to the idea of government, has to support some Government, and for instance on the Vietnam question this seems a distinct handicap since the mass of people who are disgusted by American bombing are unlikely to be rallied by admiration of the totalitarian Government in Hanoi.

Socialism can only be a movement of the people themselves for their own liberation, and today's communist manifesto should declare that the people and the State can have no interest in common. The State has been on the attack for too long. Isn't it time the people took the initiative?

10th July 1965   P.H.

Listen, Mr Callaghan!

An Open Letter to the Home Secretary

DEAR MR CALLAGHAN,

Homilies on principles, even if trite, simple and short, fall most oddly from the lips of members of the present Labour Government.

You were personally credited, a short time ago, with having ambitions to usurp Mr Wilson's position as Prime Minister. Whether the rumours were true or not, we on the sidelines of the game you play have no means of knowing, but we can all see that you are still there, growing in smugness if not in stature, as you wallow in the power apparently invested in your position of Home Secretary.

If they were true, and you really disapproved of the way Mr Wilson was running the Government, there were two choices open to you: you could have openly challenged his leadership with a direct confrontation or you could have resigned. You did neither. We can understand you funking the first. Mr Wilson has too many Aces up his sleeve and having got rid of the Joker he is not likely to be beaten by a Knave. But since you have chosen to talk about principles — why did you not follow the second course, and resign? Do you think you are too valuable a chap to be wasted on the back benches — even though everybody knows that if Parliament contains *any* principled men, that's where they are? Or was your job too attractive to give up just because of some disagreement with your leader?

Faithful Party-liner?

Or are you after all *not* in disagreement with your leader? Are you at one with him on all his policies? We must assume you are, since as member of the Inner Cabinet you must accept corporate responsibility for Government decisions. You therefore toe the Party line faithfully on, for example, Biafra, Vietnam, the Bomb, Labour Relations and the deliberate creation of a pool of unemployed, the Wage Freeze and many other issues. Including the cutback in building for homes, but not for prisons.

Ah, now we enter your special preserve. You, as Home Secretary, are in charge of Her Majesty's Prison Service as well as having over all say (on paper at least) for the police forces of Britain — and Northern Ireland. Perhaps it was because you are so proud of the brave new plans for building new prisons (a sort of Soviet-type Five-Year Plan, is it not?) and because you know as much as anyone about the special purposes police forces that have been created fairly recently (complete with riòt shields and, we have no doubt, ample supplies of CS gas), that you stayed in the Government in spite of its recent attempts to make strikes illegal.

After all, the job of a Government is to govern, as every Labour Prime Minister has repeatedly told his more socialistic followers, and as you are obviously an enthusiastic law-and-order supporter, and no fool, you clearly realise that if a Government is to introduce totalitarian-type anti-labour legislation, it must have the necessary force to beat down the inevitable opposition.

For the excuse to build up these forces in advance of their need, you must admit that you have to thank the Protesters and the Demonstrators. Through all the years of apathy and no-protest, even through the years of pacifist sit-downs and non-violent protest, your old traditional British Bobby was adequate — even an asset. But when contempt for your kind of policies turned to anger and anger turned to violence, then you had the reason for following your colleagues in totalitarian States. You must have watched the news-reels of the May-Days in France last year, noting the equipment and behaviour of the CRS, from a totally different standpoint from those of your fellow-countrymen with liberal or socialistic — let alone anarchistic — points of view. We imagine you sitting nodding with approval as law-and-order was reasserted, and no doubt you hurried up the plans for the British version of the CRS, since used in Northern Ireland.

The Wider Problem

In France, of course, the law-and-order problem was much wider than you have so far had to deal with here. It spread from students to workers, and like any one-time socialist (or do we presume too much?) you know that any real threat to a regime must include the working people in very large numbers. Ironically enough, it is you and your colleagues in the Cabinet who have managed to alienate more working people than any other British Government since 1926.

Those of us who have, you might say, a special interest in remembering such things, cannot remember a period in which such a wide range of workers have felt constrained to demonstrate and go on strike. Not only, predictably, dockers and railwaymen and builders, but bank clerks and teachers and nurses, have actually walked the streets with placards and taken direct action against their own exploitation!

Oddly enough, you reserve your wrath for those who protest against *other's* exploitation. Perhaps it isn't so odd, though. The professional, middle-class worker was only just getting his feet wet. He behaved with decorum and with what you must have thought was admirable restraint. Those who protest for wider issues — Vietnam, Biafra, South Africa — are hard cases in comparison, and you are right to be more concerned about containing them. They are out to destroy what you stand for; the bank clerks will shut up for a mere 7 per cent.

Just to Cause Trouble?

All the same, you shouldn't be a liar, you know. You can afford to give credit where credit is due, and if you lie, we are forced to believe that you are afraid of the truth. We have to admit that you have the power; at least you could admit that we have the principles.

But no, you even want to take that away from us. When you

came to the television cameras after your conference with your police chiefs last week, you grudgingly admitted that 'many' of the anti-Springbok demonstrators were motivated by principles, *but*, there were, of course 'the usual job lot of anarchists and renta-crowd hangers-on', who go around just to cause trouble.

Inasmuch as your smugness can slip, it slipped then, and so did your image of friendly, honest Jim. You revealed the typical spite-fulness of the power-seeking Labour politician reminded of what his Party used to stand for.

Now you listen here, politician. It is not for you and your hypocri-tical kind to criticise the anarchists on grounds of principle, and if we tend to turn up everywhere, it is because we are against every-thing that you and your kind stand for — on principle.

You and your kind, politician. When we protest against Vietnam it is because your kind in America and Saigon and Hanoi are behaving normally. When we protest about Czechoslovakia it is because your kind in the Kremlin are running true to form. It is because your kind in Pretoria bring politics into sport that we protest against the Springboks — and if anarchists are among your 'troublemakers' it is because anarchists want to stop the game, they don't just want to make a symbolic protest outside the stadium.

Local Initiatives
But get one thing straight, politician. It is not the same 'job lot' of anarchists going around causing trouble. It used to be, but not any more. Thanks to you and your kind behaving normally around the world, there are more anarchists today than ever before. There may be a very few individuals with the time and the determination enough to go where they feel they are needed, but since most of us are working people with limited means we are not as free as perhaps we would like to be to go around causing trouble for you and your kind. After all, you cause enough for us!

But we don't have to. When there is a demonstration in Swansea, South Wales anarchists take the initiative; in Aberdeen, South-ampton, London or Liverpool, local anarchists are there. Just be thankful, politician, that we cannot yet call up huge numbers. When we can, we shall stop your political games wherever we can — and we don't mean only rugger!

One final point. Anarchists fight racialism not only because it is an insult to our intelligence, our humanity and our international-ism, but also because it is a particularly vile instrument of govern-ment. We don't expect social democrats to go along with that, but

even if they lived up to their own supposed principles, there would
not be the need for anarchists to be 'the conscience of the Left',
as we have been described. Neither would there be the need for
pitiful laws to contain racialism. Anarchists do not need the Race
Relations Act — but if it had been invoked against a team quite
openly chosen on racialist grounds, then we should not need to be
'making trouble' on Saturday afternoons, either!

If you don't do your job, Mr. Callaghan, we've got to do ours!

Yours very sincerely,

6th December 1969   JUSTIN

Mr Benn's Wage Slavery

It is futile and against all common sense to expect the State to
transform the capitalist system of profit and exploitation into a
society whose people take control of their own lives. Such a prospect is contrary to the authoritarian nature of the State. And yet
today the idea of workers' control is being bandied about as one
of the solutions for solving capitalist ills.

Anthony Wedgwood Benn, who is the Government's supporter
of workers' 'participation', has authorised money for co-ops at
Meriden ('Triumph' motor-cycle factory), the *Scottish Daily News*,
and at the old Fisher-Bendix factory at Kirkby. However, what
Mr Benn seems to be more interested in is the benefit such experiments will bring to increased output. He has said that co-ops "can
unlock a considerable production potential that cannot be released
by the present authoritarian system of management. This country
could — with the same plant and equipment — produce a great
deal more on a continuing basis if the energy now wasted could
be released to permit higher real incomes."

What Mr Benn and all the supporters of the Government and
the State, whether bourgeois or socialist, want is increased productivity. As such they will also be authoritarian because real control,
and power, will lie elsewhere and will not be in the hands of the
workers themselves.

This is why Mr Benn's National Enterprise Board should be seen
for what it is, as another scheme to aid the survival of the capitalist

system. While it is true that private enterprise has virtually vanished, capitalism marches on with the aid and support of the State. Public capital will be used to invest in ailing companies. Mr. Wilson, the Prime Minister, has said that where this capital investment is used "there goes with it a corresponding degree of public ownership and control". But public ownership and control is not workers' control. Mr Wilson said that "when the City of London puts its money in, it usually wants a corresponding say in the business. Will not the State want a corresponding say?"

What we are witnessing is further moves towards a corporate State. Private capital has failed the profit motive system, and so huge investments of public money are now needed to keep the wheels of industry turning. Mr Wilson has called it good socialist doctrine as well as good capitalist doctrine. Its proper title is The Corporate State.

Mr Benn's image as a firebrand socialist is a long way off the mark. State capital means State control. While we have not yet got the repressive system of government which existed in Italy and Germany in the thirties, the increasing amount of control by the State here is following a similar pattern.

The series of take-overs which Mr Benn has supported are workers' reaction to the threat of unemployment and not the outcome of any real desire to take over their work places for themselves. It is a good tactic and the experience of running their own plants will give them and other workers the confidence that they can organise and run things without professional management, but these co-ops are a drop in the ocean. Such experiments are not a threat to capitalism; in fact the head of Jaguar cars helped the shop-stewards at Meriden to draw up their case for a co-op, but it will be watched over by Mr Benn's Ministry.

As anarchists we want people to control all aspects of their lives, of which the production of goods is but a small part. But without real workers' control power will always be in the hands of the State and those who own and control industry. As long as the profit motive rules, workers will be exploited and have little or no say or control of what is produced.

Mr Benn's National Enterprise Board, far from giving workers' control, will be out to exploit "the considerable productive potential". That might be socialism for some MPs, but as far as workers are concerned it is still wage slavery.

7th December 1974   P.T.

Prancing Bull and Bear

The *Observer* of 26th January on its front page describes how a bounding City has replaced a swinging City. In the article a stockbroker commenting on the sudden rise of share prices said that there are only two things that make a market move: fear and greed. This is to say that irrationality as well as irrelevance govern an activity that presumes to be the basis of our economic life.

It is curious that this rise in share prices seems to coincide with a rise in unemployment and the insecurity that this brings. One may well ask how a man may buy at one price and sell at a higher price the next week, shares representing the same resources, thereby making a profit without having contributed anything to those resources. The money and property nexus seems to have a catechism of its own as superstitious, as dangerous, and as destructive of real human values as any religion or dogma. Invisible earnings, liquidity, growing money, pay-today-live-tomorrow, the replacing of human care by insurance.

No doubt great efforts will be made to prop the system up, for it is the only way that social justice and equity can be avoided. The only remarkable feature about the Stock Exchange, apart from its irrelevance and irrationality, is the wealth of those who are in the club. All these features are shared with that other pillar of established society, the law, which by using the violence of the State aims to make these institutions self-perpetuating.

The rub to those who would like to see the established order remain is that the workers want a much larger share of the cake, and the economic problems in capitalist society cannot any longer in the West be solved by starving the workers. The contradiction is that having sold the consumer society to the workers with planned obsolescence and wasteful production, the shortage of basic materials is coming home to roost.

The plain fact is that middle-class environmentalists who bleat about these things have got to realise that the most important pollutant in the world human community is social injustice and human inequity. When these problems are dealt with, all other problems of resources, pollution and starvation will fall into place. Space, energy and food must be regarded as essential commodities to be shared equitably, and all whose demands on them are beyond their needs must regard themselves as contributing to the collapse of society into violence and destruction.

The growth of capitalism was accompanied by a reverence for private property and the development of the nuclear family and a society in which human needs involved a cash transaction, where insurance replaced community, and where taking thought for tomorrow, instead of resulting in a careful husbanding of resources, meant sidestepping this necessity by taking a lien on future resources.

The enveloping warmth of human contact has been superseded by the cold actuarial calculation. In the end it does not work, because the greed and fear of the Stock Exchange, in so far as these are reflected throughout society, will destroy the basic human and material resources needed to make any society work.

8th February 1975 ALAN ALBON

Waiving the Rules

The recent wave of prosecutions relating to official secrets is a reflection not only of the determination of certain courageous individuals to 'let the public know' what it is the public's right to know — and what potential enemies know anyway — but also of increasing Governmental sensitivity with regard to its own declared fields of knowledge. And by 'declared' we mean, or rather the Government means, 'restricted'.

If you accept the concept that the State has rights to official secrets for the sake of national security, then you may in your mind justify the suppression of information about bomber bases, and military installations in general. But under no circumstances can you justify the deception of the public in matters of the implementation of declared and public policy.

When Ian Smith declared UDI in Rhodesia all those years ago, it was perfectly clear that if the British Government had flown in troops to occupy Salisbury and neutralise any possible opposition, Smith's bluff could have been called and the usual careful progress towards 'democratic independence' could have been ensured, which was its stated intention. But Harold Wilson didn't want to do that, or didn't have the nerve, for fear of a backlash and relied instead on the long-term pressure of sanctions.

We now know what an absolutely dishonest, despicable and ineffective practice that has been — with the full knowledge of subsequent Conservative and Labour Governments. It is totally impossible that Edward Heath, Harold Wilson, Jim Callaghan, Margaret Thatcher, David Steel, Enoch Powell and Uncle Tom Cobbley and all, could have been ignorant of the facts of, for example, oil reaching Rhodesia through South Africa. The only surprising thing is that African politicians have not made more use of the knowledge *they must have had* to alert the British public. But then — are they not in the government business themselves?

The anarchist analysis remains true: distrust *everybody* seeking power. They are liars, cheats and murderers, be they white, black or khaki. All rule by coercion and deceit.

30th September 1978

THE GENERAL ELECTIONS

Landslide Against the People

One thing must be made plain about the Election: there is a positive 'Law' that politicians who are expected to carry out a strong policy can always do so *against* the people with whom they are identified and who have elected them, and the principles with which they are most closely associated. Thus in support of this Contradictions Law, a rebel anti-militarist of the First World War, like Mr Shinwell, could not possibly abolish conscription after the Second World War. It would possibly still be in operation had there not in the meantime been a militarist series of Ministers of War. Pacifists in power can be relied on to be ultra-militaristic. Militarists in power can afford to cut down the armed forces estimates; Tories can afford to surrender national sovereignty and, in the form of the Common Market, prepare 'to sell out to Europe'; it takes a Labour Trade Union Socialist Minister however, to get tough with the unions and the unofficial strikers.

The Labour Party cannot, by reason of its Left associations, attack the Swiss bankers or Hungarian economists so loudly as can the Tories. On much the same lines, the homosexuals in Parliament — with one or two fairly honourable exceptions — have been the loudest to denounce the Bill to relieve their disabilities, or at most have been discreetly silent. In the Balfour Government, the one member of the Cabinet to dissociate himself with the plan for a 'Jewish National Home' was, of course, a Jew. If a Government wish to bring in major infringements on personal liberty, they bring in somebody who has been brought up in the Liberal Party (the most reactionary Home Secretary was Sir John Simon).

During the war, it was necessary to try to bring the generals to heel. It had to be a militarist, and the job went to a Tory. The workers had to be disciplined, and so the Ministry of Labour went to the leading trade unionist, Ernest Bevin. The only exceptions to this rule have been in Ambassadorships (sending Cripps to Moscow and Hoare to Madrid was an instance). Those who imagine that by supporting one Party against another they are helping to bring in at least minor benefits or save minor bastions of personal liberty, are under a major delusion.

I am told that at least one former contributor to FREEDOM is supporting the Labour Party in a marginal constituency. Quite obviously, he expects that in a marginal seat he will be able to get marginal concessions. It would be logical perhaps to support a Tory if these marginal concessions are to be of a socialist character — but having stated this, is to state the nonsense of those whose idea of anarchism is not really anything more than a misunderstanding. At certain times anarchism may appear to be extreme anti-fascism or extreme liberalism or extreme revolutionism. It will attract those who are anti-fascist or liberal or revolutionary and want to be more so. They have not understood anarchism. One of the few useful aspects of an election is that it helps to show this. Anarchism may well be anti-fascist, support certain popular liberalistic causes, and be revolutionary; but it *is* anarchism. It has nothing to do with voting people into power.

The line of the comic Left is, of course, 'to vote Labour in order to expose it'. This hackneyed Trotskyist line, a leftover from the days when Lenin was desperately trying to get support outside Russia and thus hallowed with the sanctity of a credo in direct apostolic succession, floats around the lunatic fringe who 'bore the Labour Party from within' and everybody else from without. The most extreme case was one group that declared itself opposed to 'boring within' but decided that it would have a United Front with the Labour Party (without the latter's knowledge) so that it could be 'exposed'. The group itself was 'exposed'. After the Labour Party was elected, it wound itself up (and the United Front with it).

It is very easy in time of election to say — rents, Vietnam, nuclear bomb, this, that and the other . . . *do* something about it . . . *vote* . . . and never mind what for, so long as you do. The only excuse we can offer for a *Don't Vote* campaign is that this is equally effective or ineffective; here is something to '*do*' about it, and it will be neither more nor less useful than voting. At least it enables one to have the comfortable feeling afterwards of saying — 'Don't blame me, I didn't vote'. Which, we agree, is small consolation after the bomb has dropped, but is the best that can be offered in the context of a General Election. The positive things we can do are to be found in a vastly different context.

We can hardly deal with these things to the once-every-five-years man or woman whose knowledge of anarchism comes to him the first time when he or she sees a sticker on the tube saying, surprisingly, 'Don't vote!' To that dabbler in public affairs, we are after all only the odd few out, as we are at Coronation time and no doubt would be at Christmas time if we did not comfort ourselves with the knowledge that it is an old pagan pre-Christian festival.

We are the 'will not voters' — which in one recent opinion poll reached 3%, but who knows the reason why people do *not* vote? — ranging from the dictates of conscience to the pressing needs of nature. We must confess at the election to being somewhat like the avid idealist who interrupts the marriage ceremony with the call, 'Don't get married!' But at least the ceremony would then be interrupted to hear whether we have good cause to state this. We can only hope that for some now engaging in the irrelevant and inconsequential pastime of choosing between their rulers, there will be some who will pause to ask whether we have good cause to say why they should not vote. And the answer is simply that we don't think it desirable to delegate our authority to somebody else.

By the time of the next lot of elections, let us hope that more people understand our belief in a society based on full participation, which would be better than the present authoritative system based on property and privilege; at any rate, that at least those who consider themselves libertarian or revolutionary understand this.

26th March 1966   INTERNATIONALIST

You Don't Have to Vote!

Every election is an insult to our intelligence. As anarchists we say this not only because any difference between parties is reduced by the game of vote-catching to the level of childish *'Yah boo, you're another'*, but that the real thing about an election is that *we* are being asked to choose *them*.

We are the people, *they* are the Government, and we have no interest in common. Our interest is to be free from government, to run our own affairs and enjoy the fruits of our labour, freely given and freely enjoyed. It is *we* who create all wealth, *they* who exploit it. It is time we took back the right to the enjoyment of life.

The argument for the existence of government is that it is a necessary evil. This specious, lying, cheating phrase is used by all who wish to use something evil for their own preferment. Evil is never necessary; though we may have to tolerate it as long as we are not strong enough to be rid of it. But we should never choose it!

The evil of government is one that should be regarded in the same light as the evils of typhoid or smallpox. It is in fact a disease in the body of society, undermining all healthy relationships, eating away like an insidious cancer into all parts of our freedom and dignity, so that our lives waste away in futile conflict and sick irresponsibility.

Being asked to choose in an election is like being asked to choose which sickness we would prefer: typhoid or smallpox?

We Don't Have to Choose Either!
We are talking about 1970, not the dark ages. We have licked typhoid and smallpox — it is time we licked the disease of government. No doubt in the dark ages, disease was regarded as a necessary evil — one of nature's pruninghooks, God's Will and all that crap — but men arose who questioned what was and worked to eradicate the evils of disease. They were opposed by those with a vested interest in peddling God's Will — but all those with a firmer grasp of reality welcomed the attack on the evil of disease. The workers wanted to be healthy workers, and the bosses wanted healthy workers too. But this is only the health of the body; a healthy mind is something else.

For a man with a healthy mind questions 'necessary' evils and attacks disease wherever he finds it. The disease of government seeks to protect itself against examination by attacking the mind — by education, by unceasing propaganda, and by fear, lies and the spread of false information. Government, in fact, is all in the mind.

What, after all, does government contribute to society? Governments do not make anything (except a balls-up of everything they touch). The Minister of Housing (assuming we have one) does not build houses: building workers do that. The Minister of Health does not heal the sick: nurses and doctors do that. The Minister of Transport transports no one (not even with delight): railwaymen and transport workers do that. The Minister of Works doesn't, and the function of the Minister of Employment and Productivity is to whip others into greater productivity in their employment.

In other words, Governments do not make or do anything — they simply direct the exploitation of others and control the wealth that flows from that exploitation. Who needs that?

The anarchist argument is that we who create the wealth are capable of directing it; we who produce and distribute are capable of controlling the processes of production and distribution. We are therefore not interested in deciding which individuals should be in charge of the process of directing and controlling; we do not choose between old-fashioned landowners, individualist capitalists, bureaucratic managers, party caucuses or leaders of unheard-of genius.

Every leader, every Government, takes away our right to make our own decisions, run our own lives, give what we have to give and take what we need in a condition of equality, freedom and

dignity. Every Government must, by its very nature, set out to make us do things we do not want to do and stop us doing things we do want to do.

Why Vote For That?

In the early days of democracy — in this country effectively pre-1914 — there might have been some excuse for believing that men of good will in power could bring about changes in society that really mattered; that poverty could be eliminated, wars be abolished for ever from human society; freedom and equality become reality. Today, 1970, there is no excuse for such idealism. We have seen Governments of every known kind from fascist to Social Credit, expressing every known religion in some form or another. All that has flourished is hatred and fear — the basic requirements of government. All that has changed has been the scale and the techniques of government; the subtlety and the cynicism in the use of mass media and the brutality when that fails.

Each school of political thought has fouled its own nest. The capitalists have destroyed freedom; the socialists and communists have betrayed socialism. Nationalism has defeated internationalism — except among the ruling classes — and racism plays its part in the grand order of 'Divide and Rule'.

There is no Hope Through any Form of Government

In fact there is less than hope, there is only despair, the certainty of destruction. The result of the 'success' of statist forms of 'revolution' has been the emergence of the monster super-states which straddle the world today. America, Russia, Britain, France, China — all these States have at their disposal the means to destroy mankind. Their rulers profess differing shades of political creeds, but in their internal and international practices they are so similar that choosing between them is simply a matter of patriotism or faith, neither of which is good ground for revolution.

And it is revolution we are talking about. Everywhere the form of economy that exists is a kind of capitalism — 'free enterprise' or State controlled makes no difference to the exploited. And everywhere the State apparatus exists to defend that form of economy. This is why right round the globe unrest is mounting, in 'democratic', communist or fascist countries dissatisfaction is growing into disgust, and young people everywhere are finding the energy and the courage and the ideas to attack the squalid systems which seek to suppress them.

The Anarchist Alternative

One of the great features of the world-wide revolt against the status quo has been the re-emergence of libertarian ideas. All the political alternatives having been tried and found wanting, anarchism is the only constructive alternative, since it is the only social philosophy which rejects the State and the whole power structure.

Anarchism is the only social philosophy which starts with the individual and works up; which demands that personal freedom be related to social needs but never submerged by them. Anarchism is the only social philosophy which demands workers' control of industry and means just that. Not workers' participation in their own exploitation, like the Liberals, or workers' councils under the 'leadership' of the 'revolutionary workers' party' like the Trotskyists, but direct workers' control at the point of production through which the workers organise production and distribution in the interest of all — including themselves!

This clearly means the end of boss control and State control, and with that must go all the various means by which we are manipulated; the money and wages systems, minority control of mass media and propaganda machinery, repressive education systems geared to produce profit-fodder and technological yesmen, law and its repressive perversion of 'order', policemen and prisons, the Army, Navy and Air Force, the authoritarian family, religion and the anti-sex morality they depend upon, private property and the profit motive, diplomacy, secret or otherwise . . . all, all this and all the whole lot of stupid and cruel things which stem from them.

This crazy system cannot be reformed or patched up. It has to be abolished. It cannot be taken over and changed from within, as the communist regimes demonstrate only too well. The power structure has to be destroyed and nothing put in its place!

How do we do this? We create the alternative society by living to our own standards of behaviour and fighting the system wherever we can and by whatever means of direct action are appropriate. The direct action bit is important because this is something we have to do for ourselves.

Nobody Can Do It For Us

Nobody is going to give us our freedom on a plate. Nobody is going to make the better world for us. This is why we have to set out *now* to make our own society, build our own communes, make our own works councils, prepare to take over.

We are already being called a 'sub-culture' by the squares who think they are the real culture. It is up to us to so reorganise our own lives that we can demonstrate the superiority in human terms of our ideas, of our way of living.

Work now to spread ideas! Build now the alternative culture of freedom and self-discipline and responsibility! Take over now in small ways, and prepare to take over all that we want to save of existing things. Make *them* the representatives of the sub-culture! Push their slavery and loranorder and social irresponsibility down and out!

The anarchist alternative to Mr Wilson and Mr Heath is — *you*!
13th June 1970   THE EDITORS

Same Old Charade

There is now no doubt that Mr Heath has used the miners' dispute to call a General Election and therefore gain another term of office for his Party. Although spokesmen for the Labour Party have welcomed the Election — they can hardly do anything else — from a number of opinion polls it looks as though the Tories will win. But really this isn't so surprising because as we saw in France in 1968 de Gaulle was able to win another term of office after the May Days. Basically Mr Heath's case will be similar to the General's and will be fought against the threat of 'extremists' and about 'who governs' the country. Indeed, the Tories' manifesto sugars the pill and even follows de Gaulle's promise of 'participation' for workers in industry with representatives from the trade unions on the boards of directors. The whole approach is to get the support of 'moderates' against the 'extremists'. The Tory campaign is not union bashing but a courting of the 'moderate, reasonable' trade union leaders and their cooperation in setting wage levels and generally making decisions along with the employers and the Government. This is the tripartite solution which is the real ambition of all States but is attempted and achieved by the means of the kid glove or the iron fist.

We are glad that the National Union of Mineworkers' executive have rejected the Government's appeal to call off the strike during the period up to polling day. But there is considerable support by Labour Party supporters for such a truce. These people sincerely support the miners but see the issue in political and governmental terms rather than industrial. They only see change coming from reforms from above rather than relying on the tremendous initiatives and direct action from ordinary working people. It is this aspect of the struggle that is important for anarchists. We can see that real changes in power and social relationship only come when people take part in these changes. It is not just a question of exerting pressure but seeing the industrial struggle as a springboard to the social revolution.

People should not, and we hope the miners won't, be fooled by the General Election. We believe that a change of Government will not basically change a thing. Whichever Party is elected will have to settle with the miners. The Confederation of British Industry has already said as much and has put pressure on the Government to use the Relativities Report as a basis for a settlement. So now we have both — a General Election and a basis for a settlement which has the backing of the most powerful supporters of the Tories. Mr Heath and his Government might have just reached the right compromise in that they will get back into power, reach a settlement and just avoid an economic collapse. It is true that the balance of payments is and will be in the red for a long time, but profits have been high and these will recover later in the year.

Our message is that the Election is a charade which will alter nothing as far as the working class of this country is concerned. Miners will still have to dig coal while others will dictate the monetary value of that job. Class exploitation will continue under either a Labour or a Tory Government. Either would use troops to break a strike or put down an insurrection which is the real threat and what the ruling classes all over the world fear most.

The General Election will lower the temperature but anarchists have the task to show that the real power for social change and revolutionary potential lies with workers taking direct action not just for higher wages but to overthrow the existing social order and bring in a classless and Stateless society based on mutual aid and workers' control.

16th February 1974   P.T.

The Illusion of Voting

This election is almost a non-event. Everyone knows it is a re-run of an old epic they saw earlier this year; they didn't like it much then and they seem to like it even less now. Injections of new issues are tried, nationalisation didn't seem to worry many of the electors; the Common Market was brought in but it's not a great point since most of the leading politicians are in favour of it — on their own terms. Inflation was brought out as the bogey, but since every party has a sovereign remedy for it, and since nobody, not even the doctors, is interested in the real cause of the disease it's not a great selling policy except for a coalition or a Government of national unity. This coalition Government is not putting up candidates either; Edward and Jeremy each want a coalition — on their own terms. So that's not on either.

However, this is all on the superficial level of personalities on which the newspapers and politicians thrive. If the Election was fought and reported on the question of ideals and ideas there would not only be very little copy but the newspapers would not be very interested.

But illusions still persist even in the trendiest of political weeklies despite their supposed concentration on ideas and ideals.

As ever we have seen *Socialist Worker* and *The Militant* advocating voting Labour; the *Militant* doesn't go so far as to say so directly — they make certain conditions on which they will support the Labour Party; conditions of which the Labour Party will take not the slightest notice. We are used to *Socialist Worker* getting on by means of a quasi-syndicalism and finishing up as an adjunct to the Labour Party, dreaming of inheriting *Tribune*'s stooge role putting one Foot after another, but this Election things seem to have taken a dextrously sinister turn.

The *New Statesman*, mourning its lost virility, has been casting about for a new platform and a new soul. An essay in this direction (in both senses) was published in their issue of 13th September when five pages were given to Peter Sedgwick, a prominent member of International Socialists, who spilt his soul in an essay called 'Farewell Grosvenor Square' in which he made the case that politically, nothing much came out of the Campaign for Nuclear Disarmament except that it cleared the ground for the rise of IS as a new revivifying force for the Labour Left.

This arrogant assumption is still enshrined in academic respectability. Not only does Sedgwick claim that the ideas of factory occupation rose from IS advocacy but that IS is the growth of a new rank and file movement.

As has been pointed out, Sedgwick ignores the growth of the Committee of 100 and its predecessor the Direct Action Committee (which even anticipated CND), both grounded in the ideas of direct action which was the true seed-bed not only of the Committee but of factory occupations and of squatting. Sedgwick has not the nerve to claim squatting as an IS initiative — indeed squatting was once denounced by IS as 'adventurism'.

Claims made by IS to take up the leadership of the rank and file ring hollow. But the final illusion of Sedgwick is that they can maintain this stance and at the same time vote Labour.

There is no chance that the militants will extend their endorsement of Labour to any greater loyalty than the act of voting for Wilson on the mainly negative grounds of knocking the Tories and the Liberals . . . every socialist must engage, as a first call on his or her time and energy, in mass work within a real rank and file. This is, incidentally, one more reason why the committed revolutionary or radical will be unable to support the Labour Party in any other way beyond attendance at the polling booth.

If IS thinks that Harold Wilson and Co. care what 'mass work' Sedgwick and his busy beavers carry out so long as they vote for them . . . Once they get into power it is an illusion of voters that they have any further control over the Governments they have elected. Universal suffrage is one more of the illusions of liberty.
5th October 1974   JACK ROBINSON

The Negative Vote

We have until autumn, so it is now reliably assumed, to prepare ourselves for the ballyhoo and boredom of a General Election. Two by-elections have shown the usual predictable swing away from the Government Party and the class war of the winter has made it clear even to smug old Jimboy that he's not exactly the most popular man in the country.

There is always — or nearly always — a swing away from the governing Party at by-elections. If you are a supporter of the Opposition, you work like hell to get your voters out to show how unpopular the Government is. If you actually voted for the winning Party and now have to take responsibility for what it is doing, you can claim your democratic right to criticise, show your disappointment and your independence of spirit, all quite safely, in the majority of by-elections, without fear of 'bringing the Government down'.

The number of times that a Government is poised on a knife-edge in the House, as the present one is, and when a small swing in a marginal seat would destroy its precarious 'majority' is very small. Indeed, it is difficult to remember a time when a Labour Government has been maintained in office only by a semi-official alliance with the Liberals, as the Lib-Lab pact was, and the, albeit sullen, support of the Scottish and Welsh Nationalists on one side and the Ulster Unionists — led by Enoch Powell — on the other!

The precarious balance in the House of Commons has of course sprung from the steady erosion by 'consensus' politics into the so-called differences between Conservative and Labour. It is due to the pragmatic recognition by both of the main Parties that elections are won by the 'floating voters' — the middle ground who swing one way or the other according to the price of baked beans or whether or not little John or Mary passed their O-levels.

When our democracy depends upon this slender minority to choose our Government for us, then the Parties are going to converge in the centre trying to grab their votes. The dead heat in the Election is a reflection of the similarity between Labour and Conservative policies in effect — a similarity which, from time to time, makes both sides antagonise their own supporters. If there were real differences, the Parties would be much more unbalanced and party loyalties much fiercer than they are now.

The similarities between this winter's struggles by the trade unions against the Government and those of 1974 against the Heath Government, cannot have been lost on many workers, especially since in both cases the organised workers beat the Government. Unlike the more principled Ted Heath, Jim Callaghan was wily enough not to pin his colours too permanently to the mast of the good old ship of state, so the cry of 'Who governs the country?' was not raised again. Jim never made five per cent an issue of principle on which he was prepared to go to the Country.

Undoubtedly, though, he has lost a lot of face and a lot of friends too. And that means a lot of votes. But then so did Ted, and not only because of his lost battle with the miners. Heath was responsible for the abolition of Retail Price Maintenance which made it impossible for manufacturers or distributors to fix the selling price for their goods — heralding unbridled competition and phoney cut-throat discounting which appears to be great for the shopper prepared to shop around — but has driven many a small shopkeeper (traditionally the backbone of the Tory Party) to the wall. Disillusionment all round — and it remains to be seen whether Maggie Thatcher will stick to any principles of free competition when she comes to pin *her* colours to the mast.

Does it matter? In a time of 'consensus politics' there are no principles to be taken into consideration anyway. Only tactics. And the best tactic of all for opposition Parties is the simple use of the negative vote — calling on all those fed up with the Government to come out and vote against it.

Unfortunately, under our electoral system, there is no way you can vote 'No'. You can only vote 'Yes' for one of the consensus Parties, with which we include the Liberals, or one of the fringe Parties which vary only in their degree of helplessness . . . and repulsiveness. But it's still 'Yes' for someone.

The only way to make the negative vote meaningful is not to

vote at all. More than one-third of the Scots eligible to vote in the recent referendum declined to bother. And that was on an issue which *seemed* to concern them much more than any election for a Westminster Government. Yet while the Government was asking for a forty per cent vote for a Scottish Assembly — another tier of government in Edinburgh — nearly forty per cent of Scots showed that they didn't give a damn one way or the other.

Nevertheless, perhaps the only real surprise the other week was the surprise expressed by the media at the extent of the abstentionism. When the Government proposals first emerged, after all, not one of the opposition Parties at Westminster was exactly thrilled. The plans went either too far (for the Conservative Right and Labour/Jacobin Left) or not far enough (for the 'federalist' Liberals and Scottish and Welsh Nationalists). And — to hell with what the opposition Parties want anyway! — who in their right mind desires a recreation in this island of the so-called federal model of West Germany or regional Governments of Italy? Who in their right mind wants yet another tier on the already monstrously hierarchic cake of the European Community?

At all events, this abstentionism confronts Jim Callaghan with a pretty problem. In order to secure the continued support of the few Scottish Nationalist Members of Parliament, he must go ahead with plans for a Scottish Assembly — which the majority of Scottish voters have shown they either don't want or to which they are sublimely indifferent.

The Scottish Referendum result has therefore nonplussed the Government — and for anarchists this is a very creditable and praiseworthy achievement.

To vote negatively — i.e. simply to get someone out — is always counter-productive, because you always put somebody else in. Not to vote at all, while it can be purely negative, has the saving grace that you don't help to put somebody else in, except by default.

The positive side of non-voting lies in your alternatives. And that is what anarchists have — or should have! Colin Mackay, in this issue, reflects the feeling of many when he writes

Devolution yes, but why to this thing called Scotland? What is Scotland any more than Ireland, England or Wales? Devolution to the regions would be more sensible; devolution to the districts better still . . .

But because the evils of bureaucracy and authoritarianism can exist as well on a district as on a regional, national or European scale, *our* reply can be only: No to devolution from the top down,

Yes to federalism from the bottom up. No to existing local councils with their inevitably party-political basis; Yes to attempts to build from street groups into informal but decision-making neighbour-hood councils and communes. No to the hierarchical structures of trade unions, Yes to the alternatives of workers' councils.

Devolution and with it party politics — the politics of State entryism — are a boring irrelevance to modern life. The politics of the street and the workplace, the anarchist society of free and horizontal cooperation, must take their place. Anything more — or less — should indeed be treated with the apathy it deserves and, so far, has received.

10th March 1979   EDITORS

Vote For Fear?

Surprisingly enough, as we go to press the Falklands factor has played practically no part at all in the argy-bargy of the last couple of weeks (pun intended). No doubt the Tory think-tank, if that is not a contradiction in terms, has decided to leave the sweet smell of success wafting on the anniversary air to seep into the tribal subconscious of the masses and not draw too much attention to what has transpired since our glorious mini-victory and close shave.

The embarrassment that could be generated if the subject came up for intensive argument was just hinted at last week when Mrs Thatcher was appearing on the TV programme 'On the Spot', in which members of the public were screened in from different areas to ask questions. An 'ordinary woman' — i.e. just a voter — successfully pinned Maggie down on the question of the sinking of the 'Belgrano', the Argentine warship whose loss gave General Galtieri the first martyrs of the war, and which has since been found to have been some fifty miles *outside* the British-imposed exclusion zone, on the mainland side and sailing *westward* — that is, *away* from where the British fleet was waiting for it.

All this took place at a time when the Peruvian Government was trying to come between the Argentine and British Govern-ments in order to establish some kind of formula for heading off the coming armed conflict. Having sent the task force all that way, however, Thatcher was determined to get as much political kudos as possible out of this little Godsend for Glory. On the telly last week she didn't deny the facts — she just gave her own interpretation of them, which was that as head of the British State it was her bounden duty to 'protect the lives of our British sailors', threatened by this ship sailing off in the opposite direction.

We are sorry not to have caught the name of the lady asking the question (or even to note where she came from) — but she really had Maggie rattled, for she bravely pressed on with the issue and had the Prime Minister stammering and repeating herself, eyes flashing with anger, but trying hard to keep the soulful, concerned look of the Leader worried only about her followers. The fact that some hundreds of British sailors and soldiers and airmen were burned, maimed or killed as a result of the decision to sink the Belgrano — which apparently emanated from London — has got to wait some time for confirmation, for Maggie's trump card was to tell her persistent questioner that the whole truth would be made known — in 30 years' time, when the official documents could be published.

By which time, you might think, Maggie will have ensured that the great British public will have had a rather larger conflagration of its own to worry about. Such is Thatcher's anger about the current rash of Cabinet leaks that a clampdown is forecast. She probably won't even tell us about the holocaust until after we're safely dead.

You may also be asking yourself now why the Opposition hasn't seized upon the Falkland disaster to hammer the Tories with. Well, nobody lucky enough to have switched on their radio on 3rd April last year and to have heard Michael Foot's speech in the House of Commons, would need to ask themselves that question.

It was absolutely in line with Labour's traditional stance as Her Majesty's Loyal Opposition, every single member of which has bent his or her knee to take the Loyal Oath of Allegiance to Her Britannic Majesty before taking his seat in the House of Commons to represent the interests of the slum-dwellers, the halt, the sick and the lame, the homeless and the hopeless and the helpless.

Oddly enough, none of the gentlemen of the Press thought on that brave day that Michael was himself a candidate for the geriatric ward. We might have almost believed that there were moist eyes in the Press Gallery as one crabbed old backbench Tory came forward and pumped Michael's hand, grunting 'God Bless You for speaking for England!' and certainly the rest of the House, Liberals,

Social Democrats, Ulster Unionists, Methodists, Catholics, Seventh Day Adventists, Masons, Closet Deviants, ex-Fascists, ex-Communists and ex-honest individuals, all rose to their feet to cheer Foot . . . and to condemn the squalid fascist leader of a militarist junta, to whom they were selling weapons only the week before.

No wonder the poor sod can't make any political capital out of the Falklands factor now! It's a dead issue — like all the other poor sods who didn't come back.

And before we pass on to other things — have you noticed how Northern Ireland doesn't get a mention in this election? Could that be because it was a Labour Government that sent in the troops in the first place? Could that be because it was Woy Jenkins (as a Labour Minister) who extended the (Labour) anti-terrorist legislation for holding suspects? Could it be that every State's man or woman and every potential State's man or woman knows that the British State *needs* Northern Ireland as a training ground for 'low intensity operations' — i.e. suppression of the civilian population?

For come what may, the depression has some time to go yet. Thatcher did not call this Election after only four years for nothing. She knows full well that there is worse to come, that the present lull in the steady increase in the inflation rate is — just a lull. Unemployment is still steadily creeping up, if for no other reason because the technical changes that are taking place in industry demand far fewer workers. You and you and you are just not going to be wanted. But you could be a problem.

It is extremely lucky for the Tories that it is Michael Foot who happens to be Leader of the Labour Party at this particular time, for, say what you like about Mike, he has been a sincere nuclear disarmer for a long, long time. Which is more than you can say for other leaders of the Party. It so happens that (seeing many popular votes) the Labour Party at its Conference decided to throw in its lot with the re-born CND of the 80's, so the Conservatives have been able to switch the main argument in this Election — so far at least — to the issue of what they laughingly call defence, rather than the domestic economy. In this, they are helped by Labour leaders Healey and Shore, both against unilateralism, leaving Foot himself to try to explain the deliberately ambivalent Manifesto.

And in this 'defence' field, we are on to the shifting grounds of fears and consequences. The unknown territories of hypothetical questions, of assertions needing no proof, of the inbuilt xenophobia of an imperial Power that has lost its empire and whose slavish people identified — and still do identify — too strongly with their masters.

This Election is going to be won on fear. Not only the fear of unemployment — for millions already know the truth about that and those not yet unemployed know that, somehow, you can still survive. And, anyhow, what's so marvellous about work when all it means is being used for someone else's benefit?

The fear is of a future that nobody can foretell, or, perhaps, of no future at all. Of all being blown to hell — or a hell on earth. For make no mistake about it — if the Tories win this Election they will usher in the most reactionary regime this country has seen this century. And no other party is likely to win.

All the evidence shows that when fear strikes, everybody runs to Big Daddy — or, in this case, Big Mummy. The terrible thing is, that nobody believes in themselves. Our education, our conditioning, our religions, all, all are geared to make us believe that we need someone outside of ourselves. And above all: that's what our politics is all about.

Listen to your militants; to your reactionaries and your scientific revolutionaries; to the avant garde and the rearguard and the vanguard and the Coldstream Guards and the prison guards. Listen to those who say 'You must use your vote! You must choose someone to represent you! You cannot do anything yourself! You cannot take the law into your own hands! Anything else is Anarchy!'

Then you'll know.

4th June 1983

THE THATCHER YEARS

Bloody Leaders

Apart from taking one giant step forward for womankind by getting herself declared an honorary man in an Islamic country (which presumably means that she would not necessarily be publicly executed in the unlikely event of her committing adultery) so that she could appear in public, our Prime Minister has endeared herself to the accountants who run Britain by winning significant contracts for the one industry in the UK which is not affected by recession.

An initial contract for Hawk jet trainers for the United Arab Emirates is hoped to be the forerunner for much larger orders for the same plane adapted for its other role as ground attack weapon. If indeed this possibility were followed up by the Arabs, this would mean that Mrs Thatcher (who, as her statements on Brixton show, abhors violence) has helped to clinch a deal worth around £100 million for about 35 planes. And of course, that is only the beginning, for training and combat planes alike have to be maintained in tip-top condition at all times, which means adequate supplies of spares, engines and all back-up equipment and know-how. Very profitable.

Even more profitable, too, if they are actually used in combat in which, incidentally, they may well be shot down by British planes supplied in the past to the Israelis. They, though, have been naughty enough recently to have preferred certain categories of French planes — which may be why that other travelling salesman in death, President Giscard d'Estaing, was not successful in selling the Franco-German Alpha training plane to the Arabs.

The speed with which the arms deal was agreed indicates that there was some pretty satisfactory horse trading from the Arab point of view as well. It has been said that one of Thatcher's aims was to do a bargain deal on oil and ensure cheaper oil from the Middle East, but in view of the fact that Britain is now an oil-producing country it would be illogical for any bargain to be struck which did anything to bring down the price of oil world-wide — although in the privacy of Sheik Zayed's palace who knows what discount prices might have been haggled out? Cheap oil for cheap planes?

After all, Margaret Thatcher sees herself as supreme ruler of the British worker, just as Sheik Zayed is supreme ruler of Abu Dhabi and President of the UAE. They can both crack the whip — and in the present economic climate workers in ordnance factories must be more than glad to have a secure job at any price, so if arms deals entail accepting reduced wage deals, we don't expect much opposition — certainly not from the trade unions.

There is another factor which also makes Thatcher's deal significant. It is that there is pressure around the Gulf to standardise weapons systems. It follows then, that whoever gets in with the first large order stands a good chance of getting the whole lot.

What might mean something very serious is the report that in the course of Mrs Thatcher's representation of me and you to the Arab leaders, she was told in no uncertain terms that they consider a settlement of the 'Palestine' question an absolute priority. Just like that. Apparently they also told her they would not provide any local facilities for one of her favourite schemes — the 'rapid deployment force'. This is a highly mobile strike force that, while based in the UK, can be airborne to any trouble spot very quickly.

So Margaret Thatcher may be disappointed on the political field, but is undoubtedly preening herself for her commercial coup. And after all, what does it matter who gets killed as long as the British arms industry flourishes? The present massive unemployment is forcing young men and women into the army; the arms profits provide the means to arm them, on top of the budgeted arms expenditure.

The inference is obvious: that the Arabs, while happy to keep themselves armed up to the eyeballs in their own interests, are not prepared to make themselves targets in anyone else's. But it all bodes ill for Israel.

8th May 1981

Hobgoblins, Arise!

Over 160 years ago now, Black Dwarf, in a perspicacious missive to his friend the Yellow Bonze, remarked that 'In England, the great art is not to *avoid* tyranny, but to disguise it'.[1]

The wave of riots across Britain this month, however, bearing in its wake serious threats about the introduction of rubber bullets, water cannon, even tanks; the reinstatement of the Riot Act and the establishment of special riot courts and army camps for convicted rioters and looters, shows just how poor that disguise really is. Margaret Thatcher admitted as much when she said, 'The veneer of civilisation is very thin. It has to be cherished if it is to continue.' Whatever Margaret Thatcher actually means, it is certain that she was referring to a certain scale of values guaranteed by the police — or at least that large section of them who subscribe to the views of the Chief Constable of Manchester, James Anderton. These have predictably adopted the attitude that the riots were not caused by any social factor, but militarily organised by masked guerrillas on motor bikes, with London accents and CB radios. This is known as the conspiracy theory, or what Jeremy Bentham once described as the 'Hobgoblin Argument' — i.e. using the claim that we are 'close to anarchy' in order to sit tight and do nothing. Or rather, in this case, to sweep aside the hopes and ideas of community groups in favour of 'heavy policing'. Thus will the veneer of civilisation, if not the actual disguise of tyranny, be preserved.

There have, of course, been dissenting voices. The stock Labour response has been to deplore the decay of the inner cities, Tory monetarist policy and unemployment — for all the world as if unemployment had not risen continuously throughout successive Labour Governments — and to promise the complete abolition of unemployment when Labour resumes power.

Foreign newspapers and press agencies have largely blamed the Thatcher regime for the beginnings of what they see as civil war, by ignoring racism and fostering unemployment and (in the words of the Soviet press agency, Tass) 'unleashing [police] terror' in the cities; while the Afrikaner *Die Vaderland* fondly hopes that the riots will create greater sympathy among Britons for apartheid.

Sociologists have dwelt upon the problem of 'lax' parents, crea-

1. *Black Dwarf* was the paper published by Thomas Wooler, the English Radical, from 1817 to 1824.

ting children *seven* times more delinquent than others' (!) while attributing the laxity and the sevenfold delinquency to poverty and overcrowding; others have stressed the break down of traditional communal values and the frustration of expectations aroused by the consumerism of the 50s and 60s — the growth, in fact, of the society of the spectacle.

The Social Democrats, of course, with an eye to their by-elections, have managed to lay a large part of the blame on extremism of Right and Left. Denis Healey, too, from the front rank of the Labour Right, spoke of the 'criminal fantasies' of the 'mindless militants of the Left as well as the Right [note the order of emphasis here] who say that political change must be brought about on the streets rather than in Parliament'. And from the front rank of the Labour Left, Tony Benn warned that riots were not a means of 'social progress'.

Here, surely, we come closer to the heart of the matter. Not only is it a question of who controls the streets, but of what we may regard as genuine or legitimate political action.

Ironically, it is to Italy that we must turn to find a measure of good sense about the riots. In an article in one of the mass circulation dailies, *La Repubblica*, a correspondent writes

. . . it would be silly to link the height of the flames at Liverpool to the number of unemployed of the city. Great Britain, after all, has a long and vigorous tradition of street violence, so much so that in the eighteenth century the English system was described as 'a Whig oligarchy tempered by riot'. It can indeed be said that from the French Revolution onwards British politics have been dominated by the terror of 'mob rule', government by the multitude . . .

Since then, Edgardo Bartoli goes on to observe, its political system has been implicitly based on the prevention of grave social disturbance by means of a mixture of reformism and repression as laid down in Bagehot's *The English Constitution*. What the *Black Dwarf* so aptly encapsulated as not the *avoidance*, but the disguise of tyranny.

In 1780 the Frenchman, Sébastien Mercier, observing the Gordon Riots not long before the outbreak of the French Revolution, remarked that such events would be inconceivable in Paris, whereas in London, well . . .

It has been traditional to see the Gordon Riots as originating in the whipping up of prejudice by the Protestant Association against Irish Catholic immigrants; yet what can scarcely be denied is the way in which they developed into a massive attack against wealth and authority in general. In the same way, particular causes may be attributed to the recent riots in London, Manchester, Liverpool and elsewhere, yet it can scarcely be denied that they constituted, above all, an attack on authority, and even more, on *authoritarianism*. No, the rioters were saying, the streets will *not* be the terrain of the police, or the police alone.

To see this happening gives us a spontaneous, a natural sense of exhilaration. But we must also reflect upon where it leads. 'Is this the Beginning?' asked FREEDOM. Most probably not. The Gordon Riots resulted in little more than a strengthening of the police and a reinforcement of the Government executive. The Bristol riots of 1980, it is said by blacks themselves, changed nothing except that the police tried to smile a little, and stayed out of the Black and White Café. Revolutions are made by a lot more than this, and, besides, what *kind* of revolution do we want?

The recent riots, though they may lend weight to the words of Tory 'wets', and though they may well have the highly beneficial effect of bringing a sense of pride and dignity to the black, Asian and disenchanted communities, are not likely to bring the aims of anarchism itself much closer.

Perhaps, as we continue to combat authoritarianism, in whatever form, the best policy, paraphrasing *Black Dwarf*, is not to avoid conflict, but, in a certain sense, to disguise it. To go about it, that is, in such a way that we make it more difficult for governments to act repressively against us. In doing so we must remember to act coolly, intelligently and with discrimination. More specifically, to try to avoid taking the police (and soon the army?) head on. For, far more than being a direct street struggle against the police, who are the guarantors of the veneer of *their* civilisation, the anarchist struggle is against the heart of that civilisation itself.

1st August 1981   G & D

Circuses — Not Much Bread

What marvellous people the Romans were! Probably the people who live in Roma today think they still are, but of course, for the rest of us plebeians, it is the glories that *were* Rome that turn us on. That Caligula, for example! And Nero — first-rate fiddler, he. Eat your heart out, Stephane Grappelly!

Nor were other Italian provinces, in other times, less brilliant. Machiavelli spelt out the principles, or lack of them, for the proper, or at least the actual, art of government — the Borgias practised them, and, *inter alia*, as they were always saying, gave us the one and only woman Pope. And that must be good.

Brilliant or no, however, it is the Romans we must thank for establishing the solid foundations of government: Roman Law, the basis of our very own legal system to this day (the *habeas corpus* could well have meant something else in Caligula's day . . . or maybe not!) and the simple, basic principles upon which tyranny through the ages has been built.

Sorry, sorry, we didn't mean to write 'tyranny', we meant . . . er . . . something like 'government by consent', like what every good radical libertarian socialist is now saying is what is wanted in Brixton. Where were we? Oh, yes — basic principles of government by consent, then.

We do not actually have at our fingertips the name of whichever Latin genius first coined the phrase 'Divide and Rule' — but isn't it a good one! Been worked to death since Roman times, of course, but still very much alive in our very own modern trade unions etc. By a sleight of hand that Machiavelli would have been proud to have isolated and explained, our trade unions ('*Our*' trade unions? What does he mean?) have used a word that means 'bringing together' to cover an operation that effectively tears apart. If ever there was an organisation which guards its own privilege by the sedulous division of the people who pay for its upkeep, it is surely the trade union movement, in Britain. And America. And the Soviet Union. And, we are prepared to place a modest wager, in Timbuktoo as well.

And when that mould was broken, as it was, briefly, in Spain, who but the Social Democrats and the Communists and the Fascists smashed the unity of a people who would not be governed? So hold your breath, as you watch Poland today.

Thank you Romans, they all say, for 'Divide and Rule'.

And what was that other great tenet of government that came down to us from the Imperial City?

Why, of course you remember: 'Bread and Circuses'. For this, we are proud to say that we do know who first said it. *Juvenal*, that's who. No, not Juvenile, you Plebeian Britannicus, but Juvenal, AD60-130. See what you learn by reading FREEDOM from front to back?

Limit the Roman people's anxious longings, said Juvenal, 'to two things only — bread, and the games of the circus'.

Now here's a funny thing, as Max Miller might have said, but right now, at the very time we are writing, what should be going on up and down the length and breadth of our freedom-loving land, but a whole series of circuses. Trapeze artistes, bare faced liars — sorry, sorry, *bare backed riders* — jumping through hoops, noble lions, tamed and toothless; elephants balancing on one leg; acrobatic motion passers and jugglers of resolutions; strong men lifting block votes in one hand, whilst not knowing what the other doeth . . . and at the end, the Ringmaster sees us off, and the band played on, and on, and on.

Then — and both Barnum and Bailey would have been proud of this — no sooner did the first circus come to an end; no sooner was the big top folded and the starry-eyed children sleepily sent home, but — on again came the clowns in another three-ringed circus, nationwide, from North to South! The very latest in sensational claptrap from the Hooray Harries and the Lord George Brown look-alikes. Sensational somersaults and bellyflops from a great height, through flaming hoops into buckets of water, every sensational anti-climax in the history of political skullduggery!!

Legerdemain before your very eyes! Now you see it, now you don't. Sharpshooters hit the centre every time — only to find there's nothing there! Roll up, roll up! Stand up and be counted while we throw knives at you! Boomerangs stab you in the back when you're not looking! Ride a zebra through the Race Relations Act and you can swear that black is white and it'll be all right on the night.

The Islington Rope Trick, over and over again — man climbs rope, vanishes, and reappears in another party looking just like the first party. Party of the first part, says the lawyer, falling off his seat. 'And this is what you do', says Jimmy Young: 'Take one man — sorry, sorry, er — person, take one vote if you can buy one, add one bloody great pinch of salt, roly-poly it altogether now and hurl it into the air. It's probably come to earth you know not where, because you never see it again. Gone!'

Two cheers for the sinister doctor and his late bride. They're tunnelling their way to France, leading three million unemployed like the Pied Piper of Hamelin and the lost children of the land of Israel. Chosen people?

Chosen for what? Must we be the spectators *and the participants* in our own deception? Must we be forever the fall guys and dolls for the professional ponces and their professional circuses? Cruelty to animals and human animals alike!

And, dear readers (come on, wake up!) there's more to come. Madam Margaret and her crystal balls is gonna ride those white horses till the sows come home. Round and round we go, straight ahead for damnation. Soaring interest rates and no safety net for the daring little lame ducks. Cruising on Trident, she's the Big Top, folks, and doesn't care who dies of starvation — self-inflicted or in the great cause of monetarism, the thrill is the same. Just so long as the audience keeps on paying to come in, and paying, and paying.

So put your hands together, folks, for Golden Maggie, the Iron Maiden. It's easier then for her to slip the handcuffs on while *she* revives our memories of the Great Houdini — and escapes, once again. Curses!

10th October 1981   JUSTIN

FOOTNOTE:
Juvenal was good for another quotation, usually used out of context. We'll give it to you straight and you can make what you like of it: *'Pone seram, cohibe.' Sed quis custodiet ipsos Custodes? Cauta est et ab illis incipit uxor.* 'Put on a lock! Keep her in confinement! But who is to guard the guards themselves? Your wife is as cunning as you, and begins with them.' — *Satires*

Falkland Farce

If Andrew Lloyd Webber is so hooked on Argentinian politics that he ever wants to write a sequel to 'Evita' he could hardly do better than pick up a scenario from the media of last week and write songs to fit.

In fact, some of the songs are already there, with a bit of pirating, which would be appropriate. Alter the lyrics of 'Georgia On My Mind' and stir in a bit of 'Any Old Iron' and you've got the opening number with all those scrap merchants landing on South Georgia (where?) to demolish an old unused whaling station, the wind machine ruffling their hair through the vigorous dance routine, closing with back projections of Captain Ahab and the Great White Whale — Moby Dick himself — there to symbolise the spirit of natural sovereignty.

By the time you are reading this, comrade, you will probably know the end of this divertissement, for things are happening so quickly that as we go to press we can only say that the British Fleet, God Bless 'Er, is still steaming resolutely southwards towards the 200-mile circle declared out-of-bounds for Argentinian ships by the Lord High of the Admiralty here in London where everybody is still determined to hang on to the ownership of a couple of barren rocks pinched by our ancestors in the nineteenth century.

The actual origin of British sovereignty over the Falkland Islands is something that everybody (well everybody in power) is keeping very quiet about. This could be because the British just seized it in 1831 or thereabouts (nobody seems very sure when) after the Spanish, who had occupied it before that, had evacuated all their 'possessions' in the South Atlantic and claim had been laid to it by the newly emerging State of Argentina — who made the mistake of not occupying and planting a flag on the relatively barren islands, 400 miles off the eastern shores of Patagonia.

Those were still the heydays of Empire, especially the British Empire, and anybody finding the odd island floating around without a flag on it (even 8000 miles away) felt entitled to stick up their own flag and shout loudly 'THIS IS OURS' and so it was.

Unhappily, something about the deal made with the departing Spaniards made the Argentinians think the Falklands and South Georgia 'belonged' to them — and they have never — *never* — accepted British sovereignty, which was established by importing a lot of sheep farmers and populating the place rather like it was done in Northern Ireland.

Over the years, the dispute over ownership has been a running sore for the Argentinians, although they did not push too hard, for it was a matter of national pride more than anything else — as it has also been for the British, who have used the islands as a whaling station, a trading post and a jumping off point for whoever was exploring the Antarctic circle, as well of course, as a breeding ground for all those sheep — now numbering 600,000 — and their owners, now numbering 1,800.

These are the people, and these are the sheep (you can tell the difference because the people walk on only two legs) about whom, or which, all the trouble is. Or so you are asked to believe. The Falkland Islanders, like the Gibraltarians and the Protestant Northern Irelanders and no doubt the Hong Kongians and the North Borneoans and the people of the Isle of Man, all want to remain BRITISH.

And so they shall! No matter what the cost! They all may perish in the struggle, but by God, they'll perish British! Nobody perishes better than the British. We have perished in India; we have perished in Africa, we have perished in America, North and South; we have perished in Europe. There is no far-flung corner of the world in which the British have not perished. If we are good enough to perish in Northern Ireland, by God we must be good enough to perish in the Falklands!

What for, do we hear you ask? Are you mad, sir, or madam, or person? This is a matter of principle. You may have noticed in your public papers that at this very time we are handing over the complete control of their national affairs to the Canadians — but we must point out to you that this has been done by proper process of law. We have screwed the French Canadians and the remaining Indians by the due and legal processes that everybody respects — but here are these Argies simply walking in and taking over that which we walked in and took over a century-and-a-half ago. That was different!

Besides which, somebody has found oil in the seas around the Falklands. So what? Here are these 1,800 sheep farmers — no, sorry, more than half of them work for the Falkland Islands Company (subsidiary of Charrington Coal) and live in company-owned houses, but they are all free-born Britons and wish to remain and what do they know about oil under the sea? Well, frankly, nothing, which is sad, because it is their lives that may be expended

as a matter of principle to maintain British sovereignty over the Falklands.

We say 'may be' because we have to be realistic, don't we? It 'may be' that in the end of all this hullabaloo, we, the God-given British, will have to do a deal with these damned dagoes from Argentina. But we shall have to negotiate from a position of strength. It may well be going too far to actually *nuke* Buenos Aires, as one of our MPs suggested, but we certainly have to teach them Argies a lesson. They are on the Falklands. Right in Port Stanley, right? So that's where we have to winkle them out of, right? And if we have to blast Port Stanley, and the rest of the island out of the sea — so be it. Right must prevail, right? In this respect we must pay tribute to Michael Foot of the Labour Party. In the emergency debate in the House of Commons on Saturday 3rd April nobody provided a more patriotic, jingoistic and imperialist speech than Michael. He may be against nuclear weapons, but by God he really puts his faith in conventional forces. And he knows what's right!

Too bad about those Islanders, though. But then, we must admit, they wouldn't be much use when it comes to exploiting the oil between the Islands and the mainland — the area people who know are calling The New Kuwait — would they? It's the oilmen we want, the chaps who have made Aberdeen the Dallas of the North, not a lot of bloody sheep farmers.

So no doubt we can do a deal. When it comes to it, who really gives a damn about sovereignty? It's the material wealth that matters. Let the Islanders come back to Britain, they are white, after all — though under Mrs Thatcher's Nationality Bill, they will be third class citizens because most of them were not born in this country. But then, we repeat, they *are* white, and that's what really matters. Kith 'n' kin, innit?

Fifty million quid, this has cost us — before a shot has been fired. But it's all for a principle. It doesn't matter that the people of the Falkland Islands never *owned* the Falklands themselves, any more than the people of Argentina have sovereignty over all those vast lands, or the British people own Britain. All these were occupied centuries ago — by the same means that the British occupied those islands.

It so happens at the moment that Argentina is ruled by a particularly vicious 'tin-pot fascist junta' wanting to distract its citizens from its economic problems — and the Falklands are about to be defended by the rump of a nineteenth century imperialist Tory regime, wanting to distract its citizens from its economic problems and using willing recruits to do its dirty work for it. So what's new? We defend one 'sovereignty' against another? It's very convenient for the British that the present regime in Argentina is a particularly nasty fascist regime — but has that stopped Thatcher's Government from trading with it? Or selling arms to it? Or lending it money? No, it hasn't.

One of the ironies of the present situation is that the Argentine Navy has been equipped with British hardware. If it comes to a shooting match, the British Navy knows exactly what to expect — for it is its own (out-dated) equipment that will be used against it. Another irony is that, for all the deterrence that Britain has with its vast nuclear arsenal — all pointing Eastwards — it has been upstaged by a third-class power from the West, taking it by surprise.

We might feel sorry for the islanders, and for the marines, soldiers, sailors and airmen who could be killed in this exercise if it came to a shooting match. But nobody forced the servicemen to join the Forces. If they fell for the crap about a good life with the professionals; if they thought it was all glamour to learn how to kill their fellow men and women — and children — for the myths of nationality, patriotism and sovereignty, they have nobody but themselves to blame. The islanders have done well and have been cossetted by the myths of British sovereignty — now they are being presented with the bill.

As anarchists we have to say that the sovereignty that matters is *individual* sovereignty. We all live in occupied countries. This country of Britain has been occupied by a ruling class for centuries. We live on its terms; we are forced to obey its rules — which are laid down without consultation with us — we are governed by force, but we don't *have* to fight for it.

The nationality of our rulers does not matter. It is the fact that *we are ruled* that matters.

17th April 1982   P.S.

From Farce to Tragedy

Libertarian voices have scarcely been heard about the Falklands during the seven weeks since the crisis began, though there has been more need for them than ever before during the three weeks since our last issue appeared and since the crisis turned into a war.

Not that it has been much of a war yet, at least as we go to press. A few minor ships and aircraft on each side, an Argentine cruiser and a British destroyer, a few hundred Argentine and a few dozen British deaths — this hardly counts on the current scale, when elsewhere in South America and in Central America, Africa, the Middle East and South-East Asia, thousands and even millions of people can be killed without getting into the newspapers, let alone on to the television screen.

But a small war can all too easily and quickly grow into a big war, as has happened over and over again, most notably in 1914 and 1939. And this small War happens to involve this country, which is fighting for the first time since the Suez War of 1956 against an enemy outside the old British Empire and for the first time since the Korean War of the early 1950s against an enemy willing and able to fight back.

A lot of nonsense has been said during the crisis about Argentina. It is not a Fascist dictatorship, with a single autocrat ruling through a mass Party. It is a military dictatorship, with a president and a junta (committee) ruling through the three armed services. It may be a bankrupt country, but it is self-sufficient in food and well-armed. Anyway, countries don't stop fighting because they are poor or badly ruled, and no one should imagine that the British only have to huff and puff for Argentina to be blown down.

Nor should anyone imagine that such a dictatorship, however appalling its atrocities against its own people, will find it difficult to unite them behind it now. Patriotism is the first refuge of both rulers and ruled in trouble, and the War seems to be even more popular in Argentina than it is in Britain, which is saying something.

Support for the War may fall in either country when one or both sides begin to suffer serious casualties, but we must assume that we are once more in an all too familiar position, of being a minority within a minority — a tiny libertarian movement inside a small anti-war movement which includes careerist politicians and casuistic Marxists in an uneasy coalition.

The Falklands War is not about two thousand inhabitants of the Falkland Islands, or about the sovereignty over the two tiny islands, or about the principle of preventing aggression. British Governments since the Second World War have abandoned millions of people who wanted to remain British subjects (and prevented them entering 'their' country), have abandoned scores of territories which used to belong to the British Empire, and have condoned dozens of acts of aggression (Vietnam, Cambodia, Cyprus, Czechoslovakia, Hungary, Eritrea, Lebanon and so on round the world).

The Falklands War, like the beginning of the two World Wars, is about two groups of powerful but confused countries, both in economic difficulties and with imperialist ambitions, both deeply divided but strongly nationalist, one dictatorial and the other more or less democratic, which have come to blows over a minor quarrel of many years' standing, and which may drag not just their subjects and allies but everyone else into a struggle which began as a farce but is becoming a tragedy.

This is what States do, when they are no longer satisfied with suppressing their own subjects. The vast proportion of national budgets spent on 'defence' must eventually be paid for. (It is ironical that one of the greatest producers of modern weapons in the world is now fighting one of its best customers.) This is what most of the members of the United Nations do most of the time, though their organisation is now being asked to mediate. This is what has been done above all by the United States and the Soviet Union. (It is ironical that the former, only a few years out of Vietnam, was the first mediator, and that the latter, less than only a few months after sponsoring a military dictatorship in Poland, is on the verge of supporting another in Argentina.)

There is no point in arguing in favour of sending the British Armada to the South Atlantic, and then against using it, as the Labour leadership does. There is no point in arguing for an Argentine victory over Britain, as the Marxist sects do. There is no point in arguing for a British victory over Argentina, as most of our fellow-countrymen (though fewer of our fellow-countrywomen) do. There is no point in arguing for any kind of so-called 'just war', as most of the Christian denominations do.

There is no point in arguing for anything except the total libertarian message. Not just that both British and Argentine forces should get out of the Falkland Islands, but that they should get out of all islands and all oceans and all countries, including their own. The

Argentine forces have been fighting a war against their own population since they seized power six years ago. The British forces have been fighting wars against colonial populations all over the world ever since they began to seize the British Empire three centuries ago, and this fighting has been continued by Labour Governments as much as by Conservative Governments. War, as Randolph Bourne said at the end of the First World War, is the health of the State.

This is an unpopular message at this particular moment. But it must still be voiced, and it may even be heard when all the bills start coming in, when more British and Argentine bodies are taken home, when the taxes are raised to pay the hundreds of millions of pounds the War is costing, when the truth comes out about how our rulers blundered into the crisis and how they have behaved during it. The Suez War became one of the main factors in the revival of the libertarian Left twenty-five years ago. The Falklands War may do the same, but it will need a lot of hard work.

22nd May 1982

Wrapping It Up for God

God has been no more successful than man in settling the Falklands War. The priests have been as divided as the politicians, but like them have generally followed their own Governments.

Nearly half the Roman Catholics in the world live in Latin America, and the Catholic Church in Argentina — backed by those in the rest of Central and South America — has strongly supported not only the Argentine claim to, but the Argentine invasion of, the Falkland Islands. No doubt the same is true of the Catholics in Spain and Italy, which share the ancestors of the population of Argentina.

Meanwhile nearly all the Churches in Britain have supported the British Government in resisting the Argentine claim in deeds as well as in words. The Church of England has been predictably earning its position as the Established Church by defending the Christian doctrine of the Just War. This is designed in theory to justify only wars that are necessary, reasonable and moderate, but has been employed in practice to justify every war Christians have ever fought, including those fought between Christians. The

Archbishop of Canterbury, Dr Runcie, who himself won a Military Cross during the Second World War, has gone so far as to say that it would have been wrong to turn the other cheek in the Falklands, contradicting an explicit teaching of Jesus in the Gospels.

Even the Catholic Archbishop of Westminster, Cardinal Hume, has given his cautious support to the war. This endangers relations with Latin American and Continental European Catholics, which may not matter much, but also endangers relations with Rome, which matters a lot. God, working as usual in a mysterious way, arranged the Falklands War to coincide with the Pope's visit to Britain at the end of May. This is the first such visit by a reigning Pope, and it has already cost several million pounds to prepare. Could he visit a country which is at war with a Catholic country?

The Pope said that he might not come if there were serious fighting, but (probably will, finally did) come because of all the effort and money already invested in the visit. Before doing so he summoned Cardinals to Rome from both Argentina and Britain, and after doing so he may feel it necessary to visit Argentina too — and then presumably Chile as well, since it is also on the verge of war with Argentina. This could run and run.

Meanwhile the Pope arranged a mass with British and Argentine Cardinals, and appealed to the President of Argentina and the Prime Minister of Britain to stop the War. God, working in an even more mysterious way, promptly arranged the British counter-invasion of the Falklands Islands. Perhaps the real reason the Pope will have to come to Britain is that the extreme anti-Catholic Protestants have been praying that he won't do so, and that he can't let God take more notice of their prayers than his.

The Pope is making a 'pastoral' visit — that is, he is coming not as the head of a State or a Government but as the head of a (indeed, the) Church to feed his Catholic flock in Britain, much as he did in the United States three years ago. (Incidentally, it is odd that Jesus and his various human representatives should describe themselves as shepherds; of course shepherds care for their sheep, but only in order to fleece and eat them more efficiently afterwards). So he will be not just showing himself to the public and the media, and leading some religious services, but also delivering some messages. What (can, did) he say?

Pope John Paul II is the first Polish Pope, and the first non-Italian Pope for four centuries. He has been treated as a charismatic figure on his various visits to various parts of the world, but these have nearly all been to Catholic countries. The exception was the

United States, which has a strong political and social tradition of anti-Catholicism. There he insisted on maintaining the conventional hard line on the priesthood (no priests allowed to leave their orders, no married priests, no women priests, no nuns and monks in ordinary clothes) and on personal morality (no fornication or adultery, no contraception or abortion, no divorce, no homosexuality, no euthanasia or suicide). There was little overt opposition to his visit, but his message was covertly ignored.

In Britain his position is more delicate. In the sixteenth century Catholicism was repudiated, after more than a thousand years. The Catholic Church was virtually outlawed for three centuries, and is still thought to be somehow un-British — half Italian and half Irish. The Pope excommunicated and deposed Queen Elizabeth I in 1570, and that sentence has never been repealed. The United States did have a Catholic President in the end, but it is illegal for Britain to have a Catholic Monarch and it is unlikely to have a Catholic Prime Minister for a long time. Again, there is little overt opposition to his visit, except from some extreme Protestants and militant secularists (especially the National Secular Society and the Gay Humanists), but his message will be equally ignored. A call for peace in the Falklands will carry no more weight here than in Rome, and will only embarrass British Catholics.

So God has really made rather a mess of things this spring, and made himself look even sillier than he already did. No wonder more than half the population of Britain now never attends any religious ceremony at all. Yet some religious organisations have taken an unequivocal position against the war. The Society of Friends (Quakers) immediately repeated its traditional pacifist line. The United Reformed Church (a coalition of the old Puritan denominations of Presbyterians and Congregationalists) and the Methodist Church have condemned the fighting not so much on pacifist as on practical grounds. Even so, one can't help being reminded of the poem of the First World War:

> God heard the embattled nations sing and shout
> 'Gott strafe England!' and 'God save the King!'
> God this, God that, and God the other thing —
> 'Good God', said God, 'I've got my work cut out'.

29th May 1982   M.H.

Oh What a Lovely Conventional War

Without for one moment forgetting that the introduction of nuclear power into warfare (by the democratic Allies, at the end of World War Two) effectively introduced a new dimension in genocide, it seems to be time to bring to the attention of those who protest only against nuclear weapons that there has been just a little bit of progress in the destructive capacity of weapons which are referred to as 'conventional'.

The most deadly ones seem to be British made and already sold to the Argentinian State — and very sophisticated weapons they are too. As befits a country which prides itself on the quality of the goods we offer the world in our export drives (for a century we have lived with the phrase 'Export or Die'), such as Rolls Royce cars and the beautifully tailored products of Savile Row, we are now one of the world's leaders in the export of the most highly developed technology for burning people alive.

It so happens that at the present time, practically the only thriving industry in this country is the arms industry. It is certainly the only one which the Government is prepared to support against the recession. In any other industry, if a factory is not economically solvent — if it's a 'lame duck' — then let it sink or swim. The building industry is in the doldrums, the clothing industry facing disaster and farming, thanks to EEC price rigging, facing yet another bitter struggle. In other words, food, clothing and shelter — the three fundamentals for existence — are facing bankruptcies, but shipbuilding yards that make warships, and ordnance factories that make missiles, and the electronics industry which provides the sophisticated hardware are being given Government contracts for products that, up until last month, nobody thought would ever be needed.

The needs of our streamlined forces — the Professionals that stand between us and the Red Menace — are provided in part out of the enormous profits made from the sales of our sophisticated body-burning machinery to other States. When the decision was taken (in view of our reduced imperial role!) to stop production of large aircraft carriers, rather than let the shipyards fall idle production was switched to destroyers for the Home Fleet.

There was no great urgency, new technology was coming along all the time, and the real concern was to keep the shipyards open, so wages were going up all the time too. The first of the new

destroyer class — Type 42 — was HMS Sheffield, and you all know
where she is now. The cost of the Sheffield was nearly 60 per cent
more than the original estimate; the cost of the second new ship
(a Type 21 frigate, HMS Amazon) was more than twice the original
price — but it looked like coming right in the end because the
order for the next Type 42 destroyer to come off the line came in
from Argentina. Unfortunately, this had not been completely paid
for when the unpleasantness broke out, and some London banks
are still owed about £6 million on the money they lent the tinpot
fascist junta to buy that splendid British ship.

As far as Vickers, Vosper Thorneycroft, Yarrow, or Swan Hunter
are concerned, this hardware is for selling, and it's for selling to
anybody. Anybody in the market, that is. The main arms producing
countries in the world at the moment are the USA, the USSR,
Britain and France, more or less in that order, with countries like
Israel (a billion dollars a year in 1977!) and Germany (eh?) coming
along nicely, too. The four main dealers in death pretend, irrespective of political alignments, to respect each other's markets, but
in fact cut each other's throats wherever possible. Hence, when
the USA, in an outburst of morality, put an embargo on selling
arms to Latin America — where every military dictatorship wanted
the very best for killing its own people and whatever territorial
squabble it would get involved in — it opened the door for Britain
and France. In fact the Type 42 destroyer sold to Argentina was
followed by a second — manufactured there under licence with
parts supplied from the UK.

The USA policy was reversed by President Nixon in 1973 when
he yielded to pressure from the US arms manufacturers and allowed
Tiger fighters to be sold to Argentina, Brazil, Chile, Colombia
and Peru.

President Carter brought back some morality and put embargos
on those sales — enabling the Soviet Union to get some of the
trade — and also a ban on sales to South Africa, half-heartedly
supported by 'our' Labour Government.

President Reagan, a monetarist and free-enterprise champion
like Margaret Thatcher, has lifted the ban — which of course never
existed as far as Maggie was concerned, for Britain, it seems, will
sell arms to anybody, the excuse being — as it is for all traders —
that the export orders finance Britain's own 'needs'.

Perhaps the most shadowy figure in this shabby trade is the
Soviet Union. With the whole Warsaw Pact empire to supply (of
which Czechoslovakia, for one, is itself a massive arms producer),

and to keep updated, with its totalitarian control of its own economy and its paranoid fear of any of its precious secrets slipping out, it may seem that Russia would not be too pushy in the arms trade. But there is so much more to it than that.

Arms can bring influence, or they can quite simply be a cynical bargaining point — or they can buy commodities desperately needed by the manufacturing State. The astonishing thing about the Russian economy is that it is short of food — but it is not so long ago that the Ukraine was referred to as 'the breadbasket of Europe'.

It seems quite obvious that the Ukrainian peasants have never forgiven the Kremlin either for Stalin's war against them in the 1930s or Kruschev's vengeful purges after the war, and they have never accepted the enforced centralised collectivism laid upon them by the Bolsheviks. (Compare the totally different attitude of the Spanish peasants, who freely collectivised the land in 1936 under their own free communal control and rapidly increased production over the three years their revolution lasted).

Whatever the reason, however, the fact is that every year Russia has to go shopping for wheat all around the world — which effectively means the wheat-rich lands of the Americas, where their purchases push up the price for poorer countries. After the Soviet intervention in Afghanistan, the USA embargoed sales of wheat and the USSR went south to Argentina, where they found the right-wing junta quite ready to sell wheat — but at an inflated price, and not willing to barter goods other than arms.

Back in the good ole USA, the farmers are lobbying Reagan to let them sell their massive surpluses of wheat to Russia, and for their part the Russians would rather keep in with the wealthy USA than get tangled with the sweaty politics of Latin America — all of which explains why the USSR has played it so cool during the last few weeks. You would have thought, wouldn't you, that they would have snatched the chance to get in with Argentina as soon as America came out in open support of Britain? But the uneasy old men in the Kremlin have always played a waiting game — besides which there's all those billions of dollars in loans to Poland to think about, as well as all the other Comecon trade . . . Nevertheless, the Russians must have food, and if it really has to come down to Mig fighters for wheat, that's what it will be.

29th May 1982

The First Casualty

It does not take much to get the Tories to show just how skin deep is their devotion to freedom as a concept rather than as an excuse for them to take liberties.

Owing to some strange technicalities involved in getting news from the South Atlantic back to Britain — through the use of satellites which serve both the television channels and the radio and newspapers — there have been at times as much exposure of Argentinian points of view and airing of their claims, as there has been for the British side.

This reached its peak in a Panorama programme on the BBC on May 17th, which was so 'objective' that the entire Right Wing of the Conservative Party very nearly burst into flames. The presenter nowadays for Panorama is Robert Key, who is probably already on the Tories' death list for an historic series (that is, the theme was historic, not the series) last year on Ireland.

Anyway, from the Prime Minister and Home Secretary down through the wilder of the back benchers the howl went up of 'treachery', 'odious subversive travesties', 'irresponsible' and so on, from those who are staunchly against state interference or governmental control of anything . . . that might get in their own way.

The fact that the BBC prides itself upon being independent of government control — and is admired throughout the world for what is held to be objective and truthful reporting — means nothing when the Government wants its own point of view presented as the one and only truth and nothing else. The very idea that the Argentinians might have any arguments on their side is not to be considered. The fact that the Government in Buenos Aires strictly controls the output from the media there can be used as an example of how they are totalitarian — but freedom of expression here is not to be used except in the British Government's service.

This sudden concern for the output of the BBC would carry a little more weight, perhaps, if we forgot the heavy cuts the BBC has had to make recently in its overseas broadcasting as a result of government economies — thereby preventing many people in totalitarian countries from ever hearing any other point of view than that of their masters.

Mrs Thatcher is now such a Little Englander that she can have no real arguments about such divisions in the world as the Berlin

Wall, the Iron Curtain, closed frontiers and closed minds everywhere. The Stalin mentality is alive and well and living in Downing Street!

12th June 1982   P.S.

Who's Counting?

'We have made no estimates of cost' — John Nott, Minister of Defence, April 1982.

No self-respecting pukka sahib in Poona, settling into the creaking wicker and downing his chota peg before tiffin, would dream of letting a day pass without observing, 'Gad, life is cheap out here.' Since we are back in the glorious days of gunboat diplomacy, therefore, we shall not dwell on the cost in human life of the new Battle of the Falklands, since when States clash, life has to be cheap.[1] Besides which, by the time these words have appeared before your very eyes, the figures available as we write would be out of date.

Out of date, as well, will be any figures that could be calculated on the financial costs of this incredible exercise on economies which, as we all know, have been reeling from recession, inflation, unemployment, dying and bankrupt industries and, above all, monetarism.

Monetarism, inasmuch as any of us understand it at all, seems to mean that every enterprise must pay its way in terms of profit-making. Anything which does not make a money profit — like a Health Service, for example — is a failure in monetarist terms. Except of course, the institutions of the State: the Armed Services, the police and law enforcement agencies — prisons, Civil Services, etc. Even here, at the lower level, economies must be made — but, in order to retain personnel of the proper 'quality' to run the State's affairs efficiently, inflated salaries can be paid without thoughts of 'profit' in monetarist terms. Thus the recent increases

---

1. 'I am proud to have a son who died doing the job he loved for the country he loved' — Mr Harry Taylor, father of Lt Nicholas Taylor, shot down over the Falklands.

in judges' pay — up to £52,000 per annum for the Lord Chief Justice, and comparable pay for judges in general.

All that at a time when the already underpaid nurses of the National Health Service — which is not used by top people anyway — are being forced into reluctant militancy against a pay offer of about half the running rate of inflation.

So, the State looks after its own, and the taxpayer pays. When the task force was first being assembled to go down and give Galtieri a bloody nose, the financial cost was announced as being in the region of £50 million. This figure is now clearly laughable — if you feel like laughing. By the middle of May the Ministry of Defence was admitting that 'Frankly, we have nobody with time to spare to work on . . .' the question of cost. But, without even taking into account the cost of losses in ships and aircraft (a type-22 frigate cost £120 million in 1980; Harriers cost £6 million each; the two Tigerfish torpedoes that sank the General Belgrano cost £300,000 each) and our high-tech missiles, or helicopters that seem to have a habit of ditching themselves . . . without any of this throwaway cost in combat, the expenses that have been amassed simply in the creation of the task force are astronomical.

While the use of the naval ships and their crews would have been going on as usual, the sudden charge over 8000 miles has meant the burning of enormous amounts of fuel — to supply which the Government has bought the services of 11 civilian tankers, with an average of 25,000 tons of fuel oil — which the State buys duty free at about 65p a gallon. Work it out for yourself, if you know the consumption of those 75 ships in the original task force (since added to) all sailing flat out over those 8000 miles.

Nor are the sailors on this patriotic mission doing all this for nothing. The Royal Naval personnel immediately get a pay boost for going on active duty — and the civilian crews of the commandeered supply vessels have settled their fears by accepting a 150 per cent bonus for sailing south of Ascension Island. This means that men paid normally £200 a week are on £500 as soon as they are in the South Atlantic. Which can be a comfort to their widows, of course, though we are not told how many seamen in the Merchant Service are on £200 a week normally.

More ships are being commandeered by our freedom-loving Government every week (those who booked cruises on the Canberra or the QE2 have just got to put up with their disappointment) but at the time of writing the count is around 40 ships ranging from those giant luxury liners (which have had helicopter decks rapidly built on them and have had their comfy carpets covered with hardboard and their wall decorations removed) down to tugs and trawlers. Chartering costs alone are running at over £3 million a day, and on top of that there are special insurance and indemnity charges that the taxpayer will have to face.

And all this is to say nothing of the costs of losses of these requisitioned ships. As we write only (only!) the Atlantic Conveyor, a large container cargo ship has, among the larger supply vessels, gone down — with aircraft and ammunition and spares aboard, but not much loss of life. The Canberra and the QE2 are still sailing south, the latter with 3000 troops aboard . . .

Before the loss of the Sheffield, the Antelope, the Coventry and the Atlantic Conveyor, the costs, according to assessors in the City of London and the Ministry of Defence, were already rising in excess of £1000 million. We may be sure there is more yet to come. And if Britain 'wins' and thrusts the Argentinians off the Falklands, what then? It seems to be assumed by the British Government that then the junta in Buenos Aires will have to come to terms and a 'diplomatic agreement' will be finally agreed. But why should it? Why should not the Argentinians just sit back and let the British taxpayer go on, and on, and on, paying for Thatcher's pride and confidence and determination?

If Galtieri refuses to come to terms, the British will be forced to do what they have admitted they could not afford to do: maintain a sufficiently strong armed force on the Falklands to deter another Argentine invasion — all supplied from 8000 miles away — and pinned down forever, facing sporadic aerial harassment.

The only way of breaking the deadlock then would be to attack mainland Argentina — which would immediately force the rest of South America into support for Galtieri, which might bring the USA into more open, direct, support for Britain and then bring the USSR into more open support for the Argentinians.

And then . . .?

Then we might see the true cost of Margaret Thatcher's over-reaction, but nobody would ever be able to assess the price of saving her face.

12th June 1982   JUSTIN

Capitalist Patriotism

'But Not At Our Expense' - Lord Matthews

This year's season of Whitehall farces continues to milk the Falkland tragi-comedy for all it's worth.

Ever since the cad leapt out of the closet to snatch Britannia's treasure, catching, in true farcical fashion, the Foreign Office with its trousers down, the drama has been wound up for the gaping audience and the bathos laid on with a trowel as it turned out that the spear-carrying extras also carried the can.

The stars, however, have not done too badly, as is to be expected. Margaret Thatcher's own star shone brighter than ever, to such an extent that everybody expected her to call an Autumn election. She has, so it is said, decided not to — for which she undoubtedly deserves ten out of ten for not being an opportunist. And that should be worth a few votes on its own.

For the country's other leading patriots too, the pride and the passion has paid handsomely. Of the daily newspapers which supported Thatcher to hysterical proportions, none was more vociferous (with the possible exception of the execrable *Sun*) than the *Daily Express*, which always speaks for the poor dumb British people, unable to speak for themselves.

Such is the concentration of capital today that a newspaper baron is not content to be simply that   which for most of us would be quite enough. No, it so happens that Lord Matthews, who now owns the *Daily Express*, etc., also owns (or his company does) the Cunard shipping line, which sprang into its national service with eyes gleaming at the opportunity to serve the country by getting some of its laid-up ships out of mothballs and into the gravy.

The best thing that could happen to one of Cunard's ships — the Atlantic Conveyor — did in fact happen. It was sunk.

It was of course insured. It was due to get compensation from the 'Intervention Fund'. The Ministry of Defence was willing to contribute to the building of a replacement vessel — and the Department of Industry was ready with a substantial sum from the home shipbuilding credit scheme, if the new ship were to be built in Britain.

Ay, there's the rub. Having a ship built in Britain costs many millions more than getting it built in, say, Korea. So the highly patriotic Lord Matthews, whose publications screamed blue murder against the Argies (unfortunately not selling all that many extra papers every day in spite of that . . .) was not prepared to put his hand in his capacious pocket (wearing his Cunard hat) to give jobs to British shipbuilders.

It was then he uttered his immortal words: 'I am as anxious as anyone that it should be built in Britain, but not at our expense'.

Government support with public money

Then another factor entered the arena. In spite of Mrs Thatcher's appeal to the noble Lord to put patriotism before profit (ha, ha!), it was the dockers and portworkers who came out and said they would black ALL Cunard ships, including the gallant and heroic QE2, if Matthews insisted on buying Korean.

Fortunately it will not come to that. Our monetarist Government, with its hard face set firmly, as though in cold porridge, against spending public money — especially for something as unprofitable as a National Health Service — decided that, after all, in this special case, it can reach into the coffers and give Lord Matthews' company something between 10 and 15 million pounds (of *our* money!) so that he could do the decent thing and get his bloody boat built in Britain.

It would of course not be a simple replacement of the old one that was destroyed. It would be a modern, labour-saving ship and, more important, it would be of such design that it could be very rapidly converted for military use in the event of another crisis like the Falklands suddenly blowing up (no pun intended).

Meanwhile, among the lower orders, patriotism is not paying off quite so well. Merchant seamen coming back home and getting rather less than a hero's welcome, are finding that being British was a prime qualification for going to the South Atlantic battle ground — but back home it means that their rates of pay are far too high, in view of the fact that their work can be done by cheaper Asian workers. Nor will there be much help from the National Union of Seamen, since the Union gets a handout from the employers for every cheap Asian employed on a ship carrying the British flag (but not on those flying flags of convenience).

And on top of that the Government has now reneged on its promise of a big bonus for seamen going south of Ascension Island into a 'military' zone. Many are still there — but not on bonus pay.

Governments have to consist of liars, and as for patriotism? The FIRST refuge of scoundrels!

21st August 1982   P.S.

In the Back Yard

Without in any way wishing to be accused of petty spite, we have to admit to a feeling of great pleasure in being able to write in successive issues of matters that have caused our dear Prime Minister acute embarrassment.

Our Iron Lady's image is looking distinctly rusty, not to say dented, by the cavalier manner in which her favourite American President contemptuously ignored her very existence as he ordered the invasion of a British Commonwealth Caribbean island. Not that Mrs T can complain — she's pretty good at ignoring other people's existence as well, which was why the Falklands crisis was able to reach battle stations before she woke up to what was happening.

Not that even a genius like Margaret Thatcher can be expected to know *everything* that's going on in every far-flung corner of the globe — but are we not paying huge armies of diplomats, bureaucrats and other kinds of rats to keep their eyes on what those foreigners are doing everywhere? And isn't it their job to go running to her with every bit of information, every suspicion, and every suggestion from our own dirty tricks department?

Of, of course, we forgot, we don't have a dirty tricks department, do we? But there's one hell of a stench blowing eastwards at this moment from the beautiful island of Grenada which is raising not just Maggie's hackles, but a whole lot of other issues as well.

For 27 years Sir Eric Gairy ruled the island, and after 'independence' set up what would have been called a tin-pot dictatorship in a banana republic but for the fact that he had no imperialist ambitions that drew him into conflict with Britain and no left-wing leanings that could possibly panic America. In fact he was quite content to be a big fish in a little pond, using Grenada's Treasury as his own personal pocket-book, fiddling elections to maintain the facade of democracy, and ruthlessly crushing any potential rivals or popular unrest. The economy was moribund, international trade consisting practically entirely of the same products that had made the island a much-fought-for prize over the centuries: spices.

Apart from that, Grenada's only natural resources were — its nature. Geographically beautiful, with a wonderful coastline, the sparkling clear blue Caribbean lapping gently at silver beaches under the tropic sun and a desperately poor labour force. In fact ideal for tourism. But Gairy knew that this would mean sharing his power with lots of others — and you know how dictators are.

Well, in March 1979, he made the mistake many have made before — he took a trip abroad, creating an opportunity for Maurice Bishop and his 'People's Revolutionary Army' (spearhead of the 'New Jewel Movement') to stage a coup and take over.

Bishop was a self-styled Marxist (though of which tendency is not clear) and he quickly drew support with his announced intentions of revitalising the economy — primarily through tourism, for which he had to seek loans from richer countries.

Because 'our' Queen is still nominal head of the Commonwealth Bishop first approached Britain for finance to build an airport for holiday planes and hotels to house their passengers. A dazed Foreign and Commonwealth Office and Jim Callaghan with troubles of his own turned it all down. So Bishop went cap-in-hand to the USA, who also found plenty of excuses to say no — which meant that the suspect nature of his politics would mean interminable delays in getting any money out of the US Treasury, for the bureaucrats would have to be sure they were not financing some goddam pinko regime. Not that they put it quite like that, of course.

But Bishop was in a hurry. Such little party organisation as the PRA had contained more Generals than groundtroops and they pushed him in the only direction left — Cuba. The Americans had specifically told him *not* to go to Cuba for aid, but with the exception of Canada, nobody else offered anything.

So the door was then opened for, on the one hand, the rapid influx of Cuban construction workers (all of whom, through their national service conscription, had become skilled guerrilla fighters) and on the other, an angry USA, who saw Communist influence extending right in their own backyard. 'Get Bishop' was undoubtedly an order from the CIA.

After the spectacular failure of the 'Bay of Pigs' invasion, however, the American government has tried to play a rather more subtle game. Grenada, after all, is (still!) a British Commonwealth country, and the then President of America, Jimmy Carter, was not quite as trigger-happy as our present B-movie star. A waiting game followed.

Unease at the increasing Cuban presence and the supposed 'Marxism' of Bishop made many wealthy inhabitants sell up their idyllic holiday and retirement homes on Grenada and move out. The 'destabilisation' technique was working, and a 1979 population of 120,000 has now fallen to just over 100,000 — and it's the richer, employing class who have gone. The new airport is not yet built, nor are the hotels, and the tourist trade coming in on cruise ships is not nearly big enough to steady the economy.

So Bishop himself was the victim of another coup. The emerging military class (which barely existed in 1979) felt strong enough to have a go. Under the leadership of Bernard Coard and 'General' Hudson Austin, Bishop and his Government were seized, rescued by a civilian crowd, recaptured and shot. Almost within hours the US Navy was on its way to take over and restore law and order and democracy — something they had never bothered about when Gairy was running his corrupt and ruthless regime.

Coard and Austin are, as we write, still alive, but in detention. It will be extremely interesting to see what happens to them — for quite clearly it was Bishop himself that the Americans wanted out of the way.

Maurice Bishop, however, was extremely popular in Grenada. He led a more egalitarian and less corrupt regime than the people had known and gradually — *very* gradually and in the face of many difficulties — conditions for many people were improving. The revolt against him came from members of his own Party; a more 'extremist' Marxist and a military man with the Cubans to thank for his advancement, for his arms and the trained men under him. All they hadn't given him was power.

Bishop held the power — which made him a target for both the Party rebels and the Americans. And it must be admitted that for someone who had made a coup himself, he didn't seem to be looking over his own shoulder nearly carefully enough, and he should surely have been more aware of the effect the Cuban build-up was going to have on both the USA and the surrounding Caribbean states. He seems to have trusted the Cubans and not to have realised that *they* were working for *their* own interests, not his, not Grenada's.

According to reports, military activity had been building up in Barbados — jumping-off place for Grenada — for some time, and diplomatic activity had been going on between the USA, the Association of East Caribbean States, and the Governor-General of Grenada — all without the British Government getting wind of it. Without going into all the details, the Governor-General would seem to have been collaborating with a Government not his own in the invasion of his own territory, without a word either to Whitehall or Buckingham Palace; Thatcher is seen with egg on her face by having been snubbed by the President with whom she is so proud to have a 'special relationship'; the Americans have done an 'Afghanistan', and in so doing have antagonised all the states of Latin America — and Canada and parts of Europe. Was it all worth it?

Well, as far as the USA is concerned (and to hell with everybody else), if getting the Cubans out of Grenada is worth it, then we can only say that the Coard-Austin coup could not have come at a better time if the CIA planned it themselves. Perhaps they did?
5th November 1983 JUSTIN

The State of Maggie

It's a great shame, isn't it? Instead of a popular uprising of the people dislodging the most repressive Prime Minister in living memory, it is falling to a load of backbench Tory wets to give us even a slight hope that she may be riding for a fall.

Most Tories — and not just the wets — really do think that the Party stands against centralisation, against the steady encroachment of the State into everyday life. But the only way this has been expressed by Thatcher's monetarism is to attack all nationalised and municipalised industries or services and seek to put them into private hands — i.e. the rich particularly, but also the myriads of small investors (and union pension funds!) who dabble in stocks and shares and those working people who think they are making themselves freer by buying their own council houses.

'Revolt', even in quotes, is of course far too strong a word to apply to a reluctance of a handful of Thatcher's rank and file to support positively her 'rate capping' measure. This is a trick by which high-spending Labour Councils suffer cuts in order to bring them in line with the lower-spending Local Authorities. This is crude politicking by Thatcher, for the high spenders are mostly the poorer inner-city Labour Boroughs, where more people need all sorts of support in terms of benefits — while the low spenders are those middle-class Tory areas where people are better able to look after themselves and their dependants.

The Jackals
The present action by backbenchers (including ex-Ministers like

Francis Pym and Edward Heath, who has never forgiven Maggie
for ousting him from the Party leadership) is based, we would
think, less on caring for the old and needy, than for the necessity
for the individuals concerned to take the longer term view, if they
want to get back into Parliament next time. But also, it could be
that they are beginning to sense a weakness in the Iron Maiden,
and like the jackals they are, they will move in for the kill if they
see personal advantage in it. Only starry-eyed idealists believe they
are there for the public good.

For instance, is it only coincidence that this rumbling from below
has come along just at the same time that Mrs Thatcher is ever so
slightly embarrassed by the revelation that when she was in Oman
in 1981, and was incidentally trying to get a massive contract for
building a prestigious new university (yes, a whole, modern new
concrete university in the middle of the desert!) worth £300 million,
her son Mark had surprisingly found his way to Oman also — and
was acting for the one British construction firm, Cementation,
which had tendered for the job?

Not that we would dream of accusing Maggie of nepotism, using
her position for the advantage of any member of her family, or
any such nasty imputation, but, it was just a bit indiscreet, wasn't
it? And after the Parkinson affair last year, Tories are getting a
bit jumpy about discretion.

On top of which, Maggie's greatest triumph — that reason to
rejoice down in the Falklands — is turning out to be a running
sore on the national budget . . .

28th January 1984   P.S.

America, Libya and Us

The American attack on Libya on 14th April has various kinds of
significance for America and its allies in the Western world, for
Libya and its friends and enemies in the Muslim and African worlds,
for Russia and its satellites in the Communist world, and so on,
some of which demand comment a month later.

The general significance of the confrontation between the United
States of America and the Socialist People's Libyan Arab 'Jamahiriya'

(Mass State) is to be found in the context not so much of the current dispute about 'State-sponsored terrorism' — that is, terrorism carried out not by and for States (as in the normal course of international politics) but by individuals for States (as in the course of so-called intelligence and counter-intelligence) — as of the historical rise and fall of Western imperialism.

The Libyan predicament

During the Second World War Libya was the site of a crucial campaign between the British and German armies, the victory of the former being one of the turning-points of 1942. After the War Libya was administered by Britain and France under United Nations trusteeship, and in 1951 it became the first independent State created by the United Nations. But King Idris was a Western puppet, and Libya remained part of the Western imperialist system, with military control through American and British bases and economic exploitation through American and British oil companies.

In 1969 a revolution on the Egyptian model installed the military regime of Muammar Qadhafi, combining nationalism, socialism and Islam with an appearance of popular administration and the reality of tribal and ideological oppression. The system is violently authoritarian — indeed totalitarian since the further changes of 1977 — dealing ruthlessly with dissent both at home and among exiles abroad, but it wins reluctant support because of its defiance of Western imperialism which has ruined the country for nearly two centuries, and because of its opposition to Israel which is seen as a symbol of Western imperialism.

The essential factor in this situation is oil. Libya is rich in this awkwardly distributed fossil fuel, and this is the real reason why the West continues the old exploitation — thousands of Westerners, including American and British citizens still working there — and why the regime can cause so much trouble.

The American connection

The particular significance of the recent events is to be found in the role played by Britain, as part of our special relationship with the United States. Since the Second World War, in fact, Britain has been virtually absorbed into the economic, political and military system dominated by the United States. Economically, Britain is a sort of subsidiary company of America Inc. Politically Britain is a sort of fifty-first State of the Union. Militarily, Britain is a sort of aircraft carrier for the American Air Force. The military situation, which was first established during the Second World War, was quickly re-established immediately afterwards. A secret agreement was made as early as 1946 to allow the American Air Force to use bases in Britain, which it did during the Berlin Blockade crisis in 1948, and it has stayed here ever since, American nuclear weapons being based here since 1950.

The British authorities have made occasional attempts to retain some degree of independent control of the use of the American bases — especially on such questions as what weapons may be kept in and which countries may be attacked from them — but these attempts have been repeatedly frustrated. In 1952 Truman and Churchill made an informal agreement that 'the use of these bases in an emergency would be a matter for joint decision . . . in the light of the circumstances prevailing at the time', but this agreement was never formalised or ratified by either side, and in practice it depends on the good will of the American authorities. The only technical cooperation was the 'dual-control' system used for the Thor intermediate-range ballistic missiles stationed in Britain from 1958 to 1963, and all other American military systems in Britain during the past thirty-eight years have been under exclusively American command.

Some former Prime Ministers (Conservative and Labour) have claimed that they have resisted American requests to use British bases in some former crises, but there is no reason to believe that any future Prime Minister of any Party would (or could) refuse a serious request in a genuine emergency. Meanwhile there is no evidence that British doubts had any effect on American adventures in Cuba, Vietnam, Cambodia, Chile, Lebanon, Grenada and Nicaragua. On the other hand, American opposition to the last British independent adventure — the Anglo-French attack on Egypt in 1956 — quickly halted it by the threat of economic sanctions. And American support for the last British military action — the reconquest of the Falklands from Argentina in 1982 — was essential to its success.

So Britain's unique action, as the only country allowing the United States to use its bases in and fly aircraft over its territory for the attack on Libya on 14th April, may be seen partly as a direct act of repayment of the Falkland debt four years ago and partly as a vicarious act of revenge for the shooting of a policewoman from the Libyan embassy in London two years ago, but it is above all a symbolic act of submission to American foreign policy and military strategy.

The British Position

In *Nineteen Eighty-Four*, which was completed when American bases were being installed in Britain, George Orwell described this country as Airstrip One of the Western empire of Oceania, and this has been our geopolitical position for nearly forty years. There is no point expecting any of the established Political Parties to alter this position. Churchill's Coalition Government established it,

11th February 1984

Attlee's Labour Government re-established it, Churchill's Conservative Government confirmed it, and every subsequent Government — Conservative, Labour, or Labour with Liberal support — has continued it. Thatcher's Conservative Government has merely proved what it really means; the Labour, Social Democrat and Liberal Parties, however much opposition they express, would have done the same thing in the same circumstances.

The only way to alter the position is to alter the system which got us into it — not to argue about the small print of the American alliance (getting rid of the bases but staying in NATO, or vice versa, or making any other unenforceable compromise), but to leave the alliance (and all the military and economic deals involved); not to move from one side to the other (using anti-Americanism as a front for fellow-travelling with Soviet Russia and its equal but opposite imperialism, and its attacks on Hungary, Czechoslovakia, Poland and Afghanistan), but to leave both sides (and oppose them both); not to play off Washington and Moscow against each other in an opportunistic balancing act (like most of the Third World), but to cry a plague on both their houses (and mean it); not to elect a new Government at the next election (to play the same tricks as all the previous ones), but to take control of our own fate (and let other people and peoples take control of theirs). It is time to understand the nature of imperialism (Western and Eastern, Zionist and Muslim, military and economic), and to get out of it as quickly and cleanly as we can.

June 1986   F.C.

THE LABOUR PARTY IN OPPOSITION

The Poodle with the Face of Mirabeau

It was totally unheard of and, in the relatively small minds of the UK's 600-odd MPs, perhaps never imagined. Yet, on Thursday 13th November 1980 the unheard of and unimagined occurred. Black Rod, the Queen's messenger, was barred entry to the Commons by a phalanx of Labour backbenchers protesting about the Conservative proposals to increase council house rents.

The 'Gang of Three', Labour right-wingers David Owen, Shirley Williams and William Rodgers, were ostensibly beside themselves at such an insult to the authority of the Speaker, to the honour of the Commons and to the pomp and circumstance of Black Rod himself, who was there to prorogue Parliament and lead a procession to the House of Lords.

Yet was their fury not mitigated by a certain malicious pleasure? Certainly Dr Owen and Mr Rodgers lost no time in attributing to Michael Foot complete responsibility for the outrage. This marked the opening shot in their battle to save the soul of the Labour Party as they see it by causing mass defection of Labour MPs and voters with them if Foot does not mend his ways.

In their campaign the 'Gang of Three' have behind them the full weight of the daily Press, radio and television, which had done their utmost to promote Foot's closest rival Denis Healey. On 11th November, after the result was known, *The Times* actually lost its temper and described Foot's election by 10 votes over Healey (John Silkin and Peter Shore having been eliminated in the first round) as an act of 'unmitigated folly'. Using an odd mixture of images the editorial went on to refer to Foot's past as 'Mr Jack Jones's poodle' and to his leading the Party 'in a wild charge to the left' — unless, that is, his close colleagues could restrain him. Elsewhere in this august rag, Foot was transformed from wildly charging poodle into 'pre-revolutionary', a 'Mirabeau presaging a political logic from which he would personally recoil'.

The radicalism of Michael Foot has been taken just as seriously

83

at the other end of the political spectrum. Individuals on the 'Far
Left' who had previously cursed both houses, are becoming Labour
Party members or thinking seriously of voting for it at least. Those
who remember Foot in the vanguard of the CND marches of the
late 50s and early 60s are becoming members of the Campaign for
Nuclear Disarmament, whose ranks have swelled considerably over
the last few weeks. For at least some of these people Foot is indeed
a second Mirabeau, who will pit the full force of his romanticism,
idealism and oratory against the *ancien regime* and Margaret
Thatcher's Marie-Antoinette.

For an anarchist, however, who is leader is immaterial: what
matters is the fact that the Labour Party is, and will remain —
however the voting arrangements may change in the future —
fundamentally authoritarian and statist both in structure and in
conception. This is simply because no alternative exists for a Party
of Government committed to the pursuit of 'socialism' through use
and extension of State power, inevitably subject to the conservatism
of the unions on which it depends and to the power struggle of
ambitious professionals, as well as integrally a part of that elective
dictatorship that is euphemistically known as parliamentary
democracy.[1]

'In the past ten years' observed *The Times* of Michael Foot's
record since entering the shadow cabinet and then the Government,
'the balance of his thought, while maintaining his views, has shifted
from the pursuit of the ideal to the achievement of the practicable'.
This is but a gentle way of saying that all power corrupts, that Foot
has proved no exception to the rule, and that it is the machine
that must perforce change the man and not vice versa.

Several concrete examples spring to mind. Where, for instance,
was the libertarian when he refused to accept the principle of (non-
religious) conscientious objection to union membership? Where
was the Tribunite when, during his time as Secretary of State for
Employment, unemployment passed the one million mark? Where
was the anti-militarist when, though not actually a member of the
1964 Wilson Government with its pro-Vietnam War policy, he
nonetheless sustained it? Where was the eulogist of Hazlitt, Godwin
and Swift when in 1974 he took Government office, under Wilson,
for the first time? And where will the unilateral disarmer be if he
grows up to be Prime Minister while at the same time leader of a

1. For further discussion of these themes, see *The Impossibilities of Social
    Democracy*, by Vernon Richards (Freedom Press, 1978).

Party which, to survive, *must* continue to reconcile the Left and Right Wings?

One is brought, however regretfully, to the conclusion that the new Leader of the Opposition, that charging poodle with the face of Mirabeau, suffers from a case of profound schizophrenia. This can perhaps be seen most strikingly in Michael Foot's attitude to anarchism, of which I give three examples below. In his introduction to *Gulliver's Travels*, (Penguin, 1967), Foot describes it as sounding 'the trumpet of anarchistic revolt when others who did so were being dispatched to Botany Bay . . . ' In the same piece he refers to 'William Godwin, the mentor of Shelley, of Hazlitt himself, and of the long, honourable theme of English anarchism.' And most recently, in a *Sunday Times* article on Bertrand Russell and Bonar Thompson called 'The Philosopher and the Anarchist', he describes Thompson as 'of course an anarchist, although even this *most honourable title* (my emphasis) gives too feeble an indication of his comprehensive iconoclasm'.

How else can one explain such strange utterances than by schizophrenia or by an extreme form of self-delusion which all politicians who profess ideals must possess in some degree? But whatever the cause, with Foot's election anarchists must work harder than ever to show people that the affliction need not spread any further than the smoking room of the House of Commons.
22nd November 1980   GAIA

If You Care . . .

At an Extraordinary General Meeting of the Labour Party at Wembley (more often the scene of important national events like the football Cup Final, or visits from the Harlem Globe Trotters) last Saturday, a new method of electing the Leader of the Party was established. This meant the setting up of an 'Electoral College' rather like that which elects a Pope, although it is not yet clear whether smoke will emerge from anybody's nostrils or chimneys to indicate that a decision has been reached.

There are three main, recognised, parts of the Labour Party,

viz: the 'Constituency Parties' — which are the local branches of
the Party throughout the country; the Parliamentary Party — the
number of Labour Members of Parliament in the House of Commons
at any one time; and the trade unions, which originally founded
the Labour Party in 1906 to represent the workers in Parliament
(oh do stop laughing!) which remain the main source of money for
the Party and which to this day still have the privilege of nominating
candidates for election, who almost certainly go through on the
nod, both for nomination and in an election — for which they are
usually candidates in industrial areas offering safe Labour seats.

It is thus assumed that all members of trade unions are members
of the Labour Party and so at Party Conferences union delegates
are allowed to vote by the block vote system, whereby they simply
raise their union card and something like 1,284,976 votes may be
recorded. You may think this gives the unions immense power,
but since they are themselves as divided as any other family, their
immense block votes often cancel each other out.

Party Conferences have the task of drafting the Party Programme
for the following year and, together with the unions, as aforesaid,
this is where the Constituency Parties come in. They pass motions,
discuss, accept or reject amendments, go in for horse-dealing, and
vote according to the number of members in their branches. Potential candidates will certainly vote along with their Constituency
Parties — but actual Members of Parliament are not so likely to
do so because:
The Parliamentary Party is a law unto itself. Once a Member is in
the House he becomes a Representative. That is, he *represents* the
constituency in the House. *All* the constituency, including those
who voted against him in the election which put him there. He
does not therefore always follow the party line.

Further, this numerically small section of the Party has the power
to elect the Party Leader.

The Party Leader also has the power to elect his own Cabinet.
There are therefore many nice jobs to be handed out — Ministers
for This and Chancellors for That — in the course of which many
profitable contacts are made and many jolly good sensible, practical
and pragmatic ideas can be absorbed. Not only, therefore, is a job
in the Cabinet valuable in itself in terms of salary, expenses,
privilege and power, but it opens doors to a safe future in the event
of *not* winning a seat in an election.

This is how it was in the good old days before last Saturday.

Now things are vastly different, so we are told. It had been decided at the usual Annual Conference last autumn that changes must be made in the procedure for electing the Party's Leader and that the power to do that should be taken out of the hands of the Parliamentary Party. This decision in itself was enough to raise howls of pain from the extreme moderates of the Party who saw the move to give greater control of their Members of Parliament to the rank and file of the Party as a deep laid plot by extreme extremists to introduce Trotskyist dictatorship by the back door.

Part of the joke of course is that this is precisely what it is. Since the four-way split in the old Revolutionary Communist Party in 1948, there has been a faction practising 'entryism' boring from within. You cannot be a member of the Labour Party and any Bolshevik Party as well, but the Trots are careful (unlike the Communist Party, for instance) not to be a Party. Trots love tendencies, so what they are is the Militant Tendency.

Inside the Party, general dissatisfaction with increasingly reactionary leaderships and the patently undemocratic structure of the Party have given the Militants their opportunity to bring pressure

to bear from below in favour of changes giving the rank and file more control of their MPs. Smug establishment figures like Shirley Williams reacted hotly against the very suggestion that MPs should be expected to face their own supporters every election time and be reassessed for reselection — a fairly mild and sober suggestion you might think.

Anyway, to cut a long and boring (sic) story short, a resolution on reselection was passed last year, as also was one making the choosing of the Party's Leader a matter for the whole Party and not only the Parliamentary Party. This week's special meeting was arranged to settle the procedure by which the Leader is to be elected.

Several balances of power between the three sections of the Party were proposed, and of course there was a lot of horse-dealing in smoke-filled hotel rooms. The one that carried the day was immediately hailed by the Press (which has had a jamboree lately about the extreme Left capturing the Party and that devil Tony Benn, etc, etc) with a particularly loud shriek about a Left triumph.

Do you know what it was? It was a decision that gave 40 per cent of the votes in the Electoral College to the trade unions, 30 per cent to the Constituency Parties, and 30 per cent to the Parliamentary Party.

The only way in which this can be construed as a victory for the Left is if you think of the unions as leftish! Now it is true that the structure of most unions and the apathy of most of their rank and file membership makes it possible for 'militants' to sway resolutions, just as the Trots have been able to do in the Constituency Parties. But in the unions, the Communist Party (Stalinist) have their infiltrators and 'militants' and there's no way they will collaborate with the Trots in the local Parties — so they cancel each other out.

Anybody who proclaims the Trades Union Congress as 'left' either wants their head examined or is looking for bogey men. So, really, the Right of the Party is still safe. But having shot their mouths off so strongly, the 'Gang of Four' (Shirley Williams, David Owen, William Rodgers — joined now by Roy Jenkins, fresh back from a cushy job in Brussels) have got to make their own arguments stand up — so they are in process of forming another 'Centre' Party.

All this by way of a caption for the cartoon showing William Rodgers (left), and David Owen, ex-Foreign Minister in the last Labour Government, who faithfully maintained his support for the Shah of Iran after the Iranians had toppled him from his vile dictatorship and right up to the time the Shah fled the country with all

that money. Owen proved himself more faithful to the Shah in adversity than he has to the Labour Party. If you care about such things, that must tell you something.
30th January 1981   P.S.

Entryism

The Right Honourable Mr Norman Tebbit was to be heard a few weeks back on the radio saying that 'What the British system demands is a Government moderately right-of-centre and an Opposition moderately left-of-centre'. Mr Tebbit is one of our numerous Ministers for Unemployment, a dedicated TINA-man, and is absolutely sure that the British system is here to stay forever . . . and ever . . . and ever.

As such, he is no doubt welcoming the emergence of the Social Democratic Party and in particular Mr Woy Jenkins' victory at Hillhead last week — for you could hardly wish for anyone more moderately left-of-centre than Jenkins. He has, averred his buddy Dr David Owen, not used the word 'socialism' for years, not even in connection with the system by which an enormous amount of claret is blended and bottled through cooperatives in the Bordeaux area — a system by which many peasant producers make use communally of equipment they could not afford themselves. Isn't that socialistic? But probably Woy drinks only chateau-bottled clawet.

This cosy concept, however, of consensus politics going on and on forever, perpetually fobbing off the electorate with meaningless shufflings, must come to an end sometime. The initiative has come already, with the Trotskyist infiltration of the Labour Party and the consequent driving out of the moderates. The Trots' theory of 'entryism' is nothing new and stems from the four-way split in 1948 of the old Revolutionary Communist Party, one faction (or was it two?) of which decided that the Labour Party was where the working class was, and so that was where they should be. One of the other factions became the WRP . . . but we mustn't get involved in dusty history like 1948.

One of the fallacies of entryism was that the Labour Party would quietly stand still and be taken over. Another was that the media would not notice what was going on, and yet another was that the electorate (and remember it's the 'floating voters' who win elections) would also stand still and vote for the Labour Party no matter what it said or did, or what the media said or did.

The Labour Party's Parliamentary Party is basically a party of carpetbaggers, who have hung on as long as they could see no other alternative for a comfortable ride. Some are sponsored by trade unions, the leaders of which have had their troubles with 'The Left' in the past and have seen them off. Some have swung from Left to Right themselves in the interests of not rocking a boat for a Labour Government and have no thought other than remaining as well-paid labour representatives in a capitalist world. Although the Conservative Party has to maintain its traditions of hostility to the unions, most of the largest capitalist companies have been more than happy to embrace the closed shop in exchange for a quiet life; it is noticeable that when a storm blows up over the issue of the closed shop, it is the union which is seen as being in the wrong, while the bosses sit back chuckling.

The unions, through their political levy, are the paymasters of the Labour Party, and they are quite capable of pulling the rug out from beneath anybody who looks like rocking the boat too violently from their entrenched position of moderate left-of-centre.

The battle has not yet been joined between the Labour Party proper and the Militants. What has happened is that the more frightened carpetbaggers have packed their bags and fled — and this must be something the Militants didn't bargain for: that any significant section of the Party could just get up and walk away from them, taking the voters with them. Slowly but surely the Labour Party leadership is going to be forced into the position of taking action against the Trots — and the moment they do, the voters will come streaming back. And if they don't, and Labour fades away — what's the betting that the trade unions will look to the Social Democrats as their parliamentary friends?

And while all this political cleverness is going on, what is the State doing? Is it sitting back, like a hopeful virgin (male or female), waiting to be taken over — with permission of course? Like hell it is.

The State is arming itself to crush the perpetual enemy within: the people. The State's first line of defence, the police, are on the offensive, and getting more offensive every day. Following last year's relatively small outbursts on the streets, our lads in blue are collecting lethal plastic bullets, water cannon, CS gas, new laws, new powers, a new ruthless use of the media and a new entry into politics. Ho, ho, comrades — a new twist on entryism emerges, as the police chiefs declare their determination to be a law unto themselves. Even in Lambeth, where they are trying to live down the damning effect of the Scarman Report and are promising to tell the local community leaders what they are going to do, they are putting qualifications to their promises, like 'If there's time . . .!'

A word on yet one more fallacy in 'entryism'. Like all attempts to change THE SYSTEM from within, it depends on the system not only standing still while it is changed — but allowing itself to be used against itself. This supreme underestimation of your enemy could be fatal. Like the man said, 'If voting could change the system it would be illegal'.

One final point. In their desire to be identified with the underdog and to be populist, the Trots are antagonising the police. Why don't they come out and tell the truth — that in a Leninist-Marxist State the police would really come into their own — in cooperation with the Party, of course.

4th April 1982   P.S.

Labour Pains

The first resignation of a real grass-roots Labour Party Member of Parliament has again brought bubbling to the surface the seething undercurrents within the Labour Party.

Mr Robert Mellish has been a member of the Party since 1927 — 55 years. And for nearly 37 of those years he has been a Member of Parliament for a dockland constituency in South-East London — Bermondsey.

A great contribution of service to the working class, you might think — if you think that the Labour Party operates in the interest of the working class, which we don't.

In his time Bob Mellish has never achieved highest office in the Party but in the various Labour Governments that have ruled us during the years he has been a faithful party hack — and he did reach the dizzying heights of becoming Chief Whip (that's the man who rounds up Members to vote in the House whenever there is a 'vital' vote) from 1969 to 1976, and he chaired the London Labour Party for 21 years.

Being a faithful party hack, he built up a faithful party constituency who voted for him by the tens of thousands, election after election. He had one of the 20 or so safest seats in the country, clocking up a majority of over 38% at the last election.

Being such an enormous Labour majority and thus looking such a safe Labour seat, Bermondsey has been a prime target for the 'Militant' Tendency, who must also have been taking into account the fact that Mellish is getting to retiring age — and the tiring age too. This tends to make people complacent and to think that their positions are unassailable, after such a record of service, but the younger Militants are impatient and the faithful but dull Mellish no longer satisfies them as their Parliamentary representative.

Besides which, they were moving into the Labour Party in order to take it over, and it was the safe seats with massive majorities that seemed to offer the best chances.

Labour's last annual conference established the procedure for making every MP re-present himself as a candidate for every election — a blow for such as Mellish, who had just been automatically accepted time after time. Short of coming out as a gay, being found in bed with Margaret Thatcher or uncovered as a supporter of some Northern football club, it was unthinkable that Bermondsey would even think of another candidate — until the Militant Mafia (as Mellish now calls them) moved in.

Operating the now properly constitutional procedure, the Constituency Labour Party elected young Mr Peter Tatchell as their favoured candidate for the next election — only to be roundly condemned by the party leader Michael Foot (who has, in his day, spoken alongside anarchists on public platforms) following a speech by Tatchell in which he pledged his faith in parliamentary democracy but did not rule out extra-parliamentary methods in the struggle against capitalism in general and the Conservatives in particular.

By the use of purely Parliamentary methods (like the Central Committee having the right to squash any rebellious local Parties) the Party managed to hold back Tatchell's nomination — until, still fuming about the mafia in the local Party, Mellish came out in support of three local candidates in a local Council election who had themselves fallen foul of the same mafia and were now standing as 'Independents' — Mellish apparently believing that these ex-Labour members would serve the local people, and incidentally the *real* Labour Party, better than the new boys.

As it transpired, the Independents were successful, presumably because they had a record of work in the local community whereas the new 'Militant' candidates did not — to say nothing of the campaigns in the media against the Militant Tendency and all its devil work. But Mellish's support for Independents instead of for the official Labour candidates, was enough to get him into constitutional hot water from which even his friends in Westminster could not save him, the National Executive Committee now having to allow a fresh selection conference in Bermondsey for their favourite candidate in the next General Election. And no prizes are offered for guessing who that might be, Tatchell having won last time by 59 votes to 7.

So Mellish has decided to chuck it in, fed up with all the backstairs politicking with which he is not at all suited to compete and which no doubt hurts him deeply, faithful servant of the Party that he is.

So, in the interests of all the 'decent people of Bermondsey' he has resigned from the Labour Party, saying that it is no longer the Party that he joined all those years ago. He is going to continue sitting in Parliament as an Independent until the local Party has chosen their new official candidate, when he will resign and fight a by-election to give all those decent people of Bermondsey a chance to put down the new man and send good ole Bob back to Parliament with flying colours.

Which of course they may, for oddly enough he might be supported not only by the out-manoeuvred Right and Centre in the local Party, but also by some young leftists (supposedly of the decent Tribune tendency) who actually called on Michael Foot to boot out young Tatchell when he was first chosen — threatening to raise hell themselves if he didn't — so he did. It all depends on whether party faithfuls who hate the Militants will support the man who they know or the Party they used to think they knew . . . to say nothing of being influenced by the furious campaign of hatred that the media will mount against Tatchell, though strictly speaking that ought to rally them to his side. Either way, it will be amusing to watch.

Of rather more fundamental interest, however, is Mellish's remark about the Labour Party not being the Party that he joined all those years ago. Well, of course it isn't; it wasn't then the Party it was when it was first founded 20 years before that. And Bob Mellish is not the same today as when he first joined.

Below we reproduce a quote from *The Observer* showing what Labour leaders were saying fifty years ago, when the Party had already lived through its ditching of its internationalism and anti-militarism during the First World War and its collaboration with the Tories in Ramsay MacDonald's coalition 'National' Government in 1929.

Sir Stafford Cripps went on to serve in Churchill's wartime coalition Government (with its governmental conscription for industry as well as for the Forces) and in 1942 went to India to talk the (then neutral) Congress Party of Gandhi and Pandit Nehru & Co, into collaboration with the British in return for independence after the war. The pacifist Indian leaders maintained official neutrality, but allowed British troops to travel through India to get at the Japanese in Burma . . . while after the war Attlee's government had to be forcefully nudged by massive riots and demonstrations before they would fulfil Churchill's reluctant bargain.

The Labour Party probably never was the Party Mellish thought he joined in 1927. It has changed over the years so that Cripps' statement below is today unthinkable as cabinet policy. It is certainly much nearer to what the Militants are saying today — and that's enough to scare Mellish away.

The Party has changed and Mellish has changed and the fact that Militants are trying to change it again means nothing — for they too will change once they tread the corridors of power. They would not be playing the power games they are now if it was not the power they were after.

Truly, the more it changes, the more it remains the same . . .
7th August 1982   P.S.

Fifty years ago

Sir Stafford Cripps, MP, told a meeting in support of the Labour Party's crusade to obtain a million members yesterday that the first lesson of the recent election defeat was that the real issue was now between reactionary capitalism and Socialism. The second was that it was impossible to have a slow and gradual transition. On gaining power, they must be prepared to end the power of the House of Lords, nationalise the land, break down the capitalist control over money, and the stranglehold of private ownership, and place industry under social control.

Sunday 7th February 1932   THE OBSERVER

THE LIBERALS AND THE SOCIAL DEMOCRATS

Young Liberals, Disband!

One of the mysteries of British political life is the continued existence of the Young Liberals as a supposedly libertarian grouping. It is a mystery which the Liberal conference at Blackpool earlier this month heightened yet further. In vain did assembly chairman Michael Meadowcroft (to quote a *Times* reporter) remind 'everyone of the Liberals' anarchist as well as social democratic strand in their tradition'. His reference, it was noted, somewhat discomforted the Liberal leader, and was hardly greeted with enthusiasm by the assembled multitude.

Much more in keeping with the general tone was the contribution of new Liberal luminary Aubrey Jones, late of the Prices and Incomes Board and of the Conservative Party. Clearly the latter is going through too classic Liberal a phase for the taste of a Tory of the old school. Aubrey Jones has decided that the Liberals are very much a Party of the State and moreover the best one to halt the alienation of workers from capitalism. Mr Jones was most definitely *not* going to make Mr Steel squirm in his chair.

Leaving aside the pre-conference attempt on the part of some pathetic grass-roots members to persuade their leaders to support CND, and leaving aside the predictable vote against unilateral disarmament, what does this Conference show us — and what should it show those Young Liberals who still aspire towards the more discomforting side of Liberal tradition as Michael Meadowcroft portrayed it?

David Steel is aware that some of his flock still cling to the conception of a Liberal golden age. He thus called on them to 'break free from the past'. In a speech that can rarely have been excelled for *double entendre* and which apparently drew much applause, he told them: don't be so purist and exclusive (i.e. forget the liberal side of your Liberalism); give the lead to a broad radical movement (i.e. press on to soggy centrism); show the way towards a well-educated, compassionate, healthy and harmonious society (i.e. aim for a yet more comprehensive Welfare State in which all conflict has ceased — a participatory paradise of capitalism).

To achieve this the Liberal leadership possibly still entertains the faint hope of a Labour split — although it now looks as though the fixing of union block votes in James Callaghan's favour at the Labour Party Conference in Blackpool a few days hence will keep Shirley Williams and her fellow 'gangsters' within the fold. Failing the recruiting of the 'Gang of Three' Steel hopes that renegade Labour right-winger and EEC Commission President Roy Jenkins may yet form an alliance with him for the next election. This could win sufficient votes to enable him to insist on electoral reform — i.e. proportional representation. This, it is hoped, would in turn lead to endless coalition Governments in which he, Steel, has considerable powers of manipulation — plus a Minister or two like the Liberal Police Minister of West Germany, Gerhart Baum. He can sink with a sigh of relief into a sensible centre morass (the *marais* as the French call it) of parliamentary politics — that vague and indeterminate marshland which deters the extremes of Right and Left from moving very far in any direction . . . What a noble (if somewhat static) vision! But what has it to do with Liberalism?

The answer, of course, is everything. David Steel is no traitor to his Party (as Aubrey Jones, appealing to the ghost of Gladstone, was at pains to point out to any radicals who had not yet gone to drown their sorrows at the bar). He is, on the contrary, its apotheosis. For, Young Liberals, ponder awhile on the history of Liberalism. Think back to the illuminati of the past, Locke and Mill, and read them carefully and you will see that (granted their good points, and the necessary liberal elements in anarchism) the values of freedom with which they are associated are those of a freedom that is always bestowed from above and heavily fringed about with ifs and buts. Liberalism has always been the ideology of freedoms with an 's' but not of *freedom* in the singular. The history of Liberalism over the centuries has been one of an increasing acceptance and justification of State intervention in all fields until, with Green and Bosanquet, came the concept of the organic State. And with that, Young Liberals, the seeds of both left- and right-wing fascist ideology were sprung.

Young Liberals, who like to sprinkle your texts with titillating quotations from Kropotkin and Bakunin, who like to scare your elders just a little with the word 'anarchism' and play a little with the idea of 'community politics', ask yourselves once and for all, who do you think you're kidding? Do you really believe in Steel's swampland of consensus politics? Do you really believe that a libertarian society, in which freedom and social justice combine, can ever come about without conflict, or indeed that it would not entail *perpetual* conflict and rebellion against the will to power and domination which your own leaders so transparently display?

Young post-Blackpool 1980 Liberals, disband at once or relinquish for ever the illusion, the deceit — whatever it may be — of libertarian politics!

27th September 1980   GAIA

A Touch of Anarchism

Why has there been so much mention of anarchism in the Press recently? What can it possibly have to do with any of the political parties, let alone with the 'Gang of Four' and the newly-fledged Council for Social Democracy?

Before such questions are dismissed as meaningless we might give them a small thought. For the strange, the distasteful, the rather improbable and the mildly amusing fact is that over the last few months of upheaval within the Labour Party an ideological battle of sorts has been waged on the basis of anarchist ideas.

This odd business can be traced back at least to the day Dr David Owen became Foreign Secretary in the Callaghan Government and when he appeared on television to reveal that there were actually two main schools of socialism — one which followed Marx, but — wait for it! — another which followed Proudhon. He thereupon announced that he was Proudhon's man, a champion of decentralisation as opposed to Marxist centralism. But, of course, he was careful not to mention the word 'anarchism'.

It was later the turn of Shirley Williams. In her reply to an earlier *Times* article by Eric Heffer (Liverpool, Walton) this second Gang member defended her socialist ideals. She reminded Mr Heffer that she too wanted equality, full employment and a united Europe, and said that Marx was not a bad sort of a fellow, but after all he was still fallible. After quoting from Anthony Crosland on the virtues of political democracy she then adminstered her *coup de grâce*:

The doctrine that, I believe, distorted and eventually defiled Marxism was the dictatorship of the proletariat, a dictatorship that has nowhere been superseded by a classless communist State. Bakunin explained why: 'These previous workers having just become rulers or representatives of the people will cease being workers; they will look at the workers from their heights, they will represent not the people but themselves — he who doubts it does not know human nature.

And she went on to show how party bureaucracies put themselves before the people. But again, she was careful not to mention the word 'anarchism'.

Then, suddenly, in January, here is Eric Heffer, regular writer in *The Times*, devoting two of its august columns to President Reagan under the heading, 'A touch of anarchism but is it real?'.

From George Woodcock's *The Anarchist Reader*, Heffer quotes:

Anarchism is the doctrine which contends that government is the source of most of our social troubles and that there are viable alternative forms of voluntary organisation. And by further definition the anarchist is the man who sets out to create a society without government.

He then compares this definition with Reagan's inaugural speech, concluding that one could be forgiven for believing that parts of it 'were from an introduction to a treatise on anarchism'.

Heffer goes magnanimously on to point out that Reagan is 'clearly an implacable enemy of anarchism, which with all its faults is a form of non-state socialism'. However, 'like other devotees of the private enterprise system he unwittingly goes part of the way with the anarchists'.

Heffer continues with an attack on the anarchist concept of government as the root of evil. He does not, with Reagan or Thatcher, want less government, nor, with the 'true anarchist', no government, but competent and not-excessively-bureaucratic government. For,

Is government wrong to create a health service which ensures that everyone has a right to proper health care? Is government wrong to create a social security system with unemployment benefits, among others? Should government not be concerned to ensure that there is a good system of education for all and decent houses for people to live in?

This is less the place to enter into a refutation of Heffer's idea of government — which any study of anarchist theory should not make too difficult (and Heffer, besides, is here missing the point about anarchist criticism) — than to remark on the strangely convoluted way in which he expresses his apprehensions about the

Reagan administration. Why go to such lengths to equate Reagan's with anarchist concepts in the first place if at the same time he must cover himself by stating that he knows full well that Reagan is really anarchism's implacable enemy? Does this not seem an unnecessarily clumsy approach?

If, however, one remembers that the article is being written at a time when the Labour Party is under threat from a centrist alliance between Liberals and Social Democrats, and if one recalls not only Owen's remarks about Proudhon and Williams' about Bakunin but the last Liberal conference chairman, Michael Meadowcroft's, about the anarchist strand in Liberal tradition and the need for open and decentralised economic structures (thereby taking up the Kropotkin-quoting element of the Young Liberals) it all begins to make more sense.

Anarchism is the only ideology which offers a coherent critique of the centralised State socialism which Labour represents — or at least, to which many of its members aspire — and from a socialist position. Because a number of Social Democrats and Liberals wish, from a more or less left-wing perspective, to justify their dissent, they have begun to grasp (albeit in a furtive and highly selective sort of way) at anarchist ideas. It is only to be expected that Labour's faithful will retaliate by trying to show how dangerously anarchism lends itself to right-wing and reactionary forces.

The irritating thing about all this, of course, is that it gets us nowhere. It is hardly necessary to stress that, for all their references to Proudhon, Bakunin or that gentle market-gardening Prince, Council for Social Democracy members and Liberals are as 'implacably opposed' to anarchism as President Reagan, who has never heard of any of these people.

The Limehouse Declaration, with which the Council introduced itself, reveals a ragbag of contradictory aims — paying tribute to the principles of equality, classlessness, decentralisation and elimination of poverty while swearing firm allegiance to NATO, the EEC and a thriving and competitive capitalism. Truly, there is nothing in their outlook to distinguish them from the dreary David Steels of this world, and it is to Roy Jenkins' credit that he made no bones this week about the Council's electoral ambitions.

'At that [the next] election', he announced, 'working in close and friendly arrangement with the Liberals which is, I believe, our mutual desire and is certainly in our mutual interest, our aim will be no less than complete victory with a majority in the House of Commons and a Social Democratic/ Liberal Government of Britain'.

The implications of the expansion of such a centrist marshland in British politics, with the endless series of coalition Governments that this implies, is matter for a different article. Perhaps, though, the last words in this one could be left to the Leagas Delaney Partnership, the advertising firm who believe that passionate moderation is not enough.

'What a Social Democratic Party needs to establish itself', Leagas suggests, 'is an army of salesmen'. Really, does any more need to be said?

13th March 1981   GAIA

Centralising the Lib-Lab-Con Trick (or SDP)

We illustrate herewith the cover of a leaflet[1] which has been shoved through letterboxes in London (we can't speak for the rest of the country) and which could quite likely be taken to court successfully on charges of begging, misrepresentation, fraud and probably a few other things we wot not of.

As far as we know, the Social Democratic Party (sic) is not registered as a Charity, yet here it is asking for money for an aim which is not disclosed, a purpose which as yet offers you nothing more than membership of a political party which does not yet exist, a vote for a constitution and a programme which seems to be predetermined and the right to give money to a political machine created to further the personal ambitions of a handful of politically motivated persons without any Statement of Principles, Aims or Manifesto.

'Trust Us' is the message from a mere handful of known renegades whose careers have been characterised by either backing the wrong horses or feathering their own nests.

Chief among the latter is Mr Roy Jenkins, who rose to Cabinet rank in the Labour Party, becoming Home Secretary, and whose main claim to fame is that he extended the time prisoners could be kept incommunicado under the Prevention of Terrorism Act. He then took a job in Brussels at an enormous tax-free salary, furthering the interests of the great European bureaucracy.

---

1. The cover shown reads; 'Help us build a party that's in nobody's pocket by digging into your own: An invitation to join the Social Democrats'.

Most popular among the renegades is Shirley Williams, whom everybody is supposed to love, but who unfortunately lost the last election in her relatively safe Labour constituency because not enough of her constituents loved her enough.

Most disliked among the Gang of Four is undoubtedly Dr David Owen, erstwhile Foreign Secretary in Jim Callaghan's Government, who clung to his undying support for the Shah of Iran long after the people of that benighted country had thrown the vicious dictator overboard. David Owen admired the way the Shah had made his country strong against Communism by torturing his own people and buying lots of planes and tanks from Britain.

Little is known about the fourth of the Famous Four. It is thought his name is William Rodgers or something.

The most famous of our Famous Four is particularly famous at the moment because he has just won a remarkable victory by losing a by-election in a town he had not heard of before — Warrington. Most of us had only heard of Warrington, because we like to think of it as Vorrington, because Vodka is made there — which may account for the obvious soft-headedness of its voters, who clearly wanted to register a protest vote against the Tories without giving a vote to the Labour Party. So they voted for Roy Jenkins in their thousands. They must have had the shock of their little lives when he nearly got in.

Our Shirl then got her knickers in a twist because the next by-election is due to come up in the South London suburb of South Croydon and she rather fancied her chances there, as she is a 'national' figure.

Unhappily, some idiot in the SDP had agreed with the Liberals that, if they supported Jenkins in Vorrington, the Liberals could 'have' South Croydon — with SDP support. The whole nation held its breath (not a pretty sight) until Shirl, being an honest girl, or perhaps outvoted, backed off and let the local Liberal candidate, who had worked on the constituency for yonks, stay in the fight — with SDP support! Hurray!! You may all make like Kermit introducing Rudolph Nureyev . . . Local candidate's name is William Pitt. He will presumably be known as Pitt the Youngest.

Whether the con trick will work and the Liberal-SDP alliance will bring him victory remains to be seen. All we know for sure is that it is going to be the good old mixture as before.

Why? Because wise-guy Owen tends to let the cat out of the bag when he is faced with unrehearsed questions on the telly. In an idle moment we were watching the goggle-box when he was

being interviewed by psephologist Bob Mackenzie. We were the
ones to begin goggling, except we are much too sophisticated of
course to do any such thing, when the conversation began to go
like this:

Mackenzie: Many SDP supporters want out of the EEC. The leadership
want in. Many SDP supporters want unilateral nuclear disarmament. The
leadership don't. Doesn't this smack of elitism?
Owen: The Common Market is not an open question, neither is nuclear
disarmament. The SDP is founded on:
1. EEC membership.
2. Multilateral nuclear disarmament.
    The Party can have members who disagree — but these two points are
essential factors!

There, you may think, you have it. You may join this 'Party', in
which the principle of 'One Member, One Vote' is to be enshrined
— but at least two essential factors are already decided by the
founders. All they want from you is your money, to support *their*
path to power.
    Inside the leaflet we read:

'. . . while the two main parties fiddle with outdated philosophies and
dogmas the country burns with indignation.[2]
    Today the Social Democrats invite you to do something about it.
    Britain needs a new political party and it needs it now.
    But if you want it, you'll have to pay for it.'

On another radio programme, we heard a paid organiser saying,
'We must have the party machine first. Without that, the policy is
worth nothing!'
    Perhaps Owen's final words with Bob Mackenzie are worth signing
off with: 'Lloyd George's Liberalism is exactly the sort of left-of-
centre radicalism we stand for!'
    A *new* party, Dr Owen? Who exactly are you trying to con?
    15th August 1981   P.S.

PS:
Since the above article was written there has been a little trouble
in Paradise. Preparing for their grand slam through the country at
the next General Election and to prevent bickering at by-elections,

---

2. This is prophetic, being written before the riots.

the Liberal Party and the ghostly SDP are trying to agree on how to decide who fights what.

The SDP leaders (and after all, it seems to consist of only leaders) want to put up 300 candidates and want the share out of seats to be arranged at 'national level', while the Liberals (so strong on 'community' politics, don't you know) want it to be agreed at local, or at most regional level.

The latter is not apparently acceptable to the SDP leaders, who, while prepared to accept 'local or regional input' (note the computerised language!) seem to be insisting that final decisions must be made at national level and enforced by the leaders of both Parties.

So at last we are beginning to know what social democracy means.

PPS:
Whatever happened to Lloyd George?

FASCISM

British Road to Fascism

The British ruling class is one of the most — if not *the* most — securely entrenched of any in the world. It is over 300 years since Civil War ended Royal oligarchy and introduced democracy under the specious name of the 'Commonwealth' and a puritan dictator who promptly reneged on all the promises he had made to the men who fought for him, and made democracy the sham it has been ever since.

What has made British democracy so secure, however, has precisely been that sham — a system of carefully constructed checks and balances manipulated by cynical and brilliant elites who have successfully circumscribed freedom within a thousand civil liberties, privileges and carefully controlled 'rights'.

Behind the sham, black slavery was profitably operated and then sanctimoniously ended when no longer needed (compare Enoch Powell's recruitment of 'Commonwealth' labour when he needed it as Minister of Health — and rejection when no longer needed!); Nelson's victorious Navy was manned by press-gang methods; Earl Haig's victims were conscripted to their graves in Flanders; the common lands enclosed and the rural poor herded into urban industrial bondage with hanging, flogging and deportation for dissidents, the workhouse the reward for loyal service.

In the three hundred years since the birth of the Mother of Parliaments a mighty Empire has waxed and waned, an industrial revolution has changed the face of the earth, Britain has been involved in not only two world wars but more minor conflicts than any other country, depressions have come and gone and come again, Mother has looked blankly at other countries torn by revolution — but has never had cause to blink at any tremor likely to disturb her own stability.

Throughout all this fantastic history, the might of the British State has rested upon one particular British characteristic: compromise. Just as the Catholic Church, with an equally successful and bloodstained history, has survived through its ability to bend with the wind, so too, the cynical and brilliant British elites have known how to learn — and the most important lesson has been to know when to give way on unimportant issues whilst retaining the essential power. Think of the 'rights' of trade unions and of women's suffrage!

If there is one dirty word in the English language of ruling class diplomacy it is 'extremism'. Thanks to the grand concept of Empire, Britain has been able to export its greatest misery; its more extreme forms of government have been reserved for the lesser breeds beyond our shores. Although public hangings of African rebels were part and parcel of the restitution of law and order in Kenya in the 1950s, our own liberal progression has denied us the pleasure of that charming spectacle in this country for over a hundred years. Indeed, hanging even behind closed doors has now been abolished in favour of the less extreme punishment of living death in prison.

Is the British ruling class the weaker for that? Of course not, for it cannot now be despised as a ruthless dictatorship or despotism, for it is seen to be humane, while the development of the Welfare State has given the apparatus of government the aura of concern for our less fortunate fellow-citizens (the deserving poor, as the Victorians described them) but at the same time our stern parent will punish wrongdoers and protect us from them.

Although a large part of our ruling class had sympathy for the fascist and many dictators of the 1930s, we can imagine the distaste with which they viewed the excesses of those crude regimes, led by vulgar upstarts — not, we hasten to add, out of sympathy for Mussolini's or Hitler's victims, but simply because such internal violence is counter-productive. It was only the expansionist policies of those dictators, when they decided they wanted a slice of the imperial and economic cake, that brought the 'democracies' into conflict with them.

The victorious allies of 1945, remember, made no attempt to march on to liberate Spain from a fascist dictatorship.

The same attitude is present today towards South Africa. It is embarrassing enough that this one-time jewel of our Empire should have degenerated into such a crude oligarchy — but, worse, it is so bad for trade, making one tread so carefully among the potentially great markets of the third world. Those boring old Boers really are so tactless.

The great achievement of the British ruling class, however, is that it has spread its distaste for extremism right down through the classes. By being so democratic and arranging things so that there is this Official Opposition in Parliament, through which any citizen in the realm may seek justice, and by sucking the official labour movement into its own orbit, with jobs and status and monetary and meaningless rewards and honours, any disagreement or misunderstanding can be hammered out and a jolly decent compromise can be reached, leaving things very much as they were.

It is this 'leaving things as they were' which is the object of the exercise.

This is the real art of government — to appear to yield but without changing anything. Isn't this what was so damned clever about the end of the Empire and the birth of the Commonwealth (very similar, really to that first Commonwealth of Cromwell's but on a grander scale), for here, again, the long term defusing of the opposition resulted in the establishment of African and Asian regimes which owed all their expertise in ruling their peoples to the outgoing British.

And here again, you see, we have this occasional embarrassment brought on by such as Idi Amin and Mrs Gandhi — to say nothing of that shocking *faux pas* by poor old Anthony Eden when, as late as 1956, he lost his marbles and went mad over the Suez Canal!

No, the really 20th Century British way is so much more subtle than that, and it is worth noting that we have managed to teach at least one of our ex-enemies a thing or two, Clearly the present German State is *in essence* as authoritarian as the Nazis, though not in practice — Stammheim notwithstanding. Not by shouting and screaming and stamping about in jackboots; not by mass concentration camps and gross racialism, but by control of the media, by buying the labour movements, by the insidious spread of conformity — all helped, of course by the threat of the Reds at the gate and the urban guerrillas within — a *modern*, scientific, computerised police state has been gradually and quietly built up — with the help and approval of their erstwhile enemies, the 'Democratic Allies'.

And we may be very sure that the British, while teaching the Germans a better way of governing, have also learned a lot from watching how it developed there. True, Germany had the advantage of the 'economic miracle' which bought the bourgeoisie and the working class alike — but 'we' have the advantage of our history and political experience.

It is this history and the lessons that our rulers learn from it so much better than the British people do, that makes the possibility of British 'fascism', for want of a better shorthand word, so likely.

With the decline of Empire, long term problems for the capitalist system, and the impossibility of using large-scale war as a stabiliser, internal conflict becomes inevitable. And the British ruling class is obviously preparing for it.

The real threat of a fascist-type authoritarian regime here does not come from a bunch of psychopathic hoodlums being kicked into the headlines by screaming socialists — it comes from the Establishment. It comes from a Labour Home Secretary who deports journalists; from a BBC executive who bans a television play about Borstal; from a friendly neighbourhood copper who has a walkie-talkie plugged into a computer with all the facts about you, comrade; from trade union officials who denounce as extremists those who fight for trade unionism; from social democrats who are sold out on the State and want, even paternally, more state control over everything; from all those who shamefacedly know that the Labour Party has produced what Harold Macmillan demanded 20 years ago — a pool of unemployment — but cannot face up to the economic facts that automation is banging on the table.

All power-seekers who cling to the old ways and cannot let go — these are the ones who will usher in the new style scientific authoritarianism. The National Front, discredited rump of the old style, will no doubt be useful in creating civil disorder, the better to invoke 'Law and Order', but the Right Wing of all respectable Parties are the ones who will coalesce, will consign the NF to the dustbin, and, if they cannot agree on a leader from their own ranks, will beckon on to the stage that fine scholar of Greek and elegant doubletalk, Enoch Powell, even now waiting patiently in the wings.

If it is to be trod, this will be the British road to fascism. The State never has been and never can be anything but an enemy of the people. It is the main enemy and if we forget that, we allow ourselves to be sidetracked, at our peril.

4th February 1978   PHILIP SANSOM

Black on Black

It was a black week for British democracy. Without wishing to be fair to the Tories we must admit that most of the Shadow Cabinet were publicly astonished at Margaret Thatcher's sudden outburst on immigration during a TV interview, whatever they thought in private. And who is to know, without bugging their most private places, just what front-line politicians really think about anything?

It would be indelicate and ungallant and most definitely male chauvinist to say that Maggie was caught with her pants down during an unscripted interview. So we won't say it; we'll just say that for once her own thoughts came through, instead of the carefully rehearsed tranquilisers that make up her usual policy statements — delivered with a fire, sense of timing and shaft of wit that make Clement Freud's dog-food commercials sound like Groucho Marx.

But still . . . who knows? Perhaps there was more calculated use of Clement Freud's distinguished ancestor Sigmund in Maggie's use of emotive words like 'fear' of being 'swamped' . . . by people with different 'cultures' . . . Perhaps she really knew what she was doing and her apparently unrehearsed indiscretions were simply a result of her taking advantage of a situation she had been awaiting for a long time — the chance to play her hunch that there's a lot of traditional Tories going to vote National Front if the Party born to rule doesn't say the things they want said.

For the Chinese it may be that 1978 is the Year of the Horse. For the British electorate it will be something slightly less — like the Year of the Donkey, the Year of the Ass, or even the Camel — the horse designed by a committee. Or will it be the year of that more shameful animal — the Year of the Scapegoat?

The cheapest and easiest of all political con-tricks is to play the scapegoat game. You risk losing the votes only of a small and insignificant minority by blaming them for the failures of the majority itself — thus purging the majority of its own sense of failure at the same time as diverting attention from the real problems.

The scapegoat game has this double-take, too, in that it has to pretend that the small and insignificant minority is bigger than it really is. More powerful, more insidious in its pervasive influence on the sound, strong, true and rocklike traditions of this great and powerful country of ours.

The British character has had so much 'to offer the world', said Maggie, 'in democracy, in law . . .' We skip over the interesting point that she should have selected 'law' as one of the great British contributions to civilisation, only to ask how it is that this patriotic lady can have so little confidence in the British way of life that a million and a half immigrants — from previously British colonies, the majority of them professing something like Church of England Christianity — can strike terror into an indigenous population of over 50 million.

While a similar figure of one and a half million unemployed — British workers deprived of their birthright to work for a boss — is sanguinely accepted as something we shall have to live with for the rest of the century!

Of course Mrs Thatcher is scratching around to find a stick to beat the Labour Party with. The other big bogey man of the bourgeoisie — the trade union blackmailer — has been successfully rounded up by Big Jim Callaghan and his posse of faithful deputies from the TUC. So there is definitely no mileage for Maggie in union-bashing now, since nobody could pretend for one moment that the Tories could have got the unions to settle for less than 10 per cent.

So, looking over her shoulder, this nauseous madam saw the NF groping at the most revolting fringes of her own Party and thought it smart to out-smart them. While it may well have been that we have thus been granted a look inside her skull at what she really thinks, it can only be described as a failure of nerve on her part — for surely the seasoned campaigners of the Conservative Party must know that elections are still won in this country by the Centre; the extremes of both Right and Left are considered expendable by the moderate parties, and it is among the floating voters that election-winners may be found.

It is among those five million Liberal voters of 1974 that the Tories will be fishing for votes — a task made more difficult for them by the Lib-Lab pact, by the success of Callaghan's 10 per cent policy and the slowing down of inflation. It was a clever stroke then for the Tories to try to smother Maggie's crude immigrant ploy with something much more complicated to bring in the middle group — the disclosure of the so-called 'Black List' drawn up by the Government of companies which have settled wage claims with their workers over the 10 per cent guide line.

For Tories wooing the Liberals this was a gift, for not only was the Labour Government found out to be acting outside of any statutory powers, and to be wielding the hammer of sanction on small firms while the big boys were publicly getting away with it, but it was unthinkable interference with the proper business of free enterprise.

We need not weep for that, of course, but we could weep for the Labour Party faithful who have had to swallow ten per cent as well as the dawning realisation that 'their' Government had no intention of tackling unemployment — and compounds the sickness by penalising employers who are willing to pay more by refusing to renew government contracts and withholding development grants — thus creating more unemployment!

By shining the spotlight on Labour's black list rather than Maggie's anti-black flounderings, then, your actual moderate Tories sought to take the sting out of a situation which was rapidly turning sour, for when facts and figures on immigration began to emerge it was shown quite clearly that Labour had done more to restrict immigration than the Tories had! Figures were dropping and Maggie had boobed — all for the sake of a few thousand fascist votes.

Even the black list 'scandal' could be turned against the Tories too, since Callaghan could argue that by not giving government contracts to firms paying over the odds, he was in fact saving public money!

And so it goes. This is the measure of public debate in 1978. Instead of principles, even wrong ones, all sides are chanting at the tops of their voices 'Anything you can do, I can do better!' It is a strident version of consensus politics, wherein all Parties agree on basic capitalist economics, while shrieking about trivial fiscal, legal or moral reform to provide distractions from the gradual infringement of real liberty and the creeping control by the State.

Both the Tories in their way and Labour in theirs, with the Liberals scavenging for influence in the middle and the extremes of Right and Left baying for their particular dictatorial moons on the outskirts — all of these offer privileges for their supporters and penalties for their opponents. And all of them, in their fashion and in their search for power, lead us nearer to the corporate State.

18th February 1978   PHILIP SANSOM

FREEDOM OF SPEECH

Professor Eysenck's Nose

The beating up of a Jewish professor is quite like old times again — old times in Munich, Nuremberg and Berlin where an academic's right to speak was measured by the length of his nose. Dr Goebbels, himself a brilliant academic, decreed new canons of academic freedom. It is interesting that these canons of academic freedom are now beginning to be applied in the London School of Economics. The LSE boys are now, *in public*, wringing their hands — 'Oh no, it was not us! How could it be? We are the inheritors of the tradition of Harold Laski, that great master of tolerance. It was *outsiders* who caused all the trouble; the mob from Birmingham and suchlike outlandish places.' It is funny how it is always *outsiders* who cause all the trouble; Enoch Powell would tell us the same story.

And was Eysenck set upon because he is a Jewish professor, that archetypal target for the bully-boys? To some extent yes, since it is always easier to stir up the mob against a ready-made target, but that was certainly not the prime reason. He was attacked on the pretext of his theories about intelligence and genetics, but that was a pretty thin pretext. Considering the quarter from which the attack came there are other more potent reasons why the Commie bully-boys should have been nursing their knuckle-dusters. I was myself a student at LSE when Eysenck published his book *The Psychology of Politics* and remember the fury of the Commies at the time. This book is a collection of research findings compiled by a team of research workers, which among other things demonstrated that in rather a large number of ways Communists and Fascists are the same mob with a different coloured sauce. That this finding was rather old hat to all of us who had spoken on soap boxes, sold literature on the streets and had the bastards break up our meetings, made no difference. It was news to the budding young political economists at the LSE. (It had never occurred to Harold Laski). 'The Party' had at LSE at that time a beastly little propaganda agent who much resembled Squealer in *Animal Farm*, and for some time he led an anti-Eysenck crusade. But what could they do at that time? If they resorted to their usual hooligan tactics of breaking up meetings at which Eysenck spoke they would merely have drawn attention to the fact that Eysenck was right — that intolerant bullies who try to stop free speech are essentially the same whatever party label they wear.

The Commies have nursed their grudge, seeking occasion for revenge. The present smear campaign against Eysenck has provided a convenient excuse for attack. They do not wish Eysenck to have the opportunity to explain himself; they prefer to spread lies about what he is supposed to maintain. They claim that Eysenck peddles 'anti-people and anti-scientific theories of Hitlerite fascism' — they claim *this* of a liberal Jew who escaped with his life from the Hitlerite regime. Long, long ago anarchists woke up to the fact that the Leninist-Stalinist tyranny which replaced the short-lived escape from Tsarist tyranny, had some specially hideous features. Violence and murder are much the same as far as the victims are concerned, whoever wields the axe of power. But there is a curiously nightmarish quality about the totalitarian technique of declaring the *opposite* of the truth so loudly that it takes on a special quality of its own.

Let me declare my personal testimony for what it is worth. I have worked in association with Eysenck for years, and during that time I have made no secret of the fact that I am an anarchist who rejects utterly the premises on which he holds his liberal beliefs. While working in his department at the Maudsley he granted me every facility I needed to carry out my own research in my own way — including a research into anarchism in which nearly fifty anarchists participated. In my view he has all the classic faults and the classic virtues of the liberal. But I respect his integrity as an academic and his integrity as a man absolutely. In the academic world (as in the world of art, letters, music etc.) there is a good deal of bitchery, and at this game Eysenck can hold his own. But let me say this with studied deliberation: those who try to *smear* Eysenck are scum. The Commie scum we all know; their stock in trade is character assassination as well as assassination by the ice-pick method. There are also scum in quite high academic positions, and minor academic scum currying favour with their superiors by joining in the smear campaign. Such academic scum are very foolish scum indeed. They do not realise that the jolly days of Nuremberg, Munich and Berlin where an academic's right to speak depended on the length of his nose, are not so very far from our tranquil British scene. Some will be shocked (I hope) by a physical attack on a professor invited to speak on an academic platform. Maybe their turn will come next — for if it is all right to bash academics who study the interaction between heredity and environment today, tomorrow it will be all right to bash academics who are exclusively concerned with environmental influences.

In a so-called 'libertarian' publication (*Rat, Myth and Magic*) there appeared the following choice instigation to a lynch mob:

There will be a 'battle' at the British Psychological Society this April between Broadbent, Jahoda and Sedgwick: 'Psychology and Society'. This symposium has been arranged to pacify the anger discovered at last April's Ethics Symposium. *Shall we disrupt it?* (italics added)

When howling 'Two legs bad, four legs good!' and other such brilliant slogans, and physically bashing the intending speakers in case they actually speak, becomes *de rigueur* in academic circles, then presumably the publishers of this so-called 'libertarian' publication will feel they have done their bit in liberating the academic scene. But by this time other people besides Professor Eysenck will have to be concerned about the length, size, shape and consistency of their noses before they venture on an academic platform. And fashions in noses can change very rapidly.

To those accustomed to the propaganda rough and tumble of the streets, all this may appear as something of a storm in a teacup. When we speak on a soap-box about anarchism we expect to be asked by hecklers such questions as 'Who's going to clean out the sewers then, mate?' and we develop tricks of repartee to deal with such interruptions. I maintain that the verbal debate of the street corner with its wit, emotional appeal and preposterous exaggeration is a valuable and essential feature of a community struggling to live in freedom. But the freedom of debate of academics is not to be despised. Once that goes either at the hands of politically motivated thugs, or dictates of the Central Committee of the Party, much else in society alters too. Once all knowledge becomes vested in a Church, theocratic or secular, and free scientific debate and publication is repressed as heresy, then even the limited freedom of the streets which we enjoy today is withdrawn.

19th May 1973   TONY GIBSON

NOTT Freedom of Speech

Most of the readers of FREEDOM must already have noticed how thin-skinned is democracy, how fragile are the benefits it confers upon us, the lucky people who live under a Government whose first concern is the defence of our liberties.

It is this concern for our way of life which justifies Governments in their determination to destroy us all rather than let our way of life be tampered with.

'Better dead than red' is a slogan from the first round of the people's struggle against nuclear lunacy, when our then leaders were quite prepared, as they are now, to see *us* all dead rather than that *they* should be replaced by 'reds'.

For this is what 'the defence of our way of life' really means. It is *their* way of life which has been defended by *us* in every war and the only new factor to have emerged in the nuclear age has been that they stand to go up in that indiscriminate mushroom cloud along with us, the common herd.

Incidentally, perhaps we should make the anarchist position clear on this. We have not gone along with the common herd in the defence of their leaders' way of life, for we have seen the identity of Governments across the frontiers and recognised how stupid it is for the exploited of every country to be fighting and killing each other in defence of their respective ruling classes — which earlier through aristocratic dynasties and now through multi-national companies, has for centuries been the same truly international ruling class, squabbling among themselves just as families will quarrel over the will of the dear departed.

And if you think that all this has been altered by the emergence of 'workers' States' in Eastern Europe, and particularly Russia itself, then explain away the massive loans from Western banks which have now so put Poland in hock that the Soviet Government is reluctant to keep its grip upon it, or indeed the equally massive amount of 'business' and investment from the West that goes into Russia proper: the 'Vodka-Cola' economy.

What the state-capitalist regimes of Eastern Europe have provided for the 'free-enterprise' capitalist regimes of the West is precisely what 'Prussian Militarism' and the Kaiser provided in the early years of this century — the external threat that all States need to keep their people perpetually under a fear of foreign domination and thus amenable to domination at home. All forms of domination need bogeymen to keep the masses frightened and in need of protection; remember the role of 'Goldstein' in *1984*? When Governments are in charge it is known as national defence, whereas when Chicago gangsters do it, it is more honestly known simply as 'the protection racket'.

We would not be so silly as to say that there is nothing to choose between the totalitarian system of Russia and that of this country or the other 'democracies' of the West. That is to say, in the comforts of everyday life and the degrees of licence we have. Because the West was more advanced along the capitalist road than Imperial Russia was in 1917 (whose backwardness, after all, was one of the reasons for the Revolution) that advantage has been maintained, while in Russia the backwardness of technology (until very recent times, and then advances have been made only in areas which benefit the State) has been further aggravated by the dead weight of centralised bureaucracy. Capitalism, it must be admitted, has come up with the goods — i.e. the material trivia that keep the proles happy; masses of second-rate food which keeps their bellies full, and mass entertainment to dull their minds — while decent housing (at least in Britain) disappears and any sense of *involvement* in their own destinies is just as absent as in the totalitarian USSR. (Unless you claim that newspaper Bingo is 'involvement' in your own destiny'!)

At the same time the degree of licence and access to real information we have, erode so slowly that nobody notices their gradual disappearance until some bomb-happy politician drops a clanger and shows the joins in his big wig.

This happened last week, when Minister for Defence John Nott (our equivalent of the USA's Defence Secretary General Haig — and that's a name that brings shivers to the spine of old soldiers in Britain) blew his cool on a radio programme[1] in which he said that criticism of the Government's nuclear weapon policy was an abuse of the freedom of speech that is one of the glories of democracy.

His claim that a campaign for nuclear disarmament was 'playing into the hands of the Russians' is hardly new, and in itself would not have made news — but his extension of the argument was sufficiently new to the ears of liberal democrats to draw fire from

1. The World at One — Radio 4 9th November 1981

a *Guardian* leader and of course its readers — though hardly novel to anarchists.

What Nott said in effect was that freedom of speech is one of our most precious possessions, but that its use can embarrass the Government and encourage the enemy (like who?), who does not allow freedom of speech like we do.

It is therefore irresponsible to use our most treasured possession, which is too precious to use, and anybody who does use it is virtually a traitor and an agent of Moscow. We must have freedom of speech because we are a democracy, unlike that beastly Soviet Union, but we must never use it to contradict our Government, of which Mr John Nott is such a distinguished member — and powerful to boot — because that would make the enemy think that our Government does not have the support of the people and thus the country is ripe for conquest and takeover.

Yes, of course, we must jealously keep and defend and fight to the death for our right to freedom of speech and even yours too, though we disapprove of what you say, but really, chaps, we mustn't actually *use* it, must we, because anything that is really *using* freedom of speech and thus may actually lead to speaking the truth instead of what we want people to believe unquestioningly and may lead to the undermining of the State's right to speak for the whole of the people without consulting them or listening to them, must be wrong and must in fact be an *abuse* of freedom of speech.

Thus, you see, in a democracy, the use of freedom of speech can so easily become an abuse, and obviously, the proper Government of the country, democratically elected, cannot allow the people to be subjected to an abuse of one of its fundamental freedoms.

In order to defend that freedom, therefore, the properly elected authority must prevent its abuse, and even, if necessary — and clearly it is becoming more necessary every day — its use. By anyone, that is, except the properly elected (or not, as the case may be) authority. QED!

Did someone say that's how it is in Russia? Well, even the Soviet Government can't be wrong about everything, can it? Or can it Nott?

21st November 1981   P.S.

THE WORKERS AND THE TRADE UNIONS

Abolish Employment!

Anyone with half an eye can see that the one great contribution that the technological revolution offers us is the abolition of hard labour. Mechanisation has always been attractive for employers because it has enabled them to get more out of their factories with fewer workers. But it should be attractive for workers too, because it enables *them* to produce more wealth with less effort.

The trouble is, of course, that the wealth then belongs to the employers, as do the machines and, in a very real sense, so do the workers, since they can live only by selling themselves to the employers.

Last week at Blackpool a Party that likes to call itself socialist at conferences and democratic at elections managed to talk for a week about most of the things which affect our lives without once questioning the essence of wage slavery — that it means the vast

majority can live only by working for a boss. We do not expect the Party gathering this week at Brighton to question it either!

Nor does this blindness stop at our two leading capitalist Parties. The servile call that went up from the Socialist Workers' Party for 'The Right to Work' might have been astonishing except that the authoritarian Left no less than the Right wants to be in the position of power, whereby workers would be controlled by employers (even if the State), the unions and, for good measure, the Party as well. *Any* authority, be it aristocratic or bureaucratic, can maintain power only by exploiting the wealth created by the workers.

The anarchists stand alone in demanding both workers' control in industry and the abolition of the wage system — in a word the end of employment as we know it. Which is why we don't join in the general bleating about irrelevancies like five per cent or even unemployment. If we did we should be demanding a three-day week as more just than the catch-as-catch-can and differential-squabbling of the unions.

But we want much more than that. We want the workers in control and free. That means the Abolition of Employment!
14th October 1978

Anarchy Still Reigns, Claims CBI Chief

Predictably, 'Anarchy' has been hitting the headlines this last three weeks. There has been 'Anarchy' on the railways as the points froze and 'Anarchy' on the picket lines as they became effective. Indeed, the frequency of the use of the word was in direct proportion to the effectiveness of the pickets — so much so that we would have thought the striking lorry drivers would have realised that 'Anarchy' is a secret weapon of great power, the very mention of which strikes terror into the hearts of the capitalists.

In some minute degree the word was used with its proper meaning. 'Is Britain becoming ungovernable?' mused *The Guardian*, agonisingly aware that it has a lot of ex-*Times* readers to nurture, and the prospect daunted Maggie Thatcher so much that she was screaming for a State of Emergency (which did not suit Callaghan's book, however) even before she had finished the first emergency tin of caviar from her well-stocked larder.

It is always instructive to see how the bold Tory defenders of individual liberty, the most vocal opponents of state interference in free enterprise, will scream like stuck pigs for state action when *their* interests are threatened. Maggie was practically demanding tanks outside every Tesco's, to defend the panic-buying house-wives' right to strip the shelves of margarine and toilet paper. Odd, some people's priorities, ain't they?

Nor was Ms Thatcher alone. The Chairman of the Confederation of British Industry (sometimes laughingly called the bosses' trade union) foretold the collapse of civilisation as some of us know it, while the head of ICI prophesied an immediate loss of £25 million a week and total closure within a month.

All this because a proportion of the nation's truck drivers stopped work! We need only to reverse the argument to see clearly that ICI *make* £25 million a week while the truck drivers are working and civilisation as the CBI likes it bowls merrily along for the same reason.

This, it would seem to us, makes the lorry drivers Very Important Persons. We wonder why it is that persons who are so vital to the running of society have to fight to get a living wage? We seem to remember that every summer Parliament closes down for over two months and life goes on. When the transport workers stop for two days, we are tottering on the brink of chaos. Could Maggie Thatcher please spell out a conclusion from that for us?

A similar assessment of importance could be made for the train drivers who staged two one-day strikes over the last two weeks. A few thousand railwaymen are responsible for millions of others getting to work every day. The cursing City commuters struggled to get to work the first two days, then obviously many of them said what they should have said straight away. 'Sod it' they said, and stayed home.

So the wheels of industry *and* commerce are kept turning by these relatively small numbers of working men and women. Whether they are transporting goods or people they are taken for granted and taken notice of only when they stop — and the commuters who scream blue murder at the inconvenience never realise that they are themselves commodities, bought and sold and carted from place to place with a cost listed in the overheads just like the margarine in the canteen or the toilet paper in the loo.

Perhaps the most piercing screams went up however when hospital workers and ambulance men stopped briefly. These workers, whose daily toil is tending the sick and comforting the dying and

the injured, suddenly became callous, heartless murderers! Newspapers and authorities, having ignored the social service workers
who have been on strike for months (or if they have mentioned
them, have dismissed their claim for a working wage on the grounds
that the country can't afford it!) suddenly became so concerned
for the sick and elderly that you couldn't believe they were the
same creeps who had called for cuts in government spending on
the social services 'for the sake of the national economy'.

In fact, the hospital workers' strike went off half-cock precisely
because the workers are so bloody decent that they couldn't put
an all-out stoppage into operation (no pun intended)! And the
lorry drivers' strike has also dragged on much longer than necessary
because they have made so many concessions that its impact has
been weakened.

The Press has been so full of stories of employers having to
traipse around getting 'permits' for their trucks to cross the picket
lines, or of violence on the part of pickets armed with pickhandles,
that attention has been drawn away from the fact that food *has*
got through; hospital supplies *have* got through; essential services
have kept running; not one single case of assault by a picket has
led to any action by the police — and in fact the only casualty we
have seen reported has been a picket knocked down by a lorry
crossing the line! And he died — with very little comment.

Two new concepts, however, have been unearthed in this wave
of strikes. The first has given us a new phrase, 'Secondary picketing'. This means briefly the picketing of places one step removed
from the actual scene of the strike — like the destination of goods
that might be carried by blackleg hauliers.

The legality of secondary picketing is now preoccupying all those
good solid democratic citizens who accept, however reluctantly,
that we must allow the right to strike in principle, but can never
support one in practice. The way striking becomes acceptable in
a democracy is to make it so hedged around by legal restrictions
that it is rendered ineffective. That way we can boast to the
Communists, for example, that our workers, unlike theirs, are free
to strike — but we make sure it does them no good.

The second concept to surface is not a new one to us, but must
have been to some readers of the bourgeois Press. It is Syndicalism!
Yes, comrades, syndicalism is alive and well and dancing on the
grave of socialism, according to a Reverend gentleman in the
correspondence column of *The Guardian*! (Betcha he's a refugee
from *The Times*!)

But rather more (superficially) intelligent arguments have been paraded based on the observation that the trade union leadership has been losing control (though that's hardly something new is it?) and the local strike committees have been taking action without consulting Head Office and indeed, in flagrant defiance of Head Office directives. We have seen TU bosses squirming on the telly trying to explain the difference between directives and directives, both of which have been ignored by the lads and lasses on the picket lines. Undoubtedly, as happens in every strike, decisions have to be made on the spot — and since it is the lads and lasses on the line who are standing out there in the cold, they are going to take tougher decisions than the officials who meet the opposition only over a boardroom table.

So, yes, decentralisation happens. Yes, that is a syndicalist principle. But we shall need a bit more than on-the-spot militancy to convince us that the coffin-club, wage-bargaining mentality, the craft-based divisionism, the clinging to differentials and one-up-manship which is what our degenerate trade unionism is today (the rail strike was an example of inter-union conflict as much as anything) before we see signs of an emergent syndicalist consciousness.

Of course there is the point that when the chips are down, direct action class-war tactics fit the bill better than the collaborationist reformism of the trade union bosses. But unless the workers go further and think in terms of ending the struggle once and for all by taking over; unless they give up ideas of fighting among themselves for crumbs, but of sharing the whole cake equally, then talk of syndicalism or socialism or anarchy is just a lot of journalistic bullshit.

10th February 1979   P.S.

Who Needs Leaders?

The widest series of strikes to hit Britain since the war is drawing to a close.

It is ending as it began: piecemeal. Which is to be expected, given the nature of our trade union movement.

Thankfully, the days when it could all have been called a 'Communist Plot' have passed, not least because nobody takes the Communist

Party seriously nowadays. But nobody has placed the 'blame' on any other Party of the so-called 'Left' either — because 'politics' whether of the Right or Left, is now so discredited that not even the frantic mouthpieces of the media, trying to justify the Establishment point of view — and what else are they there for — could find a Left Party with enough influence to substantiate their placing of the blame.

Just a vague 'Anarchy' — that's all they could scream about. And of course for them — whether they be the CBI or journalists whose jobs seem to be secure for the time being — 'Anarchy' means chaos.

People taking decisions for themselves; workers at the point of production deciding what they will do and why — this is 'chaos' for those who think that only leaders and properly elected representatives, spokesmen or usually reliable sources of information, are capable of responsible thought and action.

The idea that 'ordinary' workers — especially the low paid — dust collectors and the like — are to be taken seriously even as members of 'the nation' does not seem to occur to responsible guardians of the nation's good.

Altogether, over the past few weeks, over a million workers have been engaged in struggles to defend their standards of living against the 'five per cent' policies of the Labour Government. They have been described as bully boys, as holding the country to ransom, as though they are not part of the nation at all. As long as they do as they are told, keep their heads down and keep on working, come what may, and clamber into khaki uniform to defend their freedom if the national interest demands it — then they are the salt of the earth and jolly good Britishers, but if they practice their sense of injustice and demand a little freedom for themselves against the economic interests of their employers and their Government — then, somehow, they are no longer part of the nation.

And the *nation*, the proper, pukka, highly paid, responsible, elected, ethical, far-seeing and righteous, second-home-in-the-country, chicken-in-every-pot and two-cars-in-the-garage citizens of our property-owning democratic *nation*, closes its Christian ranks against the bad anarchic breath of those who actually do the work.

And, brothers and sisters of the Left, may we point out yet again that this includes your proper trade union leaders and your actual Labour Government no less than the more obvious class enemies of the Conservative Party and the Right in general.

In our last issue we poured some scorn on the journalistic comments of those who saw 'anarchy' in the failure of the TU leaders to control their members, and who actually went so far as to diagnose an emergence of 'syndicalism' as one of the problems. One of the dangers, indeed.

We might have appeared to be wrong, inasmuch as there was clearly a rebellion against reluctant leaderships by the rank and file, but we claim a certain amount of experience in observing and analysing these events — and we know damn well that most of the militants who spat at Jim Callaghan and ignored the directives of their leaders will nevertheless vote faithfully for the Party he leads and happily go on paying large salaries to those same union leaders.

When workers take action in the heat of the moment, and act in their own interests at last, they invariably take the right action. Unfortunately, when the situation cools down, they go back to thinking along the same old lines and take the easy way out — especially, ironically, if they have won the struggle and things don't seem so bad after all.

And there is no doubt that this is a struggle that is being won. The Labour Government's five per cent policy is in tatters — and triumphant workers are settling for magnificent 16 per cents and 8.8 per cents. Big deal! In a year's time they will be looking at each other and saying 'Why ain't we better off?' while their leaders and the politicians go on calling for sacrifice and concern for the good of the nation . . .

When workers realise that they don't need leaders at all; when they think in terms of occupying the factories and taking them over, rather than shivering outside the gates; when they demand the abolition of the whole stupid wage system and refuse to vote or work for renegade leaders of any kind — then we can talk realistically of anarchy and see syndicalism as a means to that end.

But whenever any workers go to the polls in the next election, or bother to vote for a general secretary of their union — knowing that their experience this last month has taught them that it is their own strength that matters — then we shall know the lesson has still not been learnt.

24th February 1979   THE EDITORS

Our Capitalist Unions

It is ironic that in the very season when more massive action is being planned by trade unionists than we have seen for years we should also be treated to the spectacle of vicious in-fighting in both the trade union movement and the Labour Party itself.

In-fighting which, it must be said, has nothing to do with the 'emancipation of the masses' but everything to do with either the seizure or the consolidation of leadership, the protection of the institutions of 'The Labour Movement', and the presentation of a 'respectable' face to the electorate in time for the next election.

Not that the massive action itself should not be seen as part of the in-fighting as well, for the Right Wings of the Party and the unions are very conscious that they have to maintain a credibility in the face of working class suffering that will pull the carpet from under the Militant Tendency and show that the old Party that everybody knew and loved and voted for in their millions in the past can still get up and scare the pants off the Tories — without being 'extreme' or unBritish or Marxist or anything horrible like that.

It is in fact extraordinary that the Tories should have chosen (if in fact they did choose) to stand their monetarist ground on the issue of pay for the health workers. For if there is one section of the working class that is absolutely gilt-edged in the eyes of the public it must be the nurses. There is even a TV series called 'Angels' about behind-the-scenes life in our hospitals, which, thankfully, shows that some nurses are not all that angelic in every way. But doesn't that make them more human and, thus, even more lovable?

But Mrs Thatcher and her foul Mr Fowler, Health Minister for the Upper Classes, are so besotted by their own monetarism and their devotion to duty up to and beyond the deaths of others, that they couldn't really believe that the nurses could strike *and still retain the sympathy of the public.* Like Ted Heath in choosing to do battle with the miners, with their enormous industrial muscle, they have made a serious tactical blunder which may well cost them very dear. Not only are their actions politicising a section of workers who have in the past been remarkable for putting dedication before pay (The Royal College of Nursing is now considering removing the 'no strike' clause from their rule book!) but they have provided the Centre and Right of the trade union movement with a prime opportunity to DEFY THE LAW with a tremendous weight of public opinion in secret and sly sympathy with them.

The law is of course that one recently introduced by the Conservatives which tries to ban, by making unlawful, secondary picketing or industrial action in support of somebody else's industrial action. In other words, solidarity.

We must not go overboard, however, in admiration for the new-found courage of Len Murray and Co, for they are very careful, in all their public announcements, to make clear that they are not *directing* their members to come out on 22nd September (not like they would direct them to go back to work in an unofficial strike, for instance), but that they are simply asking for gestures, in sympathy, according to individuals' inclinations or abilities or degree of militan—whoop, sorry!

If the Labour Party does not screw every possible ounce of advantage out of this situation, then it certainly does not deserve to get back to Downing Street come the next election. Mr Fowler has categorically (for the second time) said there is absolutely no more money for the health workers. If he is forced to yield, there will be only one honest way out for him: into the woods with a shot-gun. But we feel he does not have the moral fibre for that.

On the other hand, the terrible railwaymen, everybody's villains a few weeks back, could stop work for an hour in the middle of the day and hardly anybody would notice. All public transport could stop; tanker drivers take an extra hour for lunch; power workers throw the switches; miners leave the coalface an hour early; teachers cut lessons, tailors cut less cloth, bakers bake a loaf or two less, car builders build one car less, bricklayers leave out an hour's courses — all gestures from workers to show their contempt for the Government's mean policies, and all to no avail.

If Mr Leonard Murray and his newfound (?) mate Mr Frank Chapple, next Chairman of the TUC and right-wing convert from the Communist Party, really want to show their contempt for Tory policies, they would call a general strike of indeterminate length to stop once and for all the concept that a Government can dictate standards of living to working people — especially those as economically weak but as morally strong as health workers.

But the fact is that they do not have contempt for Government policies, because they are in the same game themselves: the game of controlling the workers in the national interest and the continuance of the capitalist system, with, at best, a few rough edges rubbed off.

The end of capitalism, after all, would mean the end of the *need* for trade unions, necessary only in a class-divided society where there is an employing class (private or State) and thus divided interests necessitating mediators between employers and employed. This is the role of the unions: mediators, trusted by the bosses as responsible, right-thinking and law abiding, no less than by the workers, sold on the concept of obedience and the necessity for bosses.

It is not surprising therefore to find trade unions structured just like capitalist firms, with a ladder of success up which the ambitious official can climb, paying himself, with the approval of his fellow climbers, salaries far in advance of the wages of the workers he is paid to represent and with a safe pension at the end of his days — a pension made safe by investing the funds in capitalist stocks and shares. How can you expect TU leaders to fight a system out of which they do so well?

Of course you can't, any more than you can expect politicians to fight effectively against the system which offers them position, privilege and fame which, once achieved, opens doors on to the boardrooms of capitalist companies where the idea of workers' control leaves them all rolling on the floor with laughter.

It is the myth at the back of all socialist Parties that, once *their* members have achieved power they will operate it in the interests of everybody else except themselves. Generations of backsliders in the Labour Party have not convinced the members of the Militant Tendency that their selected front-runners will not be the same in their turn. To get to the top you have to have what it takes to succeed in a centralised set-up, by which time you are convinced that you know better than anybody else what is good for them. At the best you become paternalistic, at the worst dictatorial.

The issue of syndicalism must be raised in this argument since it presents the only alternative to unionism which can be logically linked with anarchism, and representing anarchistic ideas applied to the industrial scene.

We must always be careful to draw the distinction between that — which must be accurately described as anarcho-syndicalism — and 'straight' syndicalism, which is a form of industrial unionism: a higher form of unionism in that it brings together all workers in any one industry rather than the fragmentary *trade* structure of the reformist unions we know today. Unification in industrial unions, however, can work, as it does in Germany today, for the convenience of the bosses, where these are allowed to exist.

It is only when syndicalists are guided by anarchist aims and principles that the purely structural benefits of that form of industrial organisation can be used for revolutionary ends. Those who argue that involvement in the day-to-day struggle will inevitably whittle away revolutionary consciousness had better, first, examine their own consciences about how many times they have marched with others against a particular war, against particular weapons, or — assuming we will be marching on 22nd September — for particular wage claims while in our hearts and minds we comprehensively condemn the fundamental causes of all wars, all weapons and the wages system *in toto*.

Anarchists involved in industry (and there must be *some!*) know full well that the trade unions are a sell-out. What is the alternative? If it is not ANARCHO-syndicalism, what is it?

11th September 1982   P.S.

Boring From Without

The worst thing you can do in any war is to underestimate your opponent — and if you are fighting a class war in what is laughingly called a democracy it is even more dangerous, for dirty tricks and in-fighting are more the order of the day than straight confrontation.

On the surface the Trotskyist tactic of 'boring from within', or 'Entryism' as it was officially called, was no more difficult than had been the Stalinist strategy of capturing the trade unions in the 1930s and 40s. Then, you simply had to be a better trade unionist than anybody else, more dedicated, more willing to give of your time and before long you were a shop-steward, a delegate, and in a position to push through resolutions in support of the Anglo-Bulgarian Friendship Society, arrange exhibitions of Kazakhstan dancing shoes and other matters of great moment for the British working class on its march towards freedom and democracy and the next Five Year Plan for more coal production in the Don Basin.

The Trotskyists, followers of a failed authoritarian, themselves never failed to be jealous of the successful authoritarian, Stalin, and it was very much in the mode of 'anything you can do we can do better' that one of the four splinters after the crack-up of the Revolutionary Communist Party in 1948 decided that to get at the working class you had to go where the working class was gathered in strength: the Labour Party, if you didn't know.

To be fair, this must have seemed a rather easier task in 1948 than at almost any other time, for Labour was totally in control, theoretically, of the State machine, the whole apparatus of government, the forces of law and order and the upper echelons of British industry after the war. Nationalisation of basic industries was being rushed through (though with compensation for share-holders); the egalitarianism of misery was being held to through rationing (which in clothing meant dull uniformity) and conscription, Five Year Plans were being laid down and torn up with gay abandon, while clear-cut class war was not being complicated by anybody singing 'Glad to be Gay' or being militantly feminist or racist either way. Straight on for the Socialist State!

All the Entryists had to do was to sneak into the Labour Party, show themselves to be better social democrats than thou, and the Party with all its apparatus of power and millions of votes would fall into their hands. Then, oh then, the dictatorship of the proletariat could be introduced in correct Marxist terms, in line with the historic mission of the working class emancipating itself under the proper leadership, left-wing deviationists could be dealt with as the Old Man himself had demonstrated and scientific material determinism would do the rest.

Unhappily, determined materialism in the form of a capitalist class who had also read the books, struck back and within five years the Labour Party began the decline that hasn't finished yet.

Having decided that Labour was a nest of sitting ducks, and having disguised themselves with fine feathers and seductive mating calls like 'The Right to Work!', quacked from feather-lined nests of their own, nobody was more surprised than the Entryists when half the Labour Party got up and flew away. And the other half stayed put and quacked back.

This was not how it was supposed to work at all. The soppy social democrats were supposed to fall into the clutches of the bolsheviks 'just like that', as Tommy Cooper would say.

But historical determinism was not dead yet. Someone came up with the mysterious phrase 'extra-parliamentary activity'. 'What does it mean?' everybody asked themselves and each other. 'It means anything you want it to mean', came the stern reply. And among the things someone wanted it to mean was to go where the workers were by another route. The fiendish ploy was to put moles into industry.

This time it was harder. This time it meant going to work in factories like real workers. Clocking on at 7.45 a.m. for an eight o'clock start on the assembly line, jockeying yourself into a position to become shop-steward, arguing with management and — finally — coming eyeball to eyeball with the trade union bosses. Which is where the buck stops. For these are the real professionals.

Unlike the Labour Party, which can be led by graduates from the London School of Economics, renegade doctors, daughters of suffragettes and sons of the aristocracy (none of which is intended to impugn their honesty — only their experience of all-in wrestling) the trade unions are led by individuals who have themselves clawed their way up from the factory floor, aided perhaps by Catholic or Methodist teaching, till they have reached a position where they hobnob with bosses, drive cars comparable to the boss's, live at the comfortable end of town, go to the same tailors as the bosses and but for their carefully maintained working class accents, are identical with the bosses in their *responsibility* for the running of the works. Well oiled, and not about to tolerate sand in the works.

Middle class militants may falsify their job application forms and maybe fool the Personnel Officers — but they won't fool the full-time trade union representatives. They can smell pinkos a mile off.

In the current hoo-ha about the sacking of alleged 'militants' for falsification of application forms, we have not yet seen it spelt out as to how the investigation began, how the cover was blown. Surely it can't have been as easy as the *Sun* newspaper (if that's what it is) claimed: 'They never read the *Sun*; they read the *Guardian* and talk about conditions in Nicaragua.' (Tip for any of our readers thinking of moling their way into industry: read FREEDOM and fox everybody!)

No, it is far more likely that militant action on the shop floor attracted the attention of local trade union officials, one quiet word led to another and, horror of horrors, it was discovered that some of these enthusiastic rank and file unionists were *over-qualified* for their jobs — like having been to university!

One such mole told (or sold) his story to the *Observer* last week, ('I was a mole for the SWP'), and after telling how he had helped to fight for better conditions for workers in a car factory (though without raising their class consciousness one iota) he said:

At the end of the day the trades union structure was as big a stumbling block to what we were trying to achieve as the management themselves.

In fact, I ended up with a far greater loathing for the union than for management. It was the trades unions that used to get up my nose. The

full time officials never used to take the initiative on anything and when
we did come to a really important battle over redundancy, they essentially
sabotaged our attempt to fight the threat to the industry.

And once you got involved in the union you realised just what an
undemocratic organisation it was, how much control the officials had.
Probably more of my energy went into trying to democratise the union
than in fighting the management.

All this, of course, is something that any anarcho-syndicalist
could have told him. This is not even a part of the dilemma facing
every militant who wants to work towards a greater consciousness
on the part of every worker: the question of how far you go in
fighting for better conditions here and now without becoming so
bogged down in the day-to-day struggle that you forget the eventual
aim.

The mole reported in the *Observer* ended up being more sympathetic
towards the employers than the unions — and disillusioned in the
process. This was because he had been hooked on the concept of
political in-fighting in order to gain political advantage and through
that, political power. It is a hopeless seduction to think that essentially
reformist organisations — political or industrial — can be 'taken
over' to become organs of revolution and total change.

Two aspects militate against the concept: one is that in the process
of climbing the ladder to gain influence in the organisation you
aim to control, you become corrupted yourself. The practice of
manoeuvre, of stealthily winning points and advancing your cause
little by little, just as surely, little by little, leads you into ways of
thought and practice that take you over.

The second is that the organisations are already in the hands of
sharp-eyed politicos who can see you coming. The machinery of
organisations which are worth taking over are already established,
long in the tooth and ruthless; they are already — as the *Observer*'s
mole found out — part of the problem.

As we said at the beginning, it is fatal to underestimate your
opponent. Still worse is just not to recognise him in the first place!
For anarchists, the issues are still clear: both those in power and
those struggling to achieve it — by whatever means — are equally
our enemies.

27th August 1983   PHILIP SANSOM

One Big Boss

It needs only a slender majority in the Commons to give a Party power, and this is usually achieved with a minority of votes in the country. So we are usually governed by a minority Party. Way back in 1945, an exception to this was chalked up when the Labour Party swept to power with a huge majority. The party leaders were taken by surprise, for it was taken for granted that our greatest wartime leader, Winston Churchill, would be returned to office by a nation ever-so-grateful for his leadership during the most destructive war up to that date.

The election was swung, however, by the very voters he had led so gallantly from the rear: the soldiers, sailors and airmen of the Armed Forces had voted overwhelmingly for a change. Unfortunately, what they got was the Labour Party, who hadn't got the guts to do what the electorate had obviously expected of them — a *radical* change in the British system that would have made the return to the bad old days of the 1930s impossible. Blimey mate, in those days we had more than three million unemployed! Didn't want that again, did we?

The Labour Party's idea of change was to nationalise the mines, the railways, electricity and gas. Instead of a thousand mine owners, there would be only one — a State-appointed, nationalised board of bosses. Instead of a thousand little bosses, one big boss. The miners cheered, silly sods. It must be admitted that with access to State money (i.e. public, i.e. your and my money) improvements in conditions were possible. Safety standards were improved, pit-head baths were installed, so miners did not have to walk home in their working filth to squat in a bath before the kitchen fire before crawling off to bed. But the big boss was now there. A miner blacklisted for 'disobedience' in one pit found himself blacklisted everywhere — for the same boss was everywhere.

If nationalisation ever needed its final condemnation, it got it this year — when the miners had to crawl back to work after a noble year-long struggle, behind a leader who believes in nationalisation, not in workers' control but in centralised state control.

To cast another quick backward glance to the 1945 Labour Government, one can only weep that the chance to make those radical changes was not even considered. Not that anarchists expected them, but the political power was there to introduce a much stronger say in the running of industry by the workers. Never mind about owning shares in the mining industry — giving workers a slice of the capitalist action — but *some* degree of decision-making should have been written into the nationalisation legislation, some workers' control over the closing of pits, for example. But the idea of extending, even by a little, *industrial* democracy, which would give workers some control over their working lives, did not even occur to the Labour Party — or the trade union bosses. Scargill's fight against pit closures was a bit late; for pits were already being closed in the fifties — with no opposition from the unions.

But then, the Labour Party has never been a socialist Party in any real sense of the word. Or even, for that matter, social *democratic*. It has been a centralist Party, aiming at the control of individualistic capitalism by smoothing over its rough edges; its introduction of the Welfare State was aimed at making capitalism more acceptable, not abolishing it. The welfare face of the Warfare State.

November 1985   PHILIP SANSOM

NORTHERN IRELAND

Police Brutality Everywhere!
Now it's Londonderry

Respectable opinion has been suddenly shocked out of its complacent belief that 'It couldn't happen here'. In the city of Londonderry, well within the boundaries of the 'United Kingdom' and in territory owing allegiance to our Queen and governed, most English believe, by our representatives in Westminster, a sudden baton charge backed up by water cannon has made police brutality on the pattern of Mayor Daly's Chicago and de Gaulle's Paris a living reality right here.

Suddenly we discover that housing and employment conditions are so appalling, political and religious gerrymandering so corrupt, that it is necessary to organise a 'Civil Rights' march in protest. Suddenly we are told that votes are allocated according to housing occupation, ownership and 'company law' — and the allocation of municipal housing is so rigged that thousands of 'undesirables' (i.e. of the wrong religion or politics) are kept without both houses and votes. While some favoured, well-housed individuals can clock up as many as forty votes!

The voting aspect is of little concern to us as anarchists. What is more important is the ruthless manipulation of municipal assets to keep in power a bunch of greedy bigots who operate the whole scene for their own advantage while making Northern Ireland the most depressed area in the UK.

And then, when a peaceful march is organised to draw attention to this stinking situation, the police charge with batons flailing, hitting out indiscriminately at marchers and bystanders, men and women, boys and girls, in an orgy of unrestrained violence. One special tactic they are alleged to have used was to put their batons between boys' legs and bring them smartly upwards. The march consisted of few more than 1,000 people, and the Stormont Govern-

133

ment thought it necessary to send 200 police against them, clearly with orders to terrorise such demonstrations out of existence. Fifty were injured, including Republican Labour MP Gerry Fitt who was clubbed twice for good measure and needed stitches in his head, although Ulster's Minister for Home Affairs William Craig (after saying 'I am very grateful to the police') maintains they were under strict orders to hit the legs of the marchers.

Net result of this police violence: the people of Derry are now really coming out on the streets and fighting back, with bonfire barricades and petrol bombs. It was not necessary for *them* to indulge in any provocation techniques to make the State in Northern Ireland show its true colours. What is necessary now is for them to forget their religious differences and combine to destroy O'Neill's corrupt and stinking little cesspit and take over the means of production themselves. The economy may be in a bad way, but at least they could ensure that what was produced was fairly distributed and they could go some way to meeting their own needs instead of being bemused by ignorance and governed by terror.

12th October 1968   JUSTIN

In Belfast, Like Everywhere — All Law is Gun Law

The people of Northern Ireland have just come through another winter of their discontent. The pale spring sunshine does no more than illuminate the squalor of the Belfast slums and highlight the inadequacy of the barrack-like tenements which the Government offers as an alternative. For the weary mothers of over-large families the longer, lighter evenings spell, not pleasure and leisure, but more anxiety as their ragged children dice with death under the wheels of passing traffic in the only playgrounds they know — the streets. For fathers, ill-fed and demoralised, the east wind is still too cold to leave off their threadbare overcoats on their vain daily walk to the Labour Exchange.

Belfast is an occupied city, cut in two like Berlin and like Berlin patrolled by armed soldiers. Unlike Berlin, however, nobody is concerned to make Belfast a shop window, competing to demonstrate a better way of life on one side or the other. On both sides of the

Belfast barbed wire the citizens are demoralised, bewildered, humiliated by religion and plagued by politics. Over all broods the presence of the British Army.

The confrontations of last year culminated in little enough — the election of Bernadette Devlin to Westminster and a change of Prime Ministers. Instead of effete and useless Captain O'Neill, Stormont switched to effete, useless Chichester-Clark, a new broom out of the same old broom cupboard, hoping only to sweep enough dirt under the carpet to keep the party clean. Alas for C-C — he can't even keep the party together; the pathetic reforms he professes are too much for his own right wingers who, sensing his weakness, move in for the kill behind 'tough' ex-security Minister William Craig.

What has been done?

While they have been playing politics, the people have been patiently waiting, hoping that since things could hardly get worse, perhaps they might get better. They haven't. The half of the population — the Catholic half — who welcomed the British Army's occupation last year as a shield against the threat of Protestant bully-boys have gradually come to realise that when a lid is put on a boiling pot pressure builds up. Nothing was done to relieve the pressures in Northern Ireland; the immediate result of Big Jim Callaghan's visit was not a crash programme for housing — not even the *announcement* of one — nor any government pump-priming of the run-down economy nor any constructive proposals for the people. But what was *done* was the introduction of British troops complete with riot control equipment and tear gas. In other words — repression. In other words — Law and Order.

A great sigh of relief went up from the lib-labs. A period of stability, they all agreed, was what was wanted. A cooling-off period. Have you ever noted how all constitutionalists think that a 'cooling-off period' is the answer to everything? It's a variation on thinking that if you pretend something isn't there, perhaps it will go away.

But nothing has gone away in Northern Ireland. Not the religious animosities, upon which the ruling clique play with such skill; not the fear of change in the balance of power and certainly not the grinding poverty.

What has changed is the attitude of the young. The young people — in Belfast particularly — are not as sold on religion as their elders, and have begun to embrace the besetting sin for all religious bigots: disobedience. They can see for themselves that there is no future for them in an Ulster torn and divided upon itself in the service of either religious or political loyalties. And they can see that when the British Army came in last year, it used the excuse of keeping them apart for their own good, but its real work was simply — keeping them apart.

The army's real task
This is 1970, not 1917, and however much the ministers and the priests, the oldies of Church and State, may wish to hold back the clock and keep Northern Ireland the cultural and economic backwater it is, the youngsters can see and hear and some of them can even read what is going on in the rest of the world. They must be asking themselves why they are left out, and they must be coming up with the answers. Although the animosities and fears between the communities were real enough in terms of what *is* — the authorities (who, damn them, are always one jump ahead!) knew that the real danger to Ulster's rulers (and this is what concerns the authorities) lies in the breaking down of communal barriers and a joining of hands in the face of the real, common foe: the capitalist State.

What has changed in Northern Ireland is the emergence of groups cutting across these old communal barriers. Groups which, as the struggles continued last year, were beginning to make more and more sense to the young people. Who knows but that, if the British Army had not gone in, to keep them apart, the young Protestants and Catholics would have tumbled the racket and joined together against Stormont? This is the last thing the British Government wants. Hence the rubbish about Law and Order.

Now the break has come, and the Catholics, who 'welcomed' the Army last year are stoning it and throwing molotov cocktails. This is regarded with some bitterness by General Freeland (and whose satirical genius was expressed by sending in a soldier with *that* name?) who complained that the current riots by Catholic youths is a 'kick in the back'.

What every reporter and commentator has stressed, however, in these riots, is the youth of the demonstrators, many of whom are still schoolchildren. Well, is it so surprising? Their parents are demoralised, defeated. A lifetime of savage exploitation, religious irresponsibility, poverty, unemployment, appalling housing conditions — the lot. They've had it. But there's still some fight in the youngsters. And after all, what have they got to lose?

Why Should it Stop?

If the old Marxist bit about 'nothing to lose but your chains' applies anywhere in Britain today, it's in Northern Ireland. The schoolchildren of Belfast have nothing to lose and nothing to look forward to if they don't make something for themselves out of the shambles their parents have bequeathed them. And because either they see clearly that nothing can be done the constitutional way, or they can't make themselves heard any other way, they are turning to direct action.

Unfortunately it is purely destructive direct action. And until they get the support of older, working people who are prepared to occupy factories and shipyards; who will back squatting on a large scale; who will establish communal councils with an aim to make a permanent framework for a new form of society — until, in a word, *all* the people of Northern Ireland are prepared to make a social revolution, then continued harassment, confrontation, guerrilla tactics of all kinds, will continue. Why should it stop?

General Freeland thinks he has the answer to why it should stop. He announced his readiness to fire on rioters using 'offensive weapons' on Friday 3rd April. And in doing so, showed us once again the face of the State behind the mask of Law and Order.

Behind every law stands the policeman; behind every policeman stands the soldier. In every soldier's hand is the gun. Behind the respectable concept of 'Law and Order' is the bullet.

Ultimately, every State says to every citizen: 'You obey or you will be shot'. 'Democratic' States take a longer time getting round to it than totalitarian States, that's all. When the system is challenged toughly enough, when the pot is boiling too furiously, the lid is clamped down good and hard.

When the bourgeois right to exploit, to lie and deceive, to hold us down for ever, is challenged openly and they have to make a stand or go under — then we see the real, the organised, the institutionalised violence in which they believe.

Deep down, where it really matters — all law is gun law.

11th April 1970   JUSTIN

Butter Before Guns!

It was a pity about the Nazis. They just went a bit too far, and against Europeans too. If only they could have stayed within the bounds of decent ordinary governmental repression and kept it within their own sphere of influence and played the diplomatic game just a bit more cleverly, they might have been with us yet. Their buddy Franco is, after all, and only because he has been so discreet in the international sphere. No anti-semitism helps, of course, for this tends to stir people up all over the world; Franco has had the sense to keep his firing squads busy strictly on the Spaniards, thus encroaching on no other Government's preserves.

The Nazis, however, in their own way, were too honest. They always made perfectly clear what they were after and went straight after it, slaughtering their way into a very special niche in modern history. One phrase which the Nazis coined summed up perfectly what their economy was about and what their policy was to be, and they shouted it for all the world to hear. 'Guns Before Butter!' they screamed, and summed up precisely the policy of every Government in the 20th century.

The State is Never Deprived

No British Government is ever so foolish as to state a case like that so openly. They don't have to, of course. The British people will cheerfully accept any economic policy which cuts their standard of living while leaving untouched the armaments expenditure of the State, precisely because it is never expressed in such brash terms.

Under Stafford Cripps we had austerity; under Selwyn Lloyd, restraint; under Wilson, a wage freeze. Under all of them, a steady increase in the astronomical sums allocated to the State's military 'needs'. Not one of these good democrats came right out and said 'Guns Before Butter', but the apparatus of the State, not only in terms of armaments, but in the whole range of State expenditure — police, prisons, Civil Service (no wage freezes for *them*!), secret service and political police, riot equipment, Regional Seats of Government . . . the lot, all on top of what is spent on research and production of Polaris submarines and atomic bombers and the hardware they carry, and stacks of 'conventional' arms. Governments come and Governments go, but the State goes on for ever. Forever building up and extending its own power and techniques for retaining power, from CS gas to telephone tapping.

Even in the richest countries millions of families exist in squalid conditions, millions of children are deprived of proper education, but the State never deprives itself of guns or their modern, sophisticated equivalent.

Aristocratic Gauleiters

Let us take Northern Ireland. Poorest province of rich little Great Britain, it was artificially created precisely so that Britain could retain a toe-hold in Ireland and come to terms with the rebellious republicans of the South, having first established their Knoxious fifth column of bigoted Protestants from Scotland and awarded large areas of land to a few trusted families, the Chichesters and Clarks and O'Neills, who have managed the province like gauleiters before their time. By political gerrymandering, by cruel and blatant exploitation, by divide-and-rule, these privileged few have governed and manipulated an ignorant people deliberately kept in ignorance by Christian bigots. The highest rate of unemployment in the United Kingdom — and the lowest rate of new housing development, these have been the rewards for the Northern Irishman's loyalty to the Union Jack. Isn't it pathetic to see the slums of Derry dancing with the red, white and blue bunting — the banner of those who have cheated them down through the centuries?

It is even more ironical than that. Apart from its textile industry, the staple industry of industrial Ulster has been around the dockyards of Belfast. Harland & Wolffs and Short Brothers — making ships and flying boats for the British Navy and Air Force — have been the main sources of employment for skilled and unskilled workers alike and have been very sensitive to the ups and downs of military requirements. The Northern Irish have made the guns for the British, without demanding too much butter for themselves, and when the British have said from time to time that they don't need any more guns just now thank you, the shipyards close down and a thousand families starve. Precious little bread and no butter at all.

The Military Operation

And when the people of this servile province decide not to be so servile any more, what happens? First they hit out at each other, as a direct result of two centuries of religious argy-bargy, provocation and hate. Then into their midst come marching other hirelings of the masters they have helped to arm — with their guns at the ready, behaving like occupying soldiers always behave, with contempt for the people they were putting down. It's guns before butter all right. Government runs true to form and although now, just a little bit too late, reforms are promised, nothing gets done.

If things are as bad in Ulster as we all think they are, then economic aid should have been organised with every priority, pushed through and mounted like a military operation. But no. The only thing that gets mounted like a military operation is a military operation. In go the troops, in go the riot squads, in goes the CS gas ('Not made for use against civilians in the United Kingdom', they used to say at Porton) and in go the bullets and the threat of 'something better than CS gas'. Down comes the curfew.

A typical picture of how Governments operate. A fine example of 'Guns Before Butter', the true policy of Governments every-where. On such a level there is no glimmer of hope. From the people, there is some, and directly linked with butter! Into the Bogside area, where the curfew had prevented many a family from being able to get enough food into their houses (to which they had been restricted for 35 hours) and children were going hungry — into this area came storming, ignoring an army order not to have any demonstrations, hundreds of women carrying loaves and milk and butter and packets of tea.

Here was the answer of the people: solidarity.

Here is the next step: solidarity across the religious barriers!

The Real Enemy

For Christ's sake, can't these Christians see who their real enemies are? They are not their neighbours who go to a different church on a Sunday, but the rest of the week share the same economic slum: enmity does not lie in the difference between an Irish Catholic name and a Scottish Protestant one.

The real enemy is the common enemy: the bastards who sit on all their backs and crack the whips for all of them, the bosses and the politicians and the bishops of both sides.

The most relevant thing in Northern Ireland today is no doubt what both sides in the shouting match would think of as most irrelevant: revolution! This is the one and only answer that makes sense: a sweeping away of that old landed aristocracy which has governed for so long; a rejection of any political alternative which would recreate a new ruling class; the establishment of workers' control in the factories and a collectivisation of the land, with free neighbourhood communes to ensure egalitarian distribution according to need. In other words: BUTTER BEFORE GUNS!

But if they are gathering arms and if they are arming just to fight once again the Battle of the Boyne, they will create nothing but a legacy of bitterness for another three hundred years.

Bernadette Devlin

Our readers will know our attitude towards Bernadette Devlin's politics, but we don't like to see her thrown in prison any more than we like to see her wasting her time in Westminster.

One thing stands out: the utter stupidity of the Government which arrested her in such a way as to make a martyr out of her and which lit the fires in Bogside once again. Bernadette was on her way to surrender, and as a Member of Parliament she could do nothing else, when she was arbitrarily arrested and bundled off to jail without a farewell word to her comrades.

That the Government should act as it did was an act of provocation and puts the blame for the violence and deaths that arose immediately from Bernadette's arrest fairly and squarely on their shoulders. What has our new Home Secretary to say for himself?

11th July 1970 JUSTIN

British Army — Out!

Every country with a Government and a State apparatus is an occupied country. The land and the natural resources have been requisitioned by the occupying rulers who have imposed their laws and their regulations upon the population, who are compelled by want and fear to work on the masters' terms in the masters' factories for the masters' profits.

The rights of occupation, dignified and made permanent by the word 'ownership', were originally fought for with sword and lance; now they are defended by prison and bayonet. Disraeli's description of England as 'two nations' was, and is, absolutely right. It was and is 'Us' and 'Them'. They are the occupiers, we the occupied. The myths of nationalism; the shoddy confidence trick of patriotism, misusing one's sense of identity with place and people, these smother the reality of occupation when Government and governed are of the same 'nationality'. The distinction is made abundantly clear when the occupying Forces speak a 'foreign' language, swoop by plane or ship into your familiar environment wearing unfamiliar clothes and by force of arms conquer you and compel you to obey their commands.

The British in their days of imperial glory; the Germans in France; the Americans in Vietnam; Russia's Mongolian troops in Budapest or Prague — they were and are all as unacceptable as aliens from another planet. The foreign invader sticks out like a sore thumb and can be seen as the hated, imposed, master race. When it is a *master class*, the image is blurred.

But in Northern Ireland today, the image is not blurred. Although 'the province' is part of the United Kingdom, the presence of the British Army is as insulting as if they were men from Mars — and just about as bloody helpful. Although we were assured that the original occupation was welcomed by the Catholics, the most sorely oppressed part of the community, who went in fear of the hidden arsenals of the Protestants, it is now Catholic gunmen who are escalating the conflict because the hated presence of troops has not brought — and cannot ever bring — any solution to the problems of the Northern Irish people.

All that the British Army is doing in Ulster is to try to put the lid on the boiling pot — to keep law and order. This sterile excuse for a policy was doomed to failure. The very fact of military occupation was an admission of failure.

What the Northern Irish were asking for was jobs and homes and equality between the religions in the securing of these pathetic demands. It seems that this was too much to ask for, and instead of an attempt to bring the communities together, division was institutionalised by barbed wire down the middle of the street.

This mindless occupation is now in its second year. We wrote nearly a year ago (FREEDOM, 11th April 1970 'All Law is Gun Law') that the Catholics who originally welcomed the troops were now on the streets stoning them and that disillusionment with the British occupation was setting in.

Well, the iron must really now have entered the soul of the people of Belfast and Ballymurphy. Nearly two years of tension, conflict and curfew. Nearly two years of rubber bullets and CS gas. Nearly two years of the face of the State glaring in at your window.

Now they have had the lesson; now they have had the portrait of the enemy drawn for them on the pavements outside their very own doors. Now perhaps Catholic and Protestant alike can see that the State doesn't give a rat's piss for their homes or jobs or children.

In fact the State is sending in other mothers' children to fight in the streets — for the 'soldiers' who were pulled out of a pub the other night and shot down were no more than 17 — repeat *seventeen* — years old.

Over and over again, reporters have referred to the youth of the rioters. Ugly stories have circulated about the IRA (either the 'official' IRA or the new, more militant 'provisional' IRA) pushing kids forward on to the barricades. The fact is, of course, that the kids can't be kept *off* the barricades. But the question we must ask is — what are we to think of the Christian State which sends seventeen-year-old boys into a hot spot like Belfast?

Inexperienced and innocent, these stupid children have fallen for the kid stuff about 'A Man's Life in the British Army'. Ignorant of damn nearly everything after ten years of British education and particularly ignorant of Irish politics (and no wonder, by Christ!), at an age when a girl is not allowed to decide for herself whether she can have the contraceptive pill, these boys are shovelled into uniform and into a situation seething with hate for what they stand for.

Oh yes, now we know. The British Minister responsible for the Army has decided that no soldier under 18 must be allowed to serve in Northern Ireland — or any other combat zone. Oh, big deal!

Well, WE have made a decision too. It is that NO British soldier should be serving in Northern Ireland!

We maintain that the presence of the Army has solved nothing. On the contrary it has made matters worse. It has aggravated the situation until now the population can see no other solution but that which the British Government has taught them: the gun.

Where is the education programme, where the conciliation, where the social reconstruction, where even is the cooling-off that the troops were supposed to bring about? Nowhere!

In only one way has the presence of troops done any good — and that by accident and not at all in the way the Government wanted. It has brought together *some* militants from both sides of the religious barriers in a common hatred of the troops. The soldiers have in fact presented a picture of occupation so clear that even Protestants and Catholics can recognise it. They have all had more than a glimpse of the State and can now see who the real enemy is.

Fellow workers of Northern Ireland! Can you not recognise

NOW that it is not your neighbour of different faith who is your enemy, it is the Institution which grinds you both down. The State cynically uses people just like you from this side of the Irish Sea, to keep you divided and to keep you down.

And on both sides of the water we can unite in one call, at least BRITISH ARMY OUT OF NORTHERN IRELAND — NOW!
20th March 1971   JUSTIN

The Tragedy of Ireland

Nobody likes to be associated with failure. Thus the resignation of Major Chichester-Clark from the Premiership of the Northern Ireland Government is a clear indication of the failure of that Government to solve the problems of that unhappy province. Stormont is now about to endure the failure of the third Premier in three years, for if there is one thing that is absolutely clear in this particularly messy situation, it is that there is no possible solution to be hoped for from Stormont.

By a coincidence, the British Army of Occupation is also enjoying its third Commander since it began its thankless task 19 months ago, and he is in the unenviable position of knowing that his men are regarded by both sides with resentment and hatred; that there can be no military solution any more than a governmental one, and that all he can hope for is that a worsening of the situation is not forced upon him so that he looks a failure, too.

The Army's brief in Ulster is a limited one: to maintain 'law and order'. Nothing else. It has to try to keep the warring Protestants and Catholics apart and it feels entitled to shoot anybody coming at it with lethal weapons. Its presence is supposed to be a holding operation to cool the situation and buy time for political solutions to be applied.

This is essentially a policing operation, which has to be done by the British Army because the province's own police force, the Royal Ulster Constabulary, were undisciplined and panicky, cracked under pressure, as a Protestant force were hated by the Catholics and stood everywhere for provocative repression. It was a panic shooting by the RUC of a child in the Falls Road in 1969 that led to the force being disarmed and replaced by the Army.

But as we argued last week, the very presence of the Army has aggravated the situation rather than eased it and nobody even pretends that the military has a constructive role to play.

No more has the Stormont Government, dominated as it is by bigoted Protestants determined at all costs to protect the inequalities that have put them 'on top', fostered by religious hatreds that go back three hundred years and have never been allowed to be affected by any such Christian rubbish as 'love thy neighbour' or 'forgive thine enemy'.

Add to this bigoted Protestantism the fact that the Province's Government has been dominated also by upper-crust landowners whose ownership goes back to their support for Cromwell's bloody reign of terror and who are more concerned with maintaining their privilege than solving the country's economic problems and we can see why even the pathetic reforms proposed first by Captain O'Neill and then Major Chichester-Clark have never got off the ground.

Stormont's traditional answer to any demand for change has been the Royal Ulster Constabulary. The Westminster Government's answer has been the Army! Typical governmental behaviour!

Learning the Hard Way

So: no hope from above. What hopes for constructive solutions from below? Here lies the real tragedy of the situation, for working class solidarity is so clouded by religious differences that it is easier to get workers at each other's throats than at each other's sides.

There are those comrades who see the Northern Irish situation as in some way like Vietnam, and our attitude similar inasmuch as we say in both cases 'A plague on both your houses'. In fact, however, the Ulster situation is more similar to that in the Deep South of America, where the poor whites (Protestants) resent the fight for civil rights of the blacks (Catholics) and law and order is maintained by the Federal troops (British Army). Here again the oppressed who should be joining hands against a common enemy are divided by irrational prejudices; they make their own 'divide and rule' situation.

One big difference here, though, lies in the fact that a black man cannot shed his skin, whereas the Catholic can shed his religion — although it is clearly nearly as difficult! And for the Protestant in Northern Ireland to shed *his* version of revealed truth is obviously as hard as for the Southern racist to grow out of *his* prejudice.

Yet there are glimmerings of light. Just as, in the States, the young are rejecting the old racist and patriotic junk which filled

the heads of their fathers, so in Ulster a new awareness is growing
— under the pressure of events and in the heat of battle.

Nothing, after all, could be more calculated to open the eyes of
intelligent workers than the kind of experiences which are being
forced upon the people of Northern Ireland today.

On the one side the lunatic fringe of Paisleyism, the stolid reaction
of the Protestant Government and the interests it represents; behind
and above that, the forces of the State, which offer nothing constructive
but continued exploitation. On the other side various Catholic-
dominated Parties and organisations culminating in the IRA and
its split-off, the 'Provisional IRA', whose function is nominally to
protect Catholic areas from Protestant attack, but whose long-term
work is obviously to further the interests of the Eire Government.
(By seeing it like this, there *is* an analogy with Vietnam, however
much watered down, in that the Vietcong appear as a revolutionary
movement, but are actually the fighting wing in South Vietnam
for the government of North Vietnam.)

Anarchist Interests
Those who feel some sympathy for the IRA, or the Provisional
IRA, since they are the ones escalating the struggle against the
British Army, should ask themselves whether they would like to
see Northern Ireland come under anything like the Government
of Mr Lynch in Dublin? And what it would mean in terms of civil
strife to attain that unattractive goal? While we recognise that a
revolutionary situation will inevitably entail *some* violence, unless
it is the expression of mass working-class support it can only work
in the interests of an *élite* of some kind. A 'revolutionary' militia
without a revolutionary mass is doomed to failure, as Che Guevara
found out in Bolivia.

In any case, the revolution which anarchists are interested in is
the *social* revolution, overturning the whole economic and social
structure of authoritarian society and replacing it with the free
associations of free people: workers' control in the factories, free
communes, free access to the means of life, with the abolition of
the wages and money systems and all the apparatus of government
and exploitation. It's the extension of what some of our friends
call libertarian socialism into anarchism.

Now the only organisation working to any degree in this direction,
as far as we can see from here, is People's Democracy, with whom
some of our comrades actually on the spot in Northern Ireland feel
they can work. PD certainly cuts itself off from the religious hang-

ups and stresses working-class solidarity across the religious differences. It split off from the Civil Rights Association on account of the respectability of the Members of Parliament CRA had thrown up and the pressures from its Catholic right-wing, but in describing itself as 'radicalising' the civil rights movement by its demands for 'One Man One Job' and 'One Family One House' (*Free Citizen* 16th October 1970), PD clearly shows how far short of anarchist aims are 'radical' demands in the context of Northern Ireland!

It is in that context that we have to try to assess the revolutionary potential of the situation and, bluntly, the interest it holds specifically for anarchists. We have good comrades there working to build an anarchist movement and certainly, in times of ferment like these, not only should there be much interest in ideas but anarchist action is very relevant. In fact, of course, it is only anarchism which has real relevance as a solution to the appalling problems which face the Northern Irish working class.

Only if they get rid of that shoddy crew in Stormont; only if they turn their backs on the priests and ministers; only if they can find the strength to hold out their hands in solidarity to their fellows across the barriers that the centuries of bullshit have built up; only if they *want* to solve their problems *themselves* and run their own lives *themselves*; only if they take over the factories and the docks and the railways and the land *themselves* will they ever be able to break out of the ghastly prison that the priests and the politicians have made for them.

27th March 1971   JUSTIN

Role of the Provos

Comrades,
We have just received the latest issue of FREEDOM which contains a lot of stuff on the current situation in Ireland. Firstly, it should be said that Justin's article is, as usual, a relief from the tiresome tirade of inaccuracies which generally emanate from England once the situation in Ireland is mentioned. There are two points however. Firstly, the Provisionals. It is misreading the situation to state as Justin does that their 'long-term work is to further the interests of the Eire Government'. This is not so. To the Lynch-mob in control

in Dublin, the actions of the Provos are a severe embarrassment, since Eire has not in any sense achieved economic independence from England and with the advent of the EEC for the past 10 years under both Lemass and Lynch Eire has capered like a sycophantic spaniel at Albion's heel. They are only committed on paper to 'a united Ireland' and have for long appreciated that the changing needs of capitalism necessitate an end to violence here. Since they have disavowed the Provos the latter are now in the position of an anachronism. They cannot win for even if they're successful and they eventually do get some sort of federal solution, they will be among the first to be liquidated by the new State. This they appreciate as their publications show — of late they have been denouncing Fianna Fail. Their hope had been for a Blaney-Boland takeover but now that they have been completely discredited the Provisionals are left baying to the moon. It is much more likely that the ever-pragmatic Stalinist wing, the 'officials', will be able to do some deal with any federal solution. This is official CP line today. Hence the 'National Liberation Movement'.

It was a pity, however, that Justin failed to understand the article in the *Free Citizen* which referred to the PD 'radicalising' the civil rights movement by its demands for 'One man, one job' and 'one family, one house'. The point is not that these demands are in any way revolutionary, but that the posing of them was enough to split the CR movement and remove the gombeen men from it — a useful development at the time, although it is true to say that the CRA is irrelevant today.

JOHN BELFAST

Justin replies:
I take the point re the quote from *Free Citizen* — although John Belfast's interpretation is more sophisticated than the article implied!

Re the Provos: John is right. They cannot win. If they force a 'federal' solution, the 'official' leadership takes over; if they are simply smashed in the field, the Dublin Government takes the credit for *not* supporting them. I should have written 'the long term *effect of* their work'!

17th April 1971

Towards the Social General Strike

The so-called 'general strike' by Loyalist workers in Northern Ireland has been by all accounts only half-hearted and consequently, to the British Government, basically ineffectual.

The collapse of the strike has shown to a great extent the disillusionment of the Loyalist workers towards the idea of a return to a Stormont-based Parliament, and also how deeply the present economic conditions have affected them. Whereas the strike organised in May 1974 by the Ulster Workers' Council (at that time consisting exclusively of paramilitary leaders) was wholeheartedly supported by the workers and was successful in destroying the political solution known as the Sunningdale Agreement, offered to Northern Ireland by the British Government, it is also significant to note that in 1974 Loyalist political leaders remained in the background until the strike was established. Ironically, despite manning essential power supplies and petrol stations, the British Army offered no resistance to the Loyalist workers. In the present dispute it appears that the decision of the workers at the Ballylumford power station not to give support to the strike has dealt it the final blow. Only the threat of violence and intimidation, it seems, will now prolong the strike.

The present strike organised by the United Unionist Action Council (a grouping which this time includes both paramilitary organisations and political leaders such as Rev. Ian Paisley and Ernest Baird) has been ignored because experience has shown the Loyalist workers it makes no difference who rules Northern Ireland — a Stormont-based Government or direct rule from Westminster. Whilst the majority of the workers may still cling to the idea of a protestant-dominated Parliament at Stormont they must surely realise that there will never be a return to it short of a breakaway by the Six Counties from the United Kingdom. The long held prejudices of capitalism which have sought to play Protestant against Catholic worker and give the Protestants a privileged position are still prevalent in Northern Ireland and so long as they remain so the Loyalist faction will want to remain part of the United Kingdom. Parallel to this the worsening economic situation and lowering of the standard of living plus high unemployment has shown that the problem of economic welfare has taken precedence over temporary political gain.

If we can find no other sign that the 'sectarian' deadlock is ending we can take comfort in this preference; for far from being beaten by economic conditions it shows this experience at least might have taught the Loyalist and Catholic workers that the politicians need them. And that they don't need the politicians.

After seven long years of fighting in the present troubles, all talk of an end to the problem once the terrorist violence has been defeated has been shown to be a hollow sham. The Loyalist leaders protesting for an end to the violence are quite prepared to accept the effect of the bully-boys' intimidation, despite bland statements denouncing it. Once the British Army (now standing at 17,000) has gone from Northern Ireland the real violence, a corrupt capitalist system backed by military force, will be challenged by both Loyalist and Catholic worker. Then it is that we can look forward to a lasting, social, general strike that will not need intimidation to motivate it.

14th May 1977   FRANCIS A. WRIGHT

Planning Permanent Oppression

While all good democrats in the West are pointing the finger of scorn at General Jaruzelski and his martial law in Poland, a similar condition in part of the United Kingdom has assumed the air of permanence.

Martial law, of course, has not been declared in Northern Ireland — just a jolly old 'State of Emergency' — which is the British democratic way of doing the same thing without seeming to. Both 'martial law' and 'state of emergency' are supposed to describe temporary conditions in a troubled State — conditions laid upon the people by their authorities to 'restore law and order' and then when things are back to normal (i.e. the troublemakers have been crushed) the abnormal restrictions are removed and it's business as usual.

When Jaruzelski introduced martial law in Poland he was very careful to say that it would only be temporary. Only for as long as it took to destroy Solidarity, which seems to be taking longer than he thought. When the Labour British Government sent mainland British troops over to Northern Ireland in 1969, it was to 'keep the peace' between Catholics and Protestants and the first thing they did was to erect barbed wire barricades between the two communities. It was to be a temporary measure.

The Brits are now in their thirteenth year in Ireland, and not only has their presence taken on the air of permanence but their administration is now quietly indulging in practices which are literally *building-in* the divisions they were sent to resolve.

The barbed wire barricade *is* proving to be relatively temporary — only because it is being replaced by *permanent* brick walls, 20 feet high and of a strength specified by the military who, without any statutory right, is dictating to the (probably willing) Northern Ireland Housing Executive what they want and where, in any housing projects going on.

Within pedestrian areas, 'walkways' are being made wide enough and with strong enough foundations to take heavy military vehicles; community building plans are altered — like one in the Ardoyne, which has a chronic housing shortage, where the Army demanded a group of houses removed from the plan.

And round them all, cutting off the communities that occupation has failed to pacify — those bloody great walls, establishing the boundaries of the ghettos.

Ironically, the very day after this story was reported in *The Guardian*, the BBC presented a long radio 'documentary drama' on the uprising in the Warsaw ghetto in 1943 — an event sparked off by *the building of high walls around the ghetto* by order of the Nazis. Of course Jewish and Polish workers provided the labour, just as have the Catholics and the Protestants in Belfast — building their own cages.

Twenty years later, East German workers — some of whom, after all, might have survived service in Warsaw — were themselves building the Berlin Wall, not to keep intruders out, but to keep themselves in.

But then — haven't workers always built their own prisons? And the political complexion of their Governments has never made the slightest difference.

1st May 1982   P.S.

DISASTERS

Aberfan and the Price of Coal

There is a moment in the life of an individual or of a community when grief is naked and public, when a tragedy is so unexpected and overwhelming that it defies rationalisation, and one can only weep in a company of sorrow. Nature and the sophisticated mechanics of war have made us cynical with the vagaries of death, for we have had for too long to live with the cause to feel more than a futile sense of shock when the effect is personal and not the blind or wilful destruction of others. The amoral machinery of communication long ago glazed the eye of metropolitan man and the trembling heart aches a little less with the next issue of each daily news sheet. But the death of innocence through blind and bureaucratic mismanagement screams to be heard and anger roars above the official valedictions.

At 9.15 a.m. on Friday 21st October, the children of Pantglas Junior School, within the Welsh mining village of Aberfan, sat at their desks. A grey morning made even greyer by the huge black tip of drifting slime that had for many years overshadowed the small school. For years this refuse of the local coal industry had grown inch by inch to finally take command of the village, and men and women lived out their lives within its rare shadow. But this was not the acceptance of an indifferent community, for year after year they had protested, through all those official channels, that death from a river of black slime would one day sweep down and destroy them but abstract authority brushed their untutored fears aside. At 9.10 in the morning the mountain of black slime began to flow and at 9.21 a.m. 116 small children began to drown in its inescapable maw.

There is to be an inquiry and men, of their nature, will twist and distort the facts to serve their own particular ends and some unfortunate may or may not be held to be publicly responsible for the death of these 116 children. But let us not delude ourselves. Though minor figures in this masque of death will be pilloried before the community, those who are responsible for this unnecessary tragedy will never take their place within a public dock.

It is idle to catalogue the list of all those who gave private and public testimony that this evil would take place. Tory and Labour councillors, ministers of the local Churches, schoolteachers (one of whom died within the broken school), union officials, all (over the years) added their voices to the impotent cry of protest to those in authority and nothing was done. Even when the men who daily worked upon the tip gave their warning they were told to carry on for, in all honesty, what management at a local level could dispose of thousands of tons of oozing sludge. So nothing was done.

When the men protested through their union that the telephone between the tip and the colliery was no longer in working order (the wire had been stolen) the union secretary had to inform them that it was not *compulsory* to have a telephone and so the phone that might have saved lives hung useless. Yet who among us can swear in true faith that, within his own place of employment, some item of safety equipment does not also hang useless and idle?

When mineable coal was discovered in Wales a nation dug its own grave for the landless peasants found themselves herded into the rat-runs of the earth to hack forth its wealth for a foreign market.

To the Welsh people the rich coal beneath their sweet soil became a black cancer and generation after generation of men lived out their miserable lives in the darkness of the contracted earth and they became another slum proletariat doomed to slave out their short lives within the drear valleys wherein grass refused to grow. For the mine owners were absentee owners and, were they Welsh or English, they took from the Welsh people their ill-paid labour and the coal beneath their feet and in return they robbed a people of their dignity to live as free men and to show their contempt they spewed forth the refuse of their rapacity onto the green fields of Wales and the gentle beds of its lush valleys.

Those who chose to rob the people of Wales had neither the legal obligation, the intention, or the desire to haul away the unmarketable leavings of these rich pickings from the earth and year by year these huge black monuments to the infamy of corporate greed fouled the fields and streams of a once fair country.

But the men and women of Wales were not work-animals content to eat their bitter bread in silence and without protest and the story of their industrial war became a magnificent roll call of those who fought, yea even to the very pit face, for what they held to be their heritage. When a Labour Government came into office and took the pits under State Ownership many believed that now at last the day had come when the men of Wales would control their own destinies, but all they found were new masters and the black tomb-stones of industrial refuse continued to flower like festering scabs upon the barren fields, where once the overseer for the absentee owner had first poured forth his profitless filth.

The dream of a Wales green and flowering again became once more the mocked fantasy of the romantic and the nationalist, the anarchist with his cry of the good society, and the dreaming child, while the belief that the socialist society had finally taken its stand and that now, not only would the rich coal be hauled away to feed the furnaces of that socialist society, but all the millions of tons of black filth would be hauled away to fill the crevices in some un-claimed sea bed and grass would once more grow within the valleys and sheep would graze again, became the dream of an unclaimed hour.

It was indeed an idle dream for an idle moment for the State offered the people of Wales the Old Capitalism dressed in the garb of the Man from the Ministry, and for the black and foul smelling tips Section 180 of the Coal Mines Act, that gave each colliery the legal right to leave its black spew where it lay. This is the story and the tragedy of the people of Wales and all the years of struggle appear to have been wasted, for the black slime that killed their children was laid in the evil days of private profit and it killed their children in the era of State Ownership.

If there is one man who deserves to be singled out for the finger of condemnation it is My Lord Robens, that vain and stupid man who has betrayed the trust, not of his political masters, but of the socialism nurtured over the long years within these dark valleys. Vain, because while they still fought to dig the dead children from out of the still flowing black slime, he was grinning in his new robes as the first Chancellor of the University of Surrey and stupid, because this clerk in office refused to visit the valley of the dead because his own self-created protocol decreed that he should not until he had decided that the time was ripe and fitting.

Let My Lord Robens ponder these hours and this valley for this Welsh Gethsemane is My Lord Robens's Golgotha. These children died because those who claimed the allegiance of the Welsh political Left betrayed that faith. As in the past they chose to exploit these mines within the framework of the orthodox profit system and within that system, as the old time mineowners would have told them, it was uneconomical to clear the land of these black and sterile hills of uneconomic filth and so these children died.

Yet the struggle must still be fought within these valleys for the right of men to live, to work and die in peace and dignity, and only when the grass once more grows green around the graves of these innocent dead will Wales be free.

29th October 1966   ARTHUR MOYSE

Robens and the Aberfan Dead

On 21st October 1966, 116 small children died in the ruin of Pantglas Junior School. They died because of the arrogance and the stupidity of bureaucrats in high office who knowingly and deliberately failed to carry out the functions of their highly paid office. On 26th October a tribunal was set in motion by Cledwyn Hughes, the Secretary of State for Wales, and Lord Justice Edmund Davies has now handed history its report. It is a scathing and a bitter document that cries of a *terrifying tale of bungling ineptitude* that *could and should have been prevented* and it names nine men who must bear the blame for the deaths of the 144 people who died in the village of Aberfan on that tragic day.

We who were but spectators to the publicised carnage of that day can neither demand revenge nor claim forgiveness for these men, for neither gifts are ours to dispense, only the living who were unwillingly forced to sacrifice their children can make these decisions.

Our role is but to record the facts and examine our own position in relation to these tragedies, for every man that claims a cheaper bag of coal, or sells his vote for a cheaper loaf without questioning the source of his saving, must bear his share of the responsibility for the pressures that his actions exert on those who seek political and economic power by pandering to his desires.

On the Easter of 1958 TIP 7 was started in Aberfan and slowly this mound of industrial scum rose above the village, and two years later the murmured warnings of the village streets became public, only to be brushed aside as the groundless gossip of those forced to live in the shadow of TIP 7, for, claimed authority, this was the *economic* place to tip the NCB's industrial scum.

In 1963 the NCB began to tip *tailings* onto TIP 7 and these fine particles of coal waste quickly turned into a grey quicksand because of the rain above and the hidden spring below. But still the NCB failed to investigate the repeated complaints even when there was a slide in TIP 7 in 1963. And this is the key to the tragedy, for if the NCB had halted the use of TIP 7 at that time, the 1966 disaster would not have taken place.

In January of 1964, Mrs Williams told a town planning committee of her fears concerning TIP 7, and one can only quote the tribunal who state that not only was nothing done, but there was *a sorry tale of inertia and neglect and one from which the taint of subterfuge and arrogance by the National Coal Board is not wholly absent.*

I have neither the wish nor the intention to name the nine men pilloried in the tribunal's report for they will bear their black cross until the day of their own deaths. If we have sympathies let it be for the parents of Aberfan who lost their children and for that very small minority of those nine men named in the report who, because of our human failings, will be forever damned within the communities wherein they will live.

Yet there is one man who not only deserves to be named but should be named for when this tragedy was taking place My Lord Robens was prancing along in the brand new robes of the first Chancellor of the University of Surrey. This political appointee spread out his arms to an indifferent world as the father figure of the coal industry, a man prepared to give true and honest evidence before the world and to accept the responsibilities of his highly paid office, yet when the cards were laid upon the tribunal tables he has shuffled to the political rat holes of Whitehall for comfort and advice, for this is the man whom the tribunal personally criticised for his misleading remarks on television concerning TIP 7 and the tribunal accuses Robens of deliberately misinforming the Secretary for Wales that these tips were regularly inspected when this was not so.

Whether Robens resigns or not is now a matter of indifference for this £12,000 a year hollow man is already at the head of the queue for other well-paid jobs should this particular coal caper turn sour. The Establishment has, almost to a man, decided to rally round one of its adopted sons, even to the Prime Minister, and it is claimed that all those ill-involved in the Aberfan tragedy have found their escape clause in the belief that if they offer a collective resignation then nothing will be done for one does not decimate an entire platoon of the *boys.*

It is now argued that men in authority cannot be expected to resign every time a lorry crashes or a plane fails to land right way up, but in the matter of Aberfan these are false analogies, for these minehead tips are an active, daily and self-evident part of the coal industry and must, by their very nature, form part of the policy directives of any capitalistic mine owner or State manager.

When Sir Thomas Dugdale found that his advisers within the Civil Service had let him down he resigned, and when Miss Herbison felt that the Cabinet was betraying the Party she too resigned. Whatever Robens does now is a matter of indifference, for he has earned contempt by his very hesitation. He does not need time to contemplate these matters for, like the parents of the children, he has had many months to think out his future pattern of action.

Yet when the sentimental Left accuse they do not stand on the platform of hindsight for for too many years these men and women stood on dark and windy corners propagating the New Jerusalem. Year by year, in small back-street rooms, they have poured out their dreams into the tatty leaflet that men pushed into their pockets to read in an idle hour. And in the Welsh hills and the shadowed valleys men spoke of a Wales without the industrial scabs that littered its countrysides, a Wales where men did not spit out their lives in a dark sub-world that coal might be shipped for State or Private Profit to the cancerous industrial hells that we call England, and the politicians waxed fat on these splendid dreams and brought the morality of the secondhand car market to take its place.

And when TIP 7 turned into a flowing sewer of filth to destroy the children of Aberfan, the Rt Hon Emmanuel Shinwell, MP,[1] raised his ancient social democratic head and from the London seat of power, chanted that as much as he would *like to clear away the pit-heap monstrosities, for safety and amenity reasons, the cost would be beyond our resources for some years ahead.* AND THE COST? £10,000,000 to £15,000,000 over a period of four years.

Wales, Wales, you have reason to weep when knaves and fools claim your loyalties and your allegiance and of their witless thoughtlessness mock your sacred dead.

12th August 1967   ARTHUR MOYSE

1 Chairman of the Parliamentary Labour Party in 1967; Minister of Fuel and Power when the coal mines were nationalised in 1946. For comment at the time, see *Neither Nationalisation Nor Privatisation: selections from FREEDOM 1945-1950* (Freedom Press, 1989) — Editor.

ONE-WAY TRAFFIC

What is There to Say About the Pakistan Disaster?

Every two or three years a cyclone sends a tidal wave over the delta
of the Ganges river, destroying the pitiful hovels and killing the
pitiful peasants who live there. They cannot move away because
they can't afford to live anywhere else. Someone has to live there
to grow the rice on which the East Pakistan economy depends. No
one anywhere will spend the money needed to build proper defences

against the cyclone and the sea; when disaster strikes, it takes ten days for aid to reach the stricken area — in a world which lives with the four-minute warning! Pakistan is divided by a hostile India which won't allow over-flying from West to East Pakistan, even when the East Pakistan Government swallows its pride and appeals for help. Religion, nationalism, money, governmental indifference — all conspire to make these Delta peasants trapped and classic victims of our world-wide corruption.
28th November 1970

Italians Buried by Bureaucracy

The deaths and suffering of thousands of Italians is an extreme and painful way with which to be made aware, once more, of the uselessness and danger of Governments. The earthquake that hit one of Italy's poorest areas destroyed entire villages and killed thousands of people, but left the machinery of government, its unshakable bureaucracy, still standing and functioning as inefficiently and ineptly as ever. The Italian Government is directly responsible for many thousands of deaths. Civil defence programmes for the protection of citizens after natural disasters had been approved of nine years ago, however, in the slow-moving Italian political arena, even now no-one knows how to implement them. Even journalists and migrant workers returning from Germany and Switzerland to their home towns arrived before any organised aid. And as I write people are dying from lack of proper care and attention and many originally buried alive are being dug out dead as the necessary equipment for moving the debris finally arrives. In an attempt to make their failure seem less serious the Government's official figures for the dead and missing are much lower than most observers' estimates. The final death toll could reach 20,000. Even the President of the Republic, Pertini, has condemned his Government's actions, or non-actions, as an outrage. The Minister of the Interior has tried to run for cover by submitting his resignation. This was refused by the Prime Minister and he now seems the most likely scapegoat. Meanwhile the Communist Party (PCI) is trying to make some political mileage out of the catastrophe, claiming that it should take over the Government. At the same time its lorries covered in PCI emblems rush to the earthquake victims to buy votes with tinned meat and condensed milk.

To put the uselessness of government aid into perspective, Sicily, where there was a massive earthquake in 1968, has sent 3 milliards (lira: c £1.5 million) in aid. This leaves them 347 milliards (lira: c £200 million in 1968) lining their pockets as they were given 400 milliards at the time to rebuild the devastated area. (The people of Valle di Belice, Sicily, still live in prefabs put there as temporary accommodation till the rebuilding work the aid was intended for was completed — it never started, the money disappeared.) There is a great fear that this state of affairs will be repeated and people sending money are distrustful of Government agencies, preferring to send it via Red Cross or their political party.

The Italian Government, arguably the most corrupt and inefficient in the Western World, begins to face up to a scandal that even it cannot hide, but which in one way or another it will undoubtedly survive. The Italian people, made up of friends, families and communities, fights back against the disaster as best it can. These people quite rightly berate a Government that, like all Governments, claims to be a panacea for all their ills. After all you are not supposed to be capable of organising your own lives, so it is to the Government you delegate your wishes, and it promises to look after you and make sure you don't hurt yourself. But Governments are always corrupt, morally and financially, and when asked to perform one of their supposed functions, invariably collapse in a morass of inefficiency and make their people suffer. Having made the people believe that under its umbrella no rain would fall, the people are now drowning in a tidal wave of concrete, bricks and mortar, and left to die beneath them. How ironic that these same people, when this same Government judiciously whips up feelings of patriotism, will merrily go to war. To die an unnatural death in an unnatural situation. And only complain if they lose, if more of them are killed than their 'enemies'. So conditioned to accept the control and authority of politicians and bureaucrats that they will find any excuse to live oppressed and refuse revolution. If thousands of people left to die after an earthquake will not shake the people's deep-rooted subservience and belief in the need to be led, and to follow, down the paths of destruction — what will?

8th December 1980   STEFANO

CHINA

Red Squares in China

How to keep the revolutionary fervour of a nation after the revolution has been defeated is the second major test of a revolutionary leader. There is no doubt that when communism took over in China, a revolution took place that incorporated a great feeling of land-hunger and class aspiration of the Chinese people. Mao Tse-tung was able to rise to power by passing the *first* major test of the revolutionary politician: how to make it appear that he is granting the people what they are taking for themselves. Now he faces, in his old age, the *second* test, which comes in the 'post-Thermidor' period of the Chinese revolution — the period when reaction has established itself but still has need of popular support against the outside world.

The upsurge of the young 'guards' in the 'cultural revolt of 1966' is Mao's answer. He has fallen back on the oldest trick in the book of the politician: he has called on the young, clean-living, respectable, conforming elements to rout the 'rabble'. It is not even fascism in the Hitlerian sense: more the early English fascism of the 'Bulldog Drummond' type, the Imperial Fascism of 1926 strike-breaking, the fascism associated with castor oil doses to liberal professors in Italy rather than the mass movements of Germany. The moves and slogans of these clean-limbed Chinese are depressingly familiar. Doctors who have treated foreigners (there is no doubt an ideogram for 'low swine, what?') are made to crawl in public humiliation. Chinese and foreigners who have passed slightingly by the portrait of the Leader are made to bow before his portrait. Most of all, the attack is directed against the decadent youths with long hair and fancy clothing whom everybody knows to be subversive of the ideals of the nation, in any nation, irrespective of its ideals. Shave their heads, rip their clothes — let them learn the folly of their ways at detention centres — if in the early days of the revolution they had got rid of the execution block (they did not) the Young Guards would now be petitioning to have it brought back. The

162

Decent Citizens in China are having it very much their own way, with Father Figure Mao beaming in the background, and the police standing by paternally in the manner of the Czarist police during a pogrom, ready to step in and arrest the victims if they resist, and shriek conspiracy and murder if at any moment the victims get the upper hand.

It is noticeable that at the moment the Chinese communists strike hard at their 'provo'(?) element, the Russian press beams for the first time at English youth fashions (which need not give too much hope to their own *stilyagi*). The Russians can, however, afford to relax a little — they answered the post-Thermidorian test of how to keep up the people's fervour, by falling back on patriotism — the fervent Russianism of the 'Great Patriotic War' and its subsequent reflection in space travel enthusiasm. The Chinese have no similar patriotic tradition (their attachment is traditionally to the soil itself, and to their ancestors in the land, but not to the mythical State). The Bulldog Drummond stage of Mao's cultural revolution can be seen as his equivalent to Stalin's 'Patriotic War'.

In moving against all the anti-party elements and arousing the licensed hooliganism of the Young Guards against people suspected of anti-State activity, Mao has revealed for the first time the truth about the schisms in the Chinese political scene. For too long the farce of Chiang Kai-shek in Formosa has led the world to assume that opposition was confined to the offshore island that imagined itself to be China. On the contrary, although bourgeois politics have almost disappeared from China for want of support, there are many popular organisations standing in opposition to the totalitarian State, including the anarchists. The harshness of measures taken against individuals suspected of supporting such underground movements is Mao's public testimony to their effectiveness. In simultaneously hitting out at the rebellious section of the young generation, and exposing them to the attacks of the conformists, Mao has indicated which way he assumes they are heading. Of course he will get a lot of support as a result. The sight of a Government getting tough with its rebels arouses a type of sadistic-masochistic joy in every country — heads on pikes were always a popular spectacle in this country and probably still would be if they did it. But if Mao has read half as much as he is reputed to have written, he will know that it is not a type of popularity that lasts, or upon which much reliance can be placed in time of social upheaval.

10th September 1966 INTERNATIONALIST

China and the Numbers Game

Many a compassionate person has condemned successive Governments in the UK for playing the numbers game with immigrants,
as doors have been slammed in the faces of weeping relatives
because magic quotas have been met.

Yet in fact numbers are what States are all about. Big countries
with large populations are powerful States; big countries with large
populations plus technology are super-States. Small States plus
technology are stable States; small States without technology or
resources are nowhere.

Only lucky chance, like having oil under your sand or uranium
in your mountains, can make a small State influential. Influential
means having the means to buy weapons, first to keep your own
people quiet and then to impose your views on others weaker than you.

Traditionally this 'influence' meant having large numbers of
expendable people ready to march forth and fight when the State
decided to expand, or stand and fight when some other State
decided to expand in your direction. Because statesmen are the
most reactionary of persons, these concepts — basically that big
is beautiful — die hard.

Only modern technology has offered States the opportunity of
remaining 'great' without enormous numbers of people. Modern
weaponry gives the State means of killing far more of the enemy
with fewer of your own forces than ever before, while modern
means of production make it possible for the eternal capitalist
quest for 'growth' to be achieved with a smaller workforce.

Having needed all the people it could get for the period of
imperialist expansion over the last three hundred or so years, the
capitalist West now finds people a bit of a problem. A hundred
years ago Britain would have panicked at the thought of a zero
growth in population — now the people that the economy does
not need, except as consumers, have somehow to be contained.

For anarchists, 'population control' was never geared to the needs
of the economy or the demands of the State for cannon fodder,
but to individual liberty and well-being. Of all the sections of the
Left, the anarchists were pioneers in propaganda for birth control
and for women's rights to control their own fertility — not to
balance the books of available labour nor to keep down the numbers
of undesirable elements, but to free women from the slavery of
perpetual reproduction, premature exhaustion and death.

That is why we look with a certain cynicism on the recent *volte-face* in China with regard to birth control. When Mao Tse-tung announced his 'great leap forward' it was his version of capitalist growth — industrial and economic expansion aided by an expansion in population. It was power seen in the same perspective as that of the Catholics: power through numbers. As with the Catholics, sex was astutely seen as a liberatory influence which had to be suppressed, the damned-up energy diverted into hard work and, no doubt, health-giving cold showers and exercise. As with the Catholics, birth control was banned, so that sex was linked only with reproduction and thus necessary only about once a year.

Now that Mao is dead and gone and even his widow discredited with the terrible 'Gang of Four', the equivalent of Lenin's 'New Economic Policy' of 1921 is coming in. The exiled capitalists have been invited to return, the big deal with America is signed and sealed, and China awaits delivery, not only of the armaments but also of the machine tools and the computer technology which is going to drag her into the twenty-first century.

Gone will be the backyard foundries and the bicycles; gone the blue denim uniformity and the austerity. Why, already Chinese women are being allowed to have their hair curled! Gone, you may be sure, will be the barefoot doctors and the communes. Gone, too, will be the newspapers on the walls.

There is a different writing on the walls of China now. It is quite clearly going to be a country in a hurry — where a population of 900 million is simply not needed. Suddenly we learn that the Chinese are ahead of the West in the variety of birth control techniques available. As you might expect from the nation which invented gunpowder, they have a once-a-month pill, a 'morning-after' pill, a paper pill, a 'visiting' pill, a coil that lasts ten years — to say nothing of widespread and easy abortion, sterilisation and vasectomy.

Could it be that, just like the Pope's pontification, Mao's mouthings never were taken seriously? After all, a coil said to last ten years must have been tested somewhere!

On behalf of all Chinese men and women we throw our cloth caps into the air and give three cheers for carefree Chinese fucking. On a more sinister note, however, we can't help wondering whether a harking back to more old fashioned methods of birth control might not have motivated the recent Chinese excursions into Vietnam. Some cynic once described war as "nature's pruninghook". While the losses to be incurred in Vietnam, Laos, possibly Cambodia and even in border clashes with the Russians might not make much

of a dent in a population of 900 million, every little bit helps —
and using up old-fashioned armaments clears the way for the new
American stuff too. And there's always land, power, to be gained.

For the capitalist West — and the capitalist Far East — it's going
to be a golden opportunity. The rift between so-called Communist
Russia and so-called Communist China is widened, and once the
demand for modern consumer goods, transported gadgets and silicon
chip technology gains momentum, the way will be opened for the
expected liaison between China and Japan.

Superficially this is a possibility which might not seem to suit
America's book — yet the opening up of a market for, say, Japanese
cars, in China would surely please General Motors. And we already
know that what is good for General Motors is good for America.

So, having gained its place among the nations on the strength
of its numbers, now China finds those numbers an embarrassment.
Mao used to boast that China could fight an atomic war and still
survive with enough people to remain the greatest nation on earth.
Kruschev once boasted that "Russia could bury the West". Nowadays,
ten fingers on ten buttons could bury us all.

The numbers game now has a different meaning altogether.
24th March 1979   P.S.

27th January 1968

THE VIETNAM WAR

Vietnam 'Dialogue with Death'

"It had become a tradition during the last few years that dictators acted and democracies protested, a division of labour which seemed to satisfy everybody"
Arthur Koestler: *Dialogue with Death* (1937)

This aphorism is basically as true today as when Koestler wrote it in a Spanish jail during the revolution (which he called civil war) when the German and Italian aeroplanes bombed the Spanish cities, while the democracies meekly protested. Perhaps the distinction between democracy and dictatorship is not so great today as it was thirty years ago. Nevertheless, after the black smoke rose to the sky near Hanoi and Haiphong the democracies duly protested. The time and motion man with his stop-watch and tape-recorder stood in the Grosvenor Squares of the world and reported back to his Government. 'Nothing to fear, your excellencies', he said, 'they were in good voice, a bit fractious but I daresay they are all in their beds by now'.

The Vietnam War has been going on since the end of the Second World War. The US entered after the Korean ceasefire, but basically both the purpose and the reason for these two wars are the same. Military economics demand a theatre of war somewhere, otherwise the system which is based on war production must collapse. Protesting against war is the only human thing to do, but without changing the system that needs war the condition for war remains.

Without an egalitarian system of distribution of the real wealth of the world the need for war will exist as it is the only way that you can have full employment in a capitalist economy. Should the Vietnam War cease tomorrow, a war in Thailand or some such place will start the day after.

The Chinese and Russian 'Communist' systems also need a localised war for the same reason. They have the added incentive that as long as the Vietnam War continues, they can make fiery speeches,

protests and the inevitable recruitment of Party members all over
the world.

The 'Communist' Powers are supporting North Vietnam with
brave words but with hardly any weapons. Possibly the North
Vietnamese cannot pay for the latest anti-aircraft batteries. It was
pitiful to read the 'Agence Presse' correspondent's report from
Hanoi where he observed the bombing raid on the oil dumps.

After the bombing of Hanoi the Chinese, of course, protested.
A statement by them described the raids as 'barbarous, wanton
and a criminal act of aggression and war. In accordance with the
interests and demands of the Vietnamese people we will at any
time take such actions as we deem necessary'. Words, fighting
words, dishonest words.

The war is being 'escalated' by the US Government according
to the 'scientific' formulae worked out by 'Professor' Kahn. What
stage have they reached now in their war of nerves? A year ago
there was furore when it was revealed that the Americans were
using gas warfare. Now, after the initial indignation has subsided,
gas is used constantly in Vietnam. Remember the horror with which
napalm bombs and lazy dogs were greeted? All this is now part of
modern warfare.

For a long time the Americans have talked about the possibility
of bombing Hanoi. Now they have done it and public protests have
been voiced, they will do it again. It won't be news next time.
They are already hinting that the next step is going to be the
bombing of Red River Delta with the consequent flooding of North
Vietnam. After that they may use 'tactical' nuclear weapons. And
so on.

What should anarchists do in the circumstances? We should
continue to protest but never lose an opportunity with our literature
or banners or private conversation to try to explain the cause of
war and the need for an egalitarian society.

Of course a 'crisis' situation tends to stultify thinking. Even
'comrades' urge us, like latter-day Kropotkins, to choose sides.
There are no short cuts to anarchism or to eradicating war for that
matter. If we are to stand by our principles we must be prepared
to lose a few friends.

9th July 1966   R.

The State is your Enemy

After the defeat of Napoleon the victors (and the smaller powers) at the Congress of Vienna signed a pact which 'guaranteed peace'. This, as every schoolboy knows, was the work of The Holy Alliance (although the Holy See refused to sign). Nevertheless, 'the settlement arrived at preserved Europe from any general conflagration for all but a century' (Harold Nicolson).

From a *status quo* standpoint this is a realistic statement, because such revolutions and their accompanying agitations that took place in 1848 or 1871 were irksome to Governments but after they were put down left the Powers with no less authority over their subjects.

The Powers did not wage wars against each other and were free to tackle discontent within their own boundaries. Mass movements were either ruthlessly crushed or channelled into reformism.

When the Holy Alliance broke down in 1914 it not only resulted in the mass murder of the First World War (which is of no interest to Governments) but the contracting out of one of its main props (Holy Russia). The main difficulty for the continuation of the *status quo* has ever since been how to accommodate a Power that does not profess to believe in the *status quo*.

The Second World War, which brought the Soviet Union into the fold, once more left this problem (for the Governments) still unsettled, although some understanding may have been reached (despite propaganda manifestations of the cold war) as the 1956 uprising in Hungary proved. The Soviet Union was allowed to crush the rebellion within her acknowledged sphere of influence.

In other words rebellions that can be contained may offer Governments momentary headaches but do not change the political map. Looking at it from this angle it is easier to understand why the Korean, and now the Vietnam, ' conflagration' occupy our consciences more than they affect those of Governments. For us it is a question of mutilated bodies, death, starvation; for the Governments it is merely restoring order within their sphere of influence.

Government knows that its greatest danger is not from within, because if Governments topple, whether violently or bloodlessly, another set of rulers will make sure that the State continues. Their greatest enemy is either another Power that does not 'play the game' or a set of revolutionaries who do not wish to replace Government by Government. Anarchists come within the second category and offer theoretically the only challenge to the State.

But if one wants to understand the Vietnam 'problem' the first category has to be discussed. In whose sphere of influence is Vietnam? If it were within the boundaries of only one great Power the Vietnamese would have been crushed by now just as Hungary was.

The rogue elephant is, of course, China. China does not 'play the game'. It has taken on the Soviet Union's role in this respect.

For the Great Powers the Vietnam skirmish is no more than an outlandish disorder in a far-flung province. But its continuation could result in the Third World War which is quite a different matter. World wars, as we have said before, frighten Governments not because of the terrible suffering but because of the diminishing of governmental authority and the possibility of some fish escaping the net (as did the Soviet Union after the First World War and China after the Second World War).

All the efforts of world statesmen are concentrated towards this end: to bring the Soviet Union and China back into the Holy Alliance. The ossification of the Russian Revolution has now finally reached the stage where the Soviet Union can safely be trusted as a partner in this new Holy Alliance. This is the reason behind President Johnson's present offer of economic concessions to the Soviet bloc and also the sudden spate of conferences; the one in Manila to reassert American authority and the one in Moscow to reassert the Soviet's. They must strengthen their own hand before they meet in the near future to carve up the world to their satisfaction at a new Congress of Vienna. And you can be sure that the problem of Vietnam will hardly be on the agenda.

If such a *détente* takes place between the US and the Soviet Union the encirclement of China will be complete and the long process of bringing China to toe the line will begin. Cut off from the rest of the world the Chinese may be ruled even more harshly or the masses may opt for anarchism in answer to the blockade.

What can anarchists do in the present situation? They should continue to expose and attack all sides who wish to oppress the Vietnamese people. There are those who say 'Peace in Vietnam', those who say 'Yanks out of Vietnam', and finally those who chant 'Victory to the Vietcong!' The first slogan unfortunately is no more than the continuation of the *status quo*, the second means Yanks out — Russians in! and the third Yanks, Russians out — Chinese in!

Exposing these governmental machinations is the important task — and if we did not present such a critique we would not be anarchists. Taking sides now can only mean compromise. But sooner or later the opportunity will occur when we can show our solidarity.

22nd October 1966   R.

Vietnam: Left Defends Right

In the struggle to bring peace to Vietnam, and get all foreign troops out, no one has done more to protect Harold Wilson from direct attack (for his complicity in the war) than the Left of the Labour Party. The effect of the thinking and activity of Fenner Brockway and the late Konni Zilliacus has been to direct the movement solely against US intervention and away from actual British responsibility.

The Labour Left is aided and abetted in this by the Communist Party and the various leftist sects. The motives in many individual cases are, I am sure, perfectly genuine but the leaders are playing internal power politics with Vietnam as the excuse and the means. This is shallow, vicious and disastrous to the success of the campaign. It plays directly into Wilson's hands.

May I take two recent examples? On 21st September, Iris Murdoch wrote what *seemed* to be a powerfully worded article on Vietnam on the front page of *The Listener*. In fact it let Wilson off the hook absolutely. She wrote (my emphases):

"Our Government has been a false friend of America here. We ought to use *our position of comparative detachment to make a more searching criticism of American policy* and to make moral judgements upon it where these seem appropriate. Our Government ought to dissociate itself firmly *and on clearly argued grounds* from the further prosecution of this callous war."

The *fact* is that the British Government is not at all 'detached' from the US and the war in Vietnam. It was British troops that divided Vietnam into two in 1945. It was British troops that reinstalled French power in Vietnam in the same year. It was Sir Anthony Eden who thought up and promoted the seven point secret agreement of 1954 under which the US was to stay in what was called 'retained Vietnam' despite whatever was said in the Geneva Agreements just about to be signed. The text of this agreement was later published and is to be found on pages 132-133 of Eden's *Full Circle* (1960).

It was then Douglas-Home and later Wilson who subsequently confirmed Anglo-American mutual aid in South East Asia. The basic policy is simple: US support for Britain in Malaysia in return for British support for the US in Vietnam.

In earnest of this agreement President Kennedy, in 1961, asked for Brigadier Robert Thompson from the British Army in Malaya (an expert of the strategic village idea). He went to Saigon with a Military Mission and remained there for about two years.

There is a British Ambassador in Saigon. South Vietnamese troops are trained by the British Army in Johore. In Thailand 700 British troops have finished building one military base for the Americans (nominally, of course, for the Thai Government!) and, according to my information, have recently started work on a second base. Hong Kong is at the disposal of the Americans as a very useful communications link. British military and other supplies, including hovercraft and tear gas, are used in Vietnam.

This brings me to the second point about Iris Murdoch's case. Because she either does not know, or does not want to know, about the long and close involvement of the British Government in the war in Vietnam, she thinks of dissociation in an abstract and moral way only. This kind of dissociation is meaningless. Dissociation is a deed, or a series of deeds, or it is nothing.

To dissociate from the US in Vietnam is to go through the list (certainly much longer than any of us can know) of actual physical commitments to the war on the part of this country and terminate them *physically*. To take the most obvious example — so long as those troops remain in Thailand dissociation is nonsense. Then of course it is politically naive to suppose that Britain can dissociate with the US in Vietnam and remain in NATO, SEATO and CENTO. But then again the Left fails to make this simple connection. Dissociation is so many empty words so long as US military aircraft remain at Alconbury, Lakenheath, Mildenhall, some nine other bases, and so long as Polaris submarines of the US Navy continue to use Holy Loch.

To turn to my second example of how the Left protects the Right . . . People think that the Left won a considerable victory over Wilson in the Vietnam debate at Scarborough. In fact if you look at the Cambridge resolution moved by Gerry Steele its import is exactly the same as Iris Murdoch's article. It speaks very correctly about the complete withdrawal of all American troops and covers U Thant's point, the Geneva Agreements, British dissociation, etc., but again perpetuates the absurd myth that Britain is not physically involved in the war and therefore instances no physical steps that might be taken. So Wilson and Brown have only to make a few ambiguous speeches and get away with it. This they have done since the dissociation resolution last year. They will go on doing it and Labour Party members will be allowed to cherish the illusion that they have *done* something. The only one to profit from this exercise is President Johnson.

We can only get a breakthrough on the streets (for peace in Vietnam) if first we have a breakthrough in the mind. We, in this country, share direct military and physical responsibility for war in Vietnam.

The immediate conclusion is a practical one. It concerns the Autumn Mobilisation demonstrations fixed for 21st October. The overall theme is the ending of British support for the US in Vietnam. If we can get this message across, first among ourselves, and then more generally to public opinion, we shall have done something of very considerable value.

14th October 1967   PETER CADOGAN

Neither Washington nor Hanoi
But Peace AND Freedom

In Vietnam 623,000 people have been robbed of their homes and livings by guerrilla forces and regular troops since the beginning of January 1968. 72,000 homes have been destroyed since the start of the New Year fighting. However not to worry, since both sides assure the victims it's for their own good.

The Americans are fighting there to abet a Government whose support is by no means a majority one, whose corruption is well known, and which is essentially authoritarian and militaristic. Not even the Americans are able to suggest that the régime derives its authority from the people.

Looking at the North in an equally critical manner reveals that the support for the régime at the moment is derived less from an appreciation of its policies than from the fear of invasion. The power of Ho Chi Minh is derived from feelings of nationalism amongst the masses of the people of both Vietnams. He became leader of this movement by eliminating other candidates — betraying the major figures to the French and using his 'fee' to build up his following and influence in the movement; and by the murder of all independent leftist groups, Pacifists, Trotskyists and Syndicalists. Pursuing a misplaced Marxism in a predominantly peasant society, he divided the population into rigid categories and classes and severely crushed opposition (such as the 1956 peasant insurrection in which reports give 10,000-15,000 killed and up to 12,000 sent to forced labour camps).

The National Liberation Front is a continued use of nationalism to advance the aims of a small guiding elite. The 'official' leadership covers the real directors of the movement. It undoubtedly has much support among sections of the population. Its triumph, however, would mean the 'unification' of the country under the Hanoi régime.

The majority of the Vietnamese are not committed in the present struggle, but bow to whoever is the master. In the recent offensive the Southern régime showed its 'concern' for the people by indiscriminate bombing and artillery fire in heavily populated areas. Similarly the 'liberators' executed anyone at all involved in the administration of social life — there are reports from Hué of people being shot for listening to the BBC, which was forbidden ('Panorama', 5th March — interview with students in Hué). A measure of the popular support for the two combatants is found in the reaction to the recent New Year offensive — the South Vietnam Government got no warning of NLF concentration of troops near the cities, and, equally revealing, there was no evidence of the spontaneous insurrection in the cities which the NLF expected and which the NLF units in the attack were promised. (In the 'Panorama' interview mentioned above, the student was asked whether the destruction of Hué had made it harder for him and his friends to choose between the Government and the NLF. He replied: "We don't choose between them, we just hate the war.")

Support must be given to this attitude rather than to the hypocrites of both sides.

Vietnam is one of the points where rival systems clash — "the 'Free' world that is not free, and the 'Communist' world that is not communist. One, pseudo-freedom based on economic slavery; the other, pseudo-freedom based on political slavery. One is already authoritarian, the other is becoming so." (In the words of the US Libertarian League.)

'Peace in Vietnam' must not be a slogan to cover a continuance of the war until a military victory. There is a need for non-aligned demonstrations in sympathy with the people of Vietnam.

To oppose the war in Vietnam is not enough; it is necessary to work in our society, in every way possible, to end the military and economic systems which give rise to Vietnams. *Neither Washington nor Hanoi, but peace and freedom.*

16th March 1968   EDITORS

What Critics?

It was astonishing to read John Rety's opening paragraph last week[1], telling us that 'many anarchists' have criticised our 'Neither Washington nor Hanoi' policy. Astonishing because this implies, not that anarchists question and criticise our policies, which is right and proper for anarchists to do, but that they presumably support the 'Victory for the Vietcong' line peddled by many political so-called 'revolutionary' groups.

Victory for the Vietcong can mean one or both of only two things: military victory and/or political victory.

If the Vietcong are to beat the Americans militarily, they have, quite simply, to out-gun them. They have got to kill, bomb and burn more than the Americans are doing, have done and will do or can do. Not only have the Vietcong to kill more Americans than the Americans can kill of them, but they will have to clear them out of the Vietnamese towns and villages which they now hold, which will mean more destruction of these places than the Americans have so far achieved and inevitably more destruction of the Vietnamese people, their farms and workshops and way of life than the Americans have managed to date.

Since the suffering, killing and destruction that the US forces have so far inflicted upon the Vietnamese people is already enormous — and is in fact the reason why most oppose the war — is it the wish of these 'anarchists' that all this be more than doubled so that a Communist regime may be imposed over what remains of Vietnam and its suffering population?

For this is what political victory will mean. And while you may say 'better Red than dead' in fact the killings will not stop with a political victory. The difference will be that the gallows and the firing squad will replace the napalm, as the abominable institutionalised violence of the Communist State replaces the abominable violence of American warmakers. The Vietcong will wreak their revenge upon all those South Vietnamese who did not support them, who did not answer their call to rise up during the New Year offensive.

If you are a Communist (Stalinist, Maoist, Trotskyist) you can

1. 'Neither Washington Nor Hanoi' was published just before the mass demonstration outside the American Embassy in Grosvenor Square, London, on Sunday 17th March 1968, reported by John Rety the following week — Editor.

176 THE STATE IS YOUR ENEMYTHE STATE IS YOUR ENEMY

support this kind of thing. If you play the political game from either side you must care nothing for the misery inevitable in your policies. But if you are an anarchist — that is, if you care for people more than for the establishment of an authoritarian regime of one kind or another — then you must reject both sides.

Neither the Americans nor the Vietcong care a damn for the Vietnamese people. Obviously one doesn't have to enlarge upon the role and purpose of the Americans in Vietnam, but do our critical comrades understand the role of the Vietcong?

This is quite obviously to keep the Americans in Vietnam! Then not only do they thus play into the hands of Communist propagandists and disrupt their own economy, but they are being used to serve the purposes of Chairman Mao who would not be able to maintain his position in power if there were not vast American forces fighting in Asia. The amount of unrest of which we know in China would escalate — *will* escalate — the moment the US pull out of Vietnam, unless another crisis can be engineered elsewhere, like Laos or Cambodia, to keep the pot boiling and keep the Yankee wolf at China's door.

To support one side or the other in Vietnam is to support the destruction of people for power politics. And, more to our point, it is to forget all the anarchist analysis that lies behind the words 'War is the Health of the State'.

Now to support neither side is not 'purist' or 'cynical'. (Much more cynical, surely, to support the Vietcong from a safe distance knowing that their victory could only mean continued suffering for the Vietnamese people!) That is only the negative side. The positive side is to do our damnedest to prevent the continuation of the war, and to call for a libertarian alternative to the Vietcong in Vietnam when the fighting stops. This latter is the difficult part to put into practice. The situation in Vietnam is so awful that only immense courage and organisational ability — only in fact a social revolution — can provide the answer. And after all these years of war it is hardly possible, especially as neither Washington nor Hanoi would allow the emergence of a libertarian society — which, surely, is why anarchists reject them both!

All right, so we can't do much about an anarchist alternative in Vietnam. Only the Vietnamese people can do that anyway. But we can do something about the British Government's support for the US, while our comrades in America, as we know, are doing all they can there to undermine their State's ability to make war.

The job of all anarchists outside Vietnam is to arouse public opinion to make it impossible for their Governments to support the war. This, surely, is why anarchists took part in the attack on the American Embassy — if that is what it was — without supporting Hanoi.

If anarchists are not clear about this, then they are just allowing themselves to be used once again, as so often in the past, to help somebody else into power.

30th March 1968   PHILIP SANSOM

Come Home GI!

The greatest anti-war demonstrations in American history have served notice on President Nixon and the Pentagon that millions of young Americans are sincerely and strongly opposed to the continuation of the Vietnam War by one single day.

The Moratorium and the days of demonstration last weekend showed a strength of feeling and a degree of organisation which could leave no doubt in Nixon's mind that what he is faced with is no longer the expected opposition of 'extremists', but growing disgust at his delaying tactics on the part of people of all political opinions and of none, of moderates and even of patriotic squares.

Everyone who has ever had anything to do with demonstrations knows perfectly well that the people who actually take part in them are only a small minority of the numbers sympathetic to the cause. Not that we need to be too concerned about numbers, which prove nothing about the rightness or wrongness of the cause, but they are important in as much as they impress the opposition and the uncommitted.

Dignity and self-discipline

The tactics of the American demonstrators were impressive in themselves. The March of Death, with each marcher carrying the name of a dead GI, quietly and with dignity placed in a coffin and carried through the streets of Washington, must have brought home to many of the 'silent majority' that Nixon leans on, just what the cruel and pointless struggle in Vietnam is costing the US in terms of young men's lives.

Demonstrations have several functions, but the most important

178 THE STATE IS YOUR ENEMY

should always be to convert the unconverted. Provocation and the mindless shouting of slogans seldom if ever do this, although they may have other uses, like attracting attention when your numbers are small. But the American demonstrators did not need this. They had numbers, and there is nothing more impressive and moving than a huge crowd behaving with dignity and quietness and self-discipline — especially when death and the mourning of the dead is what it is all about. Fortunately this mood prevailed. There was little chanting of the 'Victory to the Vietcong!' variety which has marred similar demonstrations in this country and which, while it tells us a lot about the chanters, does nothing to convert the unconverted. On the contrary, open sympathy with the enemy, with the very ones who are killing the vast numbers of dead who are being mourned, immediately brings hostility to a demonstration.

If public opinion is being wooed, then we have to remember that public opinion is nothing more than ignorant conformity. The silent majority are the unthinking mass of solid citizens, the apathetic, security-minded, square, conforming don't-knows who, grumbling, pay their taxes to send their sons to the slaughter and accept with pride the posthumously-awarded campaign medal.

These are the ones whose complacency has to be dented. To bend their ears with cries of 'Victory to the Vietcong!' is to strike terror into their fatty hearts. But to make them think that their sons died in vain — that their sacrifice is for nothing, this is the way to get them wavering in their support for the establishment.

'Peace with honour'
Richard Nixon himself, after all, is helping in this task. By some sleight of hand he got himself elected with the understanding that he was going to bring the Vietnam War to an end. He has gone so far as to bring back some soldiers. He is seeking some formula for 'Peace with Honour' in a situation so dishonourable that it would be a fit subject for cynical laughter were it not for the fact that every time he squirms another hundred men die.

But what Nixon has done is to betray at top level America's loss of morale. Shaken and bewildered by their inability to win a war against relatively poorly-equipped Asian peasants who, by all military standards, should have been wiped out years ago; conscious of growing world disgust and contempt, even your silent majority of middle Americans wants out. They would like to crawl away and lick their wounds in some dark corner. But when you are a mighty

World Power you live in the spotlight — and everybody is going to laugh when you take a pratfall.

'Peace with Honour' is a purely political concept, being not concerned with peace and impossible to reconcile with honour. It is a euphemism for squalid horse-dealing — the sordid deal which will eventually, one supposes, come out of the interminable Paris 'peace' talks. When these latter began, incidentally, we demonstrated our cynicism by prophesying their failure, until such time, that is, as both sides decided the war had served its purpose. We pointed out that for both the Asian Communists (together with Russia) and the Americans, the Vietnam War fulfilled very useful purposes and both sides had their reasons for keeping it going. It has been interesting to note recently that whenever the Americans, for whom the war has now genuinely outlived its usefulness, try to cool it, the Vietcong step up their offensives, making it more, not less, difficult for the 'doves' of Washington to influence the Pentagon.

The person involved
So the decision must be taken out of the hands either of the doves of Washington or the hawks of the Pentagon — or the politicians of Saigon or Hanoi. Last week's demonstrations show conclusively that very large numbers of American citizens have already decided where their country's honour lies. They do not want peace to be bought with thousands more dead American conscripts. They want their sons and lovers back where they once belonged. Back home.

If the vast majority of the demonstrators were young then there is this much to be said for them: they are of the same generation as the young GIs doing the fighting and dying in Vietnam. And the young GIs should be asking themselves what the hell they are doing there, when the whole world knows that, short of starting a nuclear war in Asia, American victory in Vietnam is impossible. They are being used, and their deaths are being used, purely in a holding operation while the politicians haggle for bargains like vultures at a rotting carcase.

There is still one voice we want to hear raised against the Vietnam War: that of the American soldier. Simply to wear black armbands, while their contemporaries demonstrate in the cities back home is not enough. The American Forces can surely no longer *believe* in the war in Vietnam; they must now — if honour means anything! — take action against it.

The GI is the person involved. He it is who does the shooting and gets shot. He it is who uses napalm, drops the bombs, perpetrates

the atrocities, destroys villages — and gets killed or mutilated for
his pains. We now know — and *he* now knows — it is for nothing
in terms of honour.

The only honourable thing for American soldiers to do is to
come home. Leave the war, leave the foxholes and the fighting,
the raping and the killing. Walk right away from it. Run away from
it. Fight your way out if need be. Seize helicopters and planes,
cars, trucks and trains. Ring down the curtain in the theatre of
war and come home!

22nd November 1969   JUSTIN

War Corrupts

If power corrupts and absolute power corrupts absolutely, then
every soldier in every army in the world becomes subject to the
process of corruption the moment he begins his training. The job
of the soldier is to overpower his enemy — by any means necessary.
In theory there are limits to the means, but in practice there are
none. The idea that modern war can be carried on with regard for
the humanities is a grim joke, just another liberal myth, for war
is the power game carried on with no holds barred, and when
masses of ordinary men are trained to kill or be killed, then
the concept of the struggle being carried on with regard for the
Queensberry Rules is ludicrous. Oddly enough, when the word
'atrocity' is brought out, it refers nearly always to killing on a face-
to-face level — to the cold-blooded shooting or bayoneting of
individuals, few or many, by soldiers in direct confrontation with
their victims; the mass murder of bombing raids, inevitably killing
civilians by the thousand, is not considered to be atrocious since
obliteration bombing is a legitimate form of warfare. This simple
example of the double-think of militarists is enough for us to
contend that the real atrocity is war itself — and it is the cause of
war that anarchists attack.

29th November 1969

'Why, It Is Quite Normal!'

For twenty years — first by the French, then by the Americans and throughout by the Vietcong — the Vietnamese people, peasants and townsfolk, men, women, children and babies, have been systematically slaughtered. Their villages have been bombed by napalm, one of the foulest of war weapons; their crops have been poisoned, their forests defoliated; their schools, hospitals, factories, homes, destroyed by one side or the other.

When the Vietcong take a village which has not supported them as they think it should have, the community's leaders are either shot in the public square, or taken as hostages — and then shot. Terror raids on villages, in city streets, markets, restaurants or cinemas, either with bombs, rockets or mortars, indiscriminately kill anybody within range.

And the world now knows how *some* Americans behave when *they* take a village which has not supported them as they think it should have.

Pinkville is now going to pass into the bibliography of atrocity, along with Amritsar, Lidice, Sharpeville . . . all those other shameful names in the history of government in this century alone. We don't have to go back to Genghis Khan, the Caesars or the Vikings for examples of man's inhumanity to man. Nearly two thousand years after gentle Jesus mouthed his bit about 'Love thy neighbour', and the Gods only know how long after the high priests of Judaism, Islam, Buddhism, Shintoism, Hinduism — all of them, began their hot gospelling on ethical behaviour and all their variations on 'do unto others' — after all this, the twentieth century is different only in the brutal efficiency of the weapons placed in the warriors' hands, and in the hypocrisy.

What do you expect?
Did anyone tut-tut at Genghis Khan when he came back home reeking of blood and laden with loot? Did anyone expect warriors to behave other than with rape and massacre, when all they had to fight with were their swords in their strong right arms?

Of course not. But when the killing could be more efficiently done from a distance it became just as important to control your own troops as to control the killing of the enemy. After all, when dealing with unwilling, conscript armies, undisciplined killing of the 'enemy' could even lead to the undisciplined killing of their own officers — whom some soldiers are said to regard as their real enemy, anyway!

It is because 'nobody can be allowed to take the law into their own hands' that rules are laid down for war as for peace. Nothing to do with humane treatment of the other side at all.

When ordered to, the airman must rain napalm bombs on civilian dwellings; when the time comes, someone will be ordered to press the button for nuclear annihilation. The rules of war are that you must do as you are told — no less and no more. Anything else is the liberal myth that you can temper authority with humanity under the law and under all circumstances.

You can't. Authority can be humane only when it is not threatened When it is threatened it must react to the limit of the threat and more, in order to win.

Add to this the corruption of the ordinary person in turning him into a soldier, and the frustration of his position. Fed up and far from home, treated like a thing in the military machine, spat at and shot at, knowing himself hated in a foreign land, forced to lean for his life on the solidarity of unwilling comrades, and seeing them shot down beside him — then it begins to dawn on him that the folks back home no longer think him the hero they said he was when he left.

A bad conscience

Is it coincidence that we have had three exposures of 'atrocities' by American troops — the girl kidnapped by a platoon on patrol into the jungle, where they all raped her and then shot her; the Green Berets' murder of an 'agent' and the cover-up by the CIA; and the present (though year-old) disclosures of the massacre at My Lai — all in recent weeks *after* the great swing in public opinion in America against the war?

The fact that some individuals are prepared to come forward now and expose these incidents, obviously at some risk to themselves, indicates that they know there will be support for them where only a year ago they might have been crushed.

America clearly now has a very bad conscience about the Vietnam war — and by Christ it's about time! No doubt great play will be made by the Communists (who close their eyes to their own atrocities) and by those who will jump on political bandwagons to make capital out of these sordid incidents.

For anarchists however, atrocity and massacre is what war is all about. War is the atrocity. There is no point in training personnel to be killers, to knock the humanity out of them, to force them to be lousy murdering bastards and then complain when this is just what they turn out to be.

To prevent atrocities you must prevent war. To prevent war you must remove its cause. The cause of war is the power political struggle which all Governments from Liberal to Fascist and Communist must play.

As one South Vietnamese said to Mark Frankland, *Observer* correspondent in Saigon, expressing surprise at the world's interest in Pinkville: 'Why,' he said, 'it is quite normal'.

29th November 1969   JUSTIN

Who Are the Guilty?

In their attempts to civilise the uncivilisable — war — Governments have, in their usual blundering way, come up with a category of 'war crimes'. Unmindful of the fact that speaking of 'war crimes' is like speaking of dishonesties involved in the process of robbing banks or illnesses occurring during the onset of cancer, the US Government has got itself involved in a fine ethical stew about William Calley, charged and sentenced for the murder of 22 Vietnamese civilians at the village of My Lai.

More than twenty years and many minor wars ago there was a trial at Nuremberg of the Nazi war leaders. It was manifestly a trial of the defeated by the victorious — who else could be the judges? Those Nazi leaders who had not committed suicide were hung or imprisoned — of those imprisoned only a feeble-minded senile Hess remains in prison guarded (by the only fragment of four-power cooperation left) in the jail at Spandau.

Many people had doubts of the usefulness of those trials but from them seemed to arise the doctrine that henceforward it was no defence in law for a soldier accused of 'war crimes' to say that he was acting under orders. This, it was thought, justified the trials and made international law once more a thing to respect.

However it had been said by the Judge Advocate during the trial of Henry Wirz, the commander of a prison camp, 'A superior officer cannot order a subordinate to do an illegal act, and if a subordinate obeys such an order and disastrous consequences result, both the superior and the subordinate must answer for it.'

Wirz, largely as a result of this finding, was convicted and executed. However, Wirz was a Southern prison camp commander in the American Civil War, at Andersonville in 1864 and 8,589 prisoners died through the neglect of Commandant Wirz. Nearly 100 years later the US is still far from accepting the doctrine of individual responsibility.

It could be argued, and many do, that since all attempts to civilise war have failed we might as well admit that 'war is hell' and either, as the hard-hats say, fight with no holds barred or, as the pacifists say, abolish war altogether. Both have concurred in protest against the sentencing of William Calley although from different motives.

There is something especially ironic in the perpetrators of the bombing of Hiroshima and Dresden putting on trial the bombers of Coventry and Pearl Harbour. Illogically enough, the persistent bombing, napalming and strafing of the peasants of Vietnam has called forth no juridical protest in America and frequently anti-communist peasants have been killed or suffered. However this is the lofty abstraction afforded by the remoteness of the bomber and helicopter. William Calley calls for especial horror in the same way that the retail murderer of the suburban sweetheart rates more column-inches than the wholesale slaughters in Vietnam.

It can easily be pointed out that North Vietnamese troops have also slaughtered peasants whom they suspected of being pro-American. They have acted on the same assumptions as the Americans, 'There are no innocents' and 'those who are not for us are against us'. The losers in Vietnam are always the people, whom — both sides assure us — they are protecting and for whose sake they are involved in this war. If the civilians of My Lai had not been killed by Calley and his men, they stood a good chance of being killed by the North Vietnamese.

Both sides welcome revelations of atrocities by the 'others', for this rallies waverers. This is the 'polarisation of conflict' about which we have heard much recently. The mock outrage expressed by many cannot be taken seriously from those who evaluate human life so cheaply that they believe in the historical inevitability of situations involving the maximum of human misery, death and destruction.

In an abstract sense we are all guilty of My Lai, in tolerating a world which allows this to happen. William Calley is not only guilty of commanding others to kill but in obeying orders to treat My Lai as a free-fire zone, to search and destroy and to maximise the body-count. As long as there are those who will obey there will be those who command.

It is only logical that President Nixon who, after all, is Commander-in-Chief, should not only decide that William Calley (in defiance of all known law) should return to his barracks, but that Nixon will decide Calley's fate. This, if it means anything at all, means that Nixon will pardon Calley. A White House spokesman not only gratuitously insulted Mohammed Ali by referring to him as a 'draft dodger on bail' but recalled Abraham Lincoln's pardon for a sleeping sentry. Lincoln did not pardon Wirz and William Calley was not sleeping.

Nixon is right, insofar as the State is an agency of murder, that he should pardon its instruments. The deaths inflicted by police and National Guard (notably those at Kent State University) go unpunished. But those who cooperate with any State in its foul deeds add, in the words of Shelley, 'the crime of murder to the crime of servitude'.

Calley's especial guilt, indeed the guilt of all of us, lay in his abdicating the responsibility for his ethical decisions to his superior officer. He utterly failed to comprehend even the ostensible reason for his being in Vietnam; even if it had not dawned upon him that this purpose was unlikely to be achieved (as it has to many), he was content to obey orders. A thinking soldier would be death to the State, an obedient soldier is the death of humanity.

10th April 1971   JACK ROBINSON

The Presidential Candidate from Quang Tri

During the early North African campaigns of the 1939-45 war, a candidate for an almost-vanished party won an English by-election on the strength of a British defeat. He became known as the member for Mersa Matruh; Senator McGovern, who succeeded in the Wisconsin US Presidential Primary, is by the same token in danger of being thought of as the President-elect from Quang Tri.

Quang Tri is part of the terrible geography lesson of modern war in Vietnam. The Vietnam War has deliberately been allowed to sink into the background of the American Election but the North Vietnamese offensive with its early successes (common to most offensives) has put the War back in the headlines and McGovern's victory in the Wisconsin Primary has been credited to his consistent anti-war policy.

The war in Vietnam has been going on so long that it has become habitual; a way of life — and death. For example *The Times* (3rd March) opened a report from its correspondent in Saigon, 'More than 1,000 South Vietnamese were killed or wounded last week in the annual North Vietnamese and Vietcong winter-spring campaign'. Robert Shaplen, the *New Yorker*'s Vietnam correspondent, wrote in a long speculative article (13th November 1971 — before Nixon's China visit), 'American commanders anticipate stepped-up action across the De-Militarized Zone, aimed at the cities of Hué and Quang Tri, after the first of the year, when the weather improves, and when the American 101st Division starts pulling out, and it is here that the South Vietnamese (reinforced by a newly formed ARVN division) may face their sternest test. The Vietnamization programme could also be severely tested, and the outcome could be significant for all of Vietnam'.

We shall not know what took place in the meetings between Nixon and Chou. It is obvious that Chiang Kai-shek was double-crossed and it is possible that both North and South Vietnam were left to their fates. The ostentatious breaking-off of the Paris peace talks was a piece of play-acting in the middle of a charade. Obviously, if Nixon had made any deal about Vietnam when he was talking to Chou, such agreements would not be negotiated in public. According to *The Guardian*, 'the anti-communist alliance that the United States has forged in Indo-China with dollars, weapons and American military power has been violently jarred in the aftermath of the President's visit to Peking' (7th March).

Andre Malraux, former Communist Indo-China revolutionary and former Minister of Culture in de Gaulle's Government, briefed President Nixon on China before the visit. He told Mr Nixon (says the Agence France Press report in *The Times*, 3rd March) that it did not matter whether the Americans pulled out of Vietnam or not. Malraux said, 'For the Chinese Vietnam represented the policies of Foster Dulles . . . but no one believes any longer that Asia's destiny is being played out in Cochin China [Vietnam]. So, whether you stay or whether you leave, what does it matter? The important thing was a Western illusion of a Chinese communism bent on conquering Asia. No one believes in the Vietnam war any more because no one any longer believes in Chinese imperialism in Asia. All serious-minded people understand that China's objective is China, as the Soviet objective was the Soviet Union'. It is not known whether President Nixon accepted these highly cynical views of a man who has been through the political spectrum and knows the price of everything and the value of nothing.

Nixon, like all politicians, is also a cynic, but he is absolutely determined to win the next election, and he realises the value of being a man of peace to the doves and at the same time a man of war to the hawks, so the policy of ground-troop withdrawal and bombing acceleration would suit his election book nicely.

The invasion of Quang Tri province and the rout of ARVN forces has, it is claimed, drawn support for Senator McGovern's 'peace' candidature. The protestations of 'peace' when a war is being lost have some attraction and McGovern's position seems rather equivocal. In an interview with Henry Brandon in *The Sunday Times* he said 'quizzically', 'The cold war is fading away, don't you think? I feel Americans see the world much less divided now. Nixon did a fine job with his China initiative and I also think he handled the Taiwan problem extraordinarily well. We won't need in future as many men, aircraft carriers or the newly-proposed B1 bomber'. These views display an alarming political naivete — or cunning? — and such pragmatic pacifism would not even be rejected by Nixon.

In the extraordinary political brawling that passes for election preliminaries in America (how much better we do these things in England! — the stab in the back rather than the messy bludgeon-ings) anything can happen. Whatever happens in Vietnam — and the defeat of ARVN is only crystal-gazing — may not only lead to an increase in the anti-war vote, but an increase in the vote for a reactionary candidate determined to avenge the stab in the back of defeat. George Wallace is coming along quite nicely — Nixon has already made concessions to him on 'bussing' and if Wallace doesn't make it, even for Vice-President, there's always the odious Edward Kennedy waiting in the wings as the presidential candidate from Quang Tri.

15th April 1972   JACK ROBINSON

Americans Vote for Peace

It is rumoured that Dr Kissinger when recently reporting the set-back due to President Thieu's hesitancy and North Vietnam's was consoled by President Nixon with the words 'Never mind about the peace, let's get on with the election'.

In any case it does not really matter how President Thieu objects, he is indeed, financially and materially, a puppet of the Americans and whatever they decide he must accept. Nevertheless there is a limit to what voters will swallow and possibly Nixon will feel that a decision on how Thieu will go would be better postponed until after the election. Even if George McGovern is elected, he will not go back on the peace negotiations, despite their Nixon origin, and despite his claim that they come too late.

One of the complaints of George McGovern could be that Richard Nixon has stolen his platform which was based on peace in Vietnam; he should have known that 'tricky Dicky' Nixon had always got this card up his sleeve.

There has been a revival of anarchist thought in the USA, as throughout the world, and it no longer falls upon us alone to expound the anarchist case in the USA. At one time our American cousins had frequently to be beseeched by us not to fall into the trap of voting for the lesser evil. Many fell by the wayside in, for example, the Goldwater-Johnson battle, when Goldwater was held up as the incarnation of absolute fascism compared to Lyndon Baines Johnson. Now every progressive child is taught to hiss at the name of LBJ — and whatever happened to Goldwater? In American politics, and you won't believe this, you have to register before you can become a voter for a particular party and some life-long anarchists registered in order to keep Goldwater out — it worked. But now American anarchism has found its own voices so we have no longer to fulfil the Cassandra bit.

Nevertheless echoes of long-ago battles recur in the pages of the *War Resisters' League News* (journal of the American War Resisters' International) for September/October 1972, when Connie Bleakley and David McReynolds debate the cons and pros (respectively) of voting, in McReynolds' case for McGovern. McReynolds admits he chose the lesser evil of LBJ and got corruption plus escalation. In 1968 he thought there was nothing to choose from between Humphrey and Nixon and so didn't vote. 'But', says McReynolds, 'the differences are great enough to make a vote urgent. Register now, so you can vote in November'.

David McReynolds' major concern, as it must be, is for peace in Vietnam, and he makes an overstrained analogy that 'the person who plants the wheat and the person who harvests it are both essential to the baking of bread'. He takes the electing and working for McGovern as the harvesting of the seeds planted by the anti-war movement. But does he really believe that this harvest will become bread?

Apart from the fact that Nixon has stolen the only possible reason for voting for McGovern, McGovern, as is the way with all candidates, has taken steps which have removed him far from the blue-eyed boy of McReynolds' dreams. McReynolds says McGovern is no Jesus Christ '. . . if he makes too many compromises then, on election day, there will be no choice for us, and we can stay home. But if, after all the compromises are made, there still remains a difference, we should go to the polls. We should be cautious of our own purity. No matter how absolute our values, we can at best only approximate them in application'.

The essential nature of political power is that one becomes not merely 'not a Jesus Christ', but definitely a Judas. McGovern has moderated his aims on 'bussing' for example; accepted Mayor Daley of Chicago on his platform; turned away his first vice-presidential choice, Eagleton, on the shoddy grounds of a past history of mental illness; accepted as vice-president a close friend of the Kennedy clan and has had on his platform the tarnished Edward Kennedy working his passage for the 1976 Democratic ticket. (*The Guardian* reports a Kennedy fan meeting McGovern and Kennedy and saying 'Oh, Senator Kennedy, I can hardly wait till 1976', and then she saw McGovern and apologised, 'I am sorry, Senator McGovern, but that's how we feel in Pittsburgh'.) The courting of such discredited politicians and programmes is one of the roads to political power.

We do not know what will be the result of the election. It may be a landslide for Nixon because of his 'peace with honour' in Vietnam, or it may be a close-run thing. All we know is that the votes of the Americans are but a poor token of a desire for peace. The real message for peace in Vietnam came from those GIs who voted with their feet.

4th November 1972   JACK ROBINSON

NINETEEN SIXTY-EIGHT

Vive les Etudiants!

Ten million workers were called out on strike in France in support of the student demands. This follows ten days of militant action by the students. Considering that the Communist hierarchy has previously denounced the students as Anarchists, Trotskyists and Maoists, this action is as much bowing to public sentiment as the sudden capitulation of the French Government. The Sorbonne is to be reopened and cleared of the hated combat police and the release of all students was promised for today (13th May).

The antecedents of the struggle go back to 26th January of this year. On that day forty members of the Nanterre University anarchist group marched into the faculty hall with comical posters ridiculing the police. The porters attacked the anarchists but were defeated. The authorities called in the police; one thousand students fought back and attended a protest meeting. The movement thus launched has grown ever since.[1] The students are determined to get rid of the uniformed and plain-clothed police that haunt the faculties.

On 3rd May a great meeting was called at the Sorbonne by the extreme Left. The rector appealed to the police to dislodge the students. As the student protest grew, the Government stepped in and closed down the Sorbonne and Nanterre University, which were occupied by the combat police. The students organised quickly and brilliantly to reoccupy the universities from the hated police. As many as 15,000 students and sympathisers fought in street battles until the capitulation of the Government.

One of the demands of the students was that Danny Cohn-Bendit

---

1. For an eye-witness account of events in Paris during May 1968, see *Paris: May 1968* (Solidarity, London, 1968; reprinted by Dark Star Press and Rebel Press, 1986).
   Freedom Press published material relevant to this section in three issues of *Anarchy* magazine: No. 89, the May Days in France; No. 90, Student Anarchy (in *Anarchy* Vol. 8, 1968) and No. 99, Anarchism in the May Movement in France (in *Anarchy* Vol. 9, 1969) — Editor.

of the Nanterre anarchist group should not be deported to Germany. There have been many conflicting accounts in the British Press about our comrade. Although Nesta Roberts of *The Guardian* has accurately described him as an anarchist, Joseph Carroll in the same paper on the same day imputed he was a Trotskyist. Margot Lyons in *The New Statesman* said he was a 'Maoist' ringleader, *The Observer* said he was the leader of the 'anarcho-Maoists'. More to the point was Mandrake in *The Sunday Telegraph* who said amongst the students were many tendencies — Marxists, two kinds of Trotskyists, Maoists, Anarchists, Castroists, situationists. 'On 22nd March they invaded the administrative offices of Nanterre University and demanded the right to hold political meetings'. The subsequent 'Movement of 22nd March' was led by Danny Cohn-Bendit and no doubt attracted others than anarchists.

Tuesday 7th May: Ten thousand students had taken possession of a vast circle round the Arc de Triomphe, their red and black flags massed on either side of the unknown soldier's tomb, singing the *Internationale*. The police kept out of the way. General de Gaulle declared that he would not tolerate any further student violence.

The students declared that they were ready for a dialogue on three conditions: withdrawal of the police forces from the Latin Quarter, release and immediate amnesty for the imprisoned students, reopening the Sorbonne and Nanterre. Four hundred and thirty-four demonstrators were that day under arrest. The police that day restored D. Cohn-Bendit's residence permit (but only for a short period).

Wednesday 8th May: Strong police forces still occupied the Sorbonne and the student union delivered an ultimatum to the Government. If the demands were not met they would 'liberate' the Sorbonne. Mongeneral changed his tune and said: 'The Government is ready to take the steps necessary for the adaptation of education to the modern world'. M. Pierre Sudreau, of the Party of Modern Democracy, said in the French Assembly that extremists had been trained in street fighting at two anarchist camps.

Thursday 9th May: The Ministry announced that until calm was restored the Sorbonne would remain closed. The students declared that as soon as they reoccupied the Sorbonne they 'would take over the premises and hold discussions day and night on the problems of the university'.

Friday 10th May: The industrial unions (Communist and Christian) have thrown their lot in with the students and called for a general strike on Monday. Beyond Paris the movement is now supported all over France. Several thousand young pupils marched through Paris with placards: 'Tomorrow we shall have the same problem'.

Saturday 11th May, saw the decisive battle and the defeat of the Government. There was ferocious fighting, barricades were set up by the students and cars were upturned to form a barrier. It was a night of the barricades which the capital had not witnessed since the Commune days of 1871. After a hurried conference with General de Gaulle, M. Pompidou, the Prime Minister, announced the concessions. The student unions were not overawed. The union described the concessions as 'extremely interesting' but they would wait until Monday to see if their comrades were to be released.

From all reports the population of the Latin Quarter was solidly backing the students. They showered debris over the police and water over the students to minimise the effect of the chlorine gas grenades. The demonstrators were themselves issued with a leaflet on how to protect themselves against tear gas. They took an anti-flu pill before demonstrating and one when the grenades started flying; carried lemon-soaked handkerchiefs and smeared bicarbonate of soda around their eyes.

The brutality of the police horrified all reporters. Photographs seen in London, but unavailable to this paper, showed policemen clubbing students to the ground, blood streaming from their faces. But the students also fought back, kicked gas grenades back to the police, and the police had to protect their faces from thrown stones with what looked like fencing masks.

The French Government is desperately trying to cope with the revolutionary situation forced by the students and now supported by the working class. The general strike is called on the tenth anniversary of de Gaulle's assumption of power, on the day that the Vietnam 'peace talks' were to provide him with added glory. The adulation in Sunday's British Press was an indication of the treatment he was to be given and still got without a reference to the upheavals!

The students will also have to fight off the dubious embrace of the Communist Party and all those who are now climbing on the bandwagon. But their cool determination hitherto to force their just demands is an inspiration to us all!

18th May 1968   JOHN RETY

Revolution Adjourned

For days France teetered on the edge of revolution. May we be forgiven for saying that it was the absence of a substantial anarchist movement there which enabled the bourgeoisie to pull it back?

Revolutions are like lettuces — for best results they must be kept growing quickly without check. In France the incipient revolution had the greatest pest of all to check its growth — the big fat rats of the Communist CGT who ate away at the roots.

For all the ingredients were there the moment the industrial workers joined the students in mass protest, strike and occupation of the factories. It would not have taken much to have turned the general strike into a *social* general strike and to have turned that into a social revolution — had that in fact been what any sizeable section of the anti-Gaullist forces wanted.

But was it? It was certainly among the students that the most revolutionary ideas were to be found. Correspondents tell us of the high level of heated discussion which went on day and night in the Sorbonne and the entire Latin Quarter — discussion interspersed with action in the bitter nightly battles with the hated CRS.

It may be said that when you are actually on the barricades it is a bit late to be trying to clarify your ideas — but no doubt the students en masse were just as surprised at what they were doing as anybody else. This is how it is with your actual spontaneous revolution. We may be quite sure that Daniel Cohn-Bendit and his forty comrades in Nanterre whose action first sparked the whole thing off could have had no idea that they would end up with eight million workers on strike, the economy at a standstill and de Gaulle, if not on his knees, at least toppled from his pedestal and made to face the seething unrest beneath the surface of his State.

For this has been the great surprise for the world and perhaps even for the French people themselves: the extent of discontent, even of hatred for the regime, that exists under the surface of an apparently stable and orderly society. And the great achievement of the French students has been to bring this out into the open, to carry their own struggle into the factories and workshops, to offer a great gulp of fresh air to the French workers and deliver a great kick to the fat backside of French bourgeois society. The regime, even if it survives the General Election, can never be the same again. Some degree of student control must be allowed in

the universities, some degree of hope, if nothing else, must persist
for the French workers.

For it is the workers who are in the sorriest plight. Contrary to
Marxist mythology, the industrial workers in modern industrial
countries are not — and never have been — the spearhead of social
revolution. They should be, perhaps. They could be, certainly. But
having been sold on reformist trade unionism, they are given no
encouragement by their own organisations to think in terms of
responsibility, of workers' control.

In France their condition is even worse than in this country. Here,
for political reasons, the Communists will agitate as an opposition
to the reformist unions; there the Communists *are* the reformist
unions. The counter-revolutionary role the Communists have played
in many revolutions has never been more perfectly exemplified
than in the events in France these last three weeks, and the only
comforting thought that can emerge from this is that surely they
must now be completely discredited among all those French workers
who were prepared to occupy their factories and shops — for what?

If they had taken over!
It was at the point of the occupation of the factories that the
revolution was almost on. When the Bourse was fired; when the
students began to change their tactics from mass confrontation to
smaller, guerrilla-type sorties to wear down the police and as a
result the police began to show signs of disaffection and the Civil
Service began to crack up, and de Gaulle apparently just sat and
sat — then, if the occupation of the factories had swung into *operation* of the factories by the workers, if they had demonstrated their
ability to organise their work without their bosses, if revolutionary
coordinating councils had emerged to run the economy, distribute
goods, maintain services — then the social revolution would have
been on! If! If!

But no. Just as the petrified leaders of the TUC in the British
General Strike of 1926 went to talk to King George V, so the slimy
Communist leaders of the CGT went to talk with Pompidou —
and came back triumphant with ten per cent!

Surely no-one imagined the workers would accept this? But it
was not primarily intended for acceptance. It was no more than a
talking point — a means towards taking the strikes off the boil, to
give the politicians time to put their clammy hands over the hot
aspirations of the people.

And so it worked. Everything went off the boil. The students took a hell of a beating and calmed down, the workers sat and sat and the politicians waited. Having been served by the unions perfectly, de Gaulle chose just the right moment and jumped. With a show of force, and just the right bait — a General Election! — to cool all but the 'extremists', like the cunning old cat he is, he jumped. And that was it.

But we are sure the lessons of 1968 will not be lost. The sincere revolutionaries among the students will have learnt valuable lessons of tactics and theory; the workers will have seen where their real friends lie; the divisions between intellectuals and workers must have closed, between them and the politician/trade union bureaucrat widened.

What of the anarchist movement? Well, isn't it the same old story? Not enough anarchists among the workers! In all the student unrest around the world now anarchists are setting the pace — or at least anarchistic methods of direct action are having effect. The French event is the only instance we have so far of workers joining in a struggle with the students, and events show that there was not a sufficient leavening of anarchist workers to get the message of workers' control across in the way that student power has been put across.

The task before us
It is of course a different set of problems. The bourgeoisie may moan about having to pay taxes to keep hooligan students in grants, but radical tampering with the economy at factory floor level is a really serious matter. Furthermore the workers themselves are not interested in ideas as the students are, and they are much more bogged down with the 'responsibilities' of domesticity, with noses to the grindstone and only superficial leisure activities as relief.

Nevertheless the task is before us as it has always been: the creation of a widespread anarchist movement in all levels of society; the creation of an anarcho-syndicalist movement in industry to educate workers in revolutionary aims and tactics so that the maximum advantage can be taken of any situation whenever the opportunity presents itself; the creation of an anarchist international for mutual aid across the frontiers.

One thing the French students and workers have done. They have put revolution back on the agenda in Western Europe. It is not over yet — it has simply been adjourned.
8th June 1968   P.S.

Elections — Treason to the Revolution!

The past weeks have seen a modern Western industrialised society rocked to its very foundations. French workers, following the initiative of the students, have occupied their places of work. This action took place spontaneously and soon spread all over France. It quickly followed the one-day token strike on Monday 13th May, called by the three trade union organisations, which proved to be a massive show of solidarity with the students.

However, the grievances were not confined to the students. The French working class has for a long time suffered an ever worsening standard of living. Wage increases and better conditions have been effectively resisted by the Gaullist regime and, in order to compete within the Common Market, its efforts to modernise the French capitalist system have caused the conditions and wages of workers to lag far behind what has been necessary to secure a reasonable standard of living. There is also growing unemployment which is not only affecting industrial workers, but also the students who are finding it increasingly difficult to find employment after leaving university.

However, the occupation of the factories, building sites, the docks, ships, and the bringing of the whole transport system to a standstill was not specifically for economic demands. As in the case of the students, these actions released all the pent up resentment against a bureaucratic and authoritarian regime which, over the years, had been subjecting the people to increasing exploitation.

The students had shown the way. They had forced concessions from the Government and the lessons of this were not lost on workers, especially the young ones. Following the token strike, students had gone to factories to explain their case and so had linked up their struggle with that of workers.

Caught off balance

When the workers took occupation of their places of work, there was no call put out for a general strike. It just happened. The Communist Party and their union, the CGT, were caught completely off balance and, in order to regain its control, it went along with the workers, bringing them out where it knew it was in firm control.

In actual membership, the trade union movement in France is very small. The CGT is the largest, but this numbers just over 1½ million members. The CFDT has under a million and the FO

500,000. So out of the working population, only about 30 per cent are organised. This has meant that trade unions are hardly recognised in many factories. Citröens have a total ban on union activities and even Renaults, which are supposed to be progressive, deny trade union activities, which are taken for granted in the average factory here.

While only a small number are organised, the strikes that paralysed France embraced ten million workers and indicates how widespread is the discontent amongst workers. The Communist Party and all the trade unions were caught out by the spontaneous series of strikes. Although originally unofficial, the unions were forced to support them. By occupying their factories, the workers asserted their claim to the social ownership and control of the means of production. This assertion has revolutionary implications and the trade unions were quick to realise this.

In the circumstances, the occupation was a natural thing to do. Many of the younger workers were well aware of the possibilities of this form of action, but the trade unions and the Communist Party were quick to impose purely economic demands for the workers. These demands cover big increases in wages, a 40-hour week, lower retiring age, recognition of trade union organisation and activities

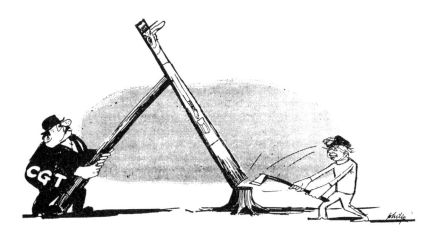

in factories and a return to the previous rates for social security benefit. They are important and justified, but diverted a revolutionary situation to an economic one, which could be handled by the present bourgeois system. Given their continued rule, these economic advances could be lost with probable devaluation of the franc and the consequences of inflation.

The Communist Party, throughout, has done nothing that in any way threatened the institutions on which the bourgeois system rests. It has at all times denounced any body or organisation which is politically to their left. It has outflanked and outmanoeuvred any movement in this direction. It has prevented, where possible, any contact or link-up between students and workers. It has played down the insurrectionary and revolutionary character of the student demonstration and the occupation of the factories. It has at all times refused to take any action which might provoke the CRS.

CGT leader booed

Once the Communist Party had gained control, the government was able to negotiate with the unions. Agreement was reached on the economic issues, but when these were put to the workers, they were overwhelmingly rejected.

The Observer says that the CGT leader, Georges Seguy, was booed by Renault workers. This rejection put the union leaders out on a limb, giving the dispute stronger political overtones. It was going further than mere economic demands.

After the revolutionary tone of Monday's march and meeting of students and workers at which André Barjonet, the ex-CGT economic adviser, said 'Revolution today is possible', the Communist Party once again reasserted its control by calling out its members and supporters on Wednesday's demonstration.

They demanded the resignation of de Gaulle and a 'Government of the people'. Hardly revolutionary, but at least political and a challenge for power which de Gaulle fully understands. Following the rejection of wage increases, a referendum was a non-starter, for who was going to print the ballot papers? Not the French printers and even Belgian workers had refused to do it.

De Gaulle has promised a general election within forty days and felt strong enough to issue a challenge that if a 'situation of force' continued to prevail (meaning revolutionary activity) 'I will have to adopt other methods than immediate elections. In any case civil action must be organised everywhere to assist the Government. Prefects of departments and regions will resume the role of

Commissioners of the Republic to ensure the livelihood of the population and the defence against subversion'. In that short speech he shattered the Left's hopes of immediate power.

De Gaulle is fighting on and has issued a challenge which, if taken, would mean civil war. The Communist Party and the socialist parties in the Parliament did not take up this challenge. Instead, they are using the ballot box. The economic concessions gained through negotiation will be used to win votes at election. The Communist Party wants only to participate in a Government of the Left. It realises it can be successful here and so a return to work is in order. Without this a General Election would be impossible.

In retreat
To continue the struggle, the Communist Party would have to move to the Left and this could once again create a revolutionary situation which, this time, it would be unable to contain. The Communist Party and the other traditional Parties of the Left are now in retreat from a revolutionary situation. By accepting elections and agreeing not to impede them, they turned away from de Gaulle's challenge.

However, in a revolutionary situation, the idea of civil war must be faced. The police and armed forces are there to protect the system and therefore have to be won over. There were signs that if such a confrontation took place, troops were not prepared to break strikes. The struggle is now moving from the streets and factories into the harmless constitutional channels of elections. Police have cleared workers from communication centres and already other workers are resuming work.

The Communists throughout have never aimed for or wanted the overthrow of the Gaullist regime, whether by violence or other means. They have been more concerned with the challenge from the extreme Left, from 'anarchist and adventurist trends'. Their concern, like all political parties, has been to strengthen their political base and support in order to gain some power by constitutional means.

De Gaulle knew this, otherwise he would not have issued his challenge. Although there was a clear political challenge when workers rejected the increases, de Gaulle knew the Communists would not carry it through.

Many Communists have been shocked by their Party's actions. The Party faces a considerable crisis here. There is also a new revolutionary movement in which anarchists have played a considerable role. It is not restricted to students, but has strong links with young trade union members. This is what is important, that the French working class responded to and supported the students. They were horrified at the treatment that the students received from the CRS and they showed where their sympathies lay.

The students alone cannot change society. They are fully aware of this. Revolution in our bureaucratic capitalist society depends on the support of the working class. Students and workers should not be divided, but should unite in such situations. It is important that they work together and that the social revolution should be their aim. These contacts have and are being made. Although, at the time of writing, work is resuming, the situation is still in a state of flux and things will never be the same in France again. Many more students and workers realise now that mere reforms are not enough. The direct action in the streets, the fighting on the barricades and the occupations of the factories have changed, educated and made many conscious of the revolutionary potential of their actions.

8th June 1968   P.T.

To Solve the 'Crisis of Democracy' — It Must Be Anarchism

We are told there is a crisis of democracy. And no wonder. For democracy has failed to deliver the goods for mankind — the material goods as well as the social goods. The much-vaunted prosperity of the West has always been a prosperity for some at the expense of the many: the so-called socialism of the East has turned out to be no more than a variation on the same theme — power for some at the expense of the many.

If the purpose of government is to provide the greatest good for the greatest number, then even by its own standard government has failed. Socialism, Communism, Fascism, like Democracy, can survive only by the slavery of the greatest number that will tolerate it. Government equals the greatest suppression of the greatest number; it is itself the greatest failure of mankind.

Democracy is, we suppose, the highest form of government that has yet been evolved. If we reject any form of despotism or totalitarianism — and any sane person with any concept of what human beings need to grow, to develop, to realise themselves, must reject it — then democracy is the best form of government we have. And it is just not good enough.

It is not good enough simply because it is only a variation on the theme of government. It is despotism disguised by a system of 'checks and balances' to give us an illusion of having a say in our own lives. But it is only an illusion, for in fact we have nothing of the kind: we are subjected to a cunning series of conjuring tricks by master illusionists who express their contempt for us by allowing us to oppose them openly in a wide variety of ways — for as long as we are ineffectual. Democracy provides 'proper', 'respectable', 'constitutional' channels for opposition — why, there is even an Official Opposition!

All of which adds up to no opposition at all because all that is offered is the means to change the personnel at the top. And while there are people at the top — i.e. while there is government — backed up, as Top People always are by the violent apparatus of the State, there is no fundamental difference between systems of government.

Consensus Politics

Two-party systems provide no alternative to one-party dictatorships. Even assuming differences in political parties, once they are in power with majorities, they become one-party Governments, with the tendency towards effective dictatorship, with government by decree, regulation or committee being merely ratified, by Parliamentary majority. We are stuck with them for their term of office — and then offered the great opportunity to replace them with the other lot who will carry on where they left off!

For in fact, just as in the economic sphere the tendency towards monopoly eliminates competition, so in the political field the tendency is towards consensus politics — the broad agreement between Parties on how best to govern the people, to run the capitalist economy, to maintain the illusions.

Who can explain for us any real differences between Democrat and Republican in America, between Christian- and Social-Democrat in Germany, between Labour and Conservative here?

What fundamental difference is there between de Gaulle's regime in France, the regime of the Colonels in Greece, that of Franco in Spain, or the variations on Stalinism practised by the Communist countries?

All are authoritarian, differing in degree only. The secure Governments allow a greater degree of latitude to their subjects, the insecure Governments are too afraid to allow any measure of liberty at all. All govern by a mixture of deceit and force. When deceit fails and the people see through it and protest, the violent institutions of the State bash them back into submission.

In every country and under every regime the ordinary people are deprived of dignity and, in varying degrees, of material well-being. Every Government, every State, can exist only through the organised and consistent robbery of its subjects by taxation, and the organised and consistent brain-washing which passes for education.

There must be an alternative to this miserable set of alternatives which are no alternatives at all. And there is. It is to break with the concept of government altogether, and to think in terms of human societies becoming self-governing communities. For many people, the crisis of democracy can be resolved only by going in the direction of more government — of resolving the apparent indecisions of 'liberal' parliamentarism by a 'strong' government. In a word, by dictatorship.

For anarchists this argument is laughable. It is like offering to cure your patient of catarrh by injecting him with pneumonia. If we have learned anything from the lessons of this century, with its massive and tragic experiments in varying forms of government, it is that dictatorship, whether of the Right or Left, can be nothing but a cruel perversion of human society, crushing individual dignity and social initiative alike.

Anarchism The Only Alternative
If the answer does not lie in more government, can we have less? Where is the Government that is prepared to relinquish any of its powers? Democracies everywhere are putting more and more power into the hands of their bureaucrats, while dictatorships — including those 'of the proletariat' — show nothing more clearly than their determination to survive. The Leninist myth of 'the withering away of the State' remains a myth.

The answer does not lie in more government or less — but in *none*! This is why anarchism — the only social philosophy which asserts the concept of no government as a means, as an immediate aim and the long-term end — this is why anarchism presents the only alternative to the crisis of democracy and its attendant threat of dictatorship.

This is why the present student revolt in so many countries is so encouraging. Whether they call themselves anarchists or not, the students are acting anarchistically since they are taking direct action in order to take their freedom. They are not crawling to their authorities and begging please to be taken notice of; they are not asking for something to be done for them — they are taking the control of their immediate environments out of the hands of their immediate authorities. They are establishing workers' control in the only way it is possible to do so — by taking control. It is as simple as that, when it comes down to it.

The politicos among the students should take note that this is happening in countries with a so-called variety of regimes. Not only does this happen in Catholic and authoritarian France and Spain, in 'permissive' and democratic Britain and America, but it is also happening in Communist Poland and Yugoslavia.

The latter country is of course one of the favourites of the 'New Left' type of socialist who refers to the degree of 'workers' control' practised in Tito's State with approval. We now see that in order to get workers' control in the universities, the Yugoslav students have to resort to exactly the same tactics as those in the capitalist democracies and fascist Police States.

Must we wait for a student revolt in Cuba before the 'New Left' will realise that a Government is a Government is a Government?

All around the world therefore, the students are showing the rest of society the simple truths of anarchism: if you want your freedom you have to take it for yourself. If you want to run your own life with dignity and a concept of self-realisation within a society of your own creation — then you simply have to set out to create it yourself.

No authority, no Government will meet your needs. Not even your material needs, since government must be a parasite on the economic productivity of society. Still less your social needs. Freedom is never given; it has to be taken.

The way out of the crisis of democracy then, is through the practise of still more direct action, still stronger rejection of the illusions of government, still more determination to seize control of our own lives to run them for our own benefit, not for the profit or power of the few.

The only alternative that breaks out of the authoritarian trap is the libertarian one — it has got to be anarchism!
15th June 1968   P.S.

Elections Provide No Answer

The predicted return to work of French workers, after the Whitsun holiday, did not take place. Instead workers have stuck to their claims and only returned when they have been satisfied. However, the trend nevertheless is back to work.

This is essential if the forthcoming General Election is to be held. With this end in view, both the Gaullist Government, its supporters and all the Left opposition Parties, including the Communists, wish to see a return to normality. But this reluctance on the part of many workers to resume work indicates that the unions do not have such a strong hold on them.

The Communists, as the strongest Party on the Left, with the CGT as the biggest union, were always frightened of being out-flanked on their Left. They did everything possible to contain the revolutionary wave that began with the students and quickly gained support amongst workers.

De Gaulle's trump card was elections and from then onwards workers have been divided up, each taking part in their separate negotiations on wages and conditions. The Communist Party was, at all times, scared stiff of two things. Firstly, of being overtaken by the revolutionary Left and, because of this, secondly of losing its own membership and supporters. Then, it was not willing to go all the way in a head-on clash with the State.

General de Gaulle's speech announcing the elections proved to be the turning point. Many of the workers who have not resumed work have increased the demands. Obviously, both the Government and employers want a quick resumption, but are reluctant to meet these increased demands. At the time of writing, metal workers, dockers, seamen, some sections of the building industry and those in the motor industry are still on strike.

Police move on Renaults
At the Renault factory at Flins, some 25 miles north-west of Paris, a thousand police took over the factory in a dawn raid. A sparsely

manned picket line offered no resistance and those inside left quietly. However, in the afternoon of the following day, workers, with the support of students, tried to regain control of the factory. The riot police used tear gas, while the workers and students threw nuts and bolts, fire-bombs and cobbles.

Much of the deadlock in these industries arises because the employers refuse to pay more than the national 10% negotiated by the top union leaders and the employers' federation. As Renault workers were probably the largest section of workers to first occupy their factories, it is thought that the Government (Renault is national-ised) might be trying to teach them a lesson.

All three trade unions have appealed for national solidarity with the Renault workers. The CGT, looking over its shoulder again, has had to give its support, but it has also said that 'wherever the essential demands of the workers were satisfied, their interest is to declare solidly in favour of a resumption of work in unity'. How this ties up with national solidarity with Renault only a Stalinist could explain. Later the CGT openly declared against any sympathy strikes in support of Renault workers.

However, all through these May days in France, the Communists have been out of touch due to the rapidness of the events. They have been as puzzled and bewildered as de Gaulle himself, because spontaneity is alien to the authoritarians. The upsurge from below, with everyone taking his or her part, gave people, for a short time, the experience of making their own decisions, of feeling a vital part of something worthwhile and of creating something new from below by their own efforts, instead of being imposed from above. The Communist Party cannot understand this, the full-flavoured wine of freedom is far too strong for them.

The French Communist Party has for a long time been working within the system. A *Times* leader quoted the following from a Communist deputy, M. Leroy, which emphasised this point.

The Communists are not in the process of preparing an insurrection. To imply that they are is a gross untruth. We are not in favour of patching up the Gaullist Government or of anarchy. What we are aiming at is the immediate satisfaction of the basic claims of manual and white collar workers. We aim at replacing a Gaullist Government by a popular govern-ment of democratic union.

So the CGT is merely a reformist trade union, working on bread and butter issues, while its political wing wants a left-wing Govern-ment with them holding some position of power.

De Gaulle has now really turned the tables on them by casting them as the menace of 'totalitarian communism' and is making the forthcoming election a choice between 'democracy and communism'. With wage negotiations still going on, the Communists have to show a little revolutionary fervour to maintain the Party's control over the more militant workers, in order not to be outflanked by what are called 'extremists on the Left' by the capitalist Press. The Communist paper *L'Humanité* calls them 'left wing groups' who use 'pseudo-revolutionary phrases' and who are opposing the workers' wish of a return to work and are 'conducting a fight not against the Government and the employers, but against the Communist Party and its policy of union among the forces of the Left'.

These tactics of de Gaulle and M. Pompidou, the Prime Minister, could well be successful. The seeking of left-wing unity by the Communists does not seem to be working out. M. Mitterand's Federation is turning, not to the Communist Party, but to the Centre for support against the Government.

A French Labour Party
Out of all these diversions, the role the French Communist Party could be seeking, one which the CGT already complements, is that of an equivalent of the Labour Party in this country. With the social democratic movement in France so divided, mostly by personalities, the Communist Party could fit in very nicely.

Whatever the outcome of the elections, the economic gains made by the workers will, by the end of the year, have been lost through higher prices and possible devaluation of the franc. They will be back to the same pre-May position. De Gaulle has promised 'participation', which he has defined as all getting 'together for the common economic task, to set an industry working by contributing either the necessary capital, or management or technique'.

He also said that 'modern society is mechanical, it enslaves man, whoever he is and whatever he does. The individual, the worker, has no grip on his own destiny any more than ants in an ant-heap'. Neither by 'totalitarian enterprise of communism, nor through capitalism' could this participation be brought about.

From these contradictory remarks, what really emerges is that, basically, the workers' position will remain the same. Government-controlled factories, like Renault, were supposed to be the most progressive and enlightened showpieces of the Fifth Republic and yet the workers from the Renault plants were some of the first to occupy their factories and make the most radical demands.

Although a revolutionary situation has been channelled to the ballot box, the signs are that the situation could repeat itself when the wage increases are lost in the ensuing inflation.

The students might be granted reforms, but the gigantic task of providing enough facilities and universities to meet their requirements is an impossible task for some time to come. On top of this, no modern State can give that control of one's destiny that de Gaulle spoke about. The State is basically an 'ant-heap' and it is this that the students came to realise they were rebelling against.

Young workers are also feeling this and a student-worker alliance is becoming a reality. Both are becoming aware that there is more in life than getting a bigger and bigger share of the goods of a consumer society. A modern technological society can do this, but it cannot provide for the human desire of men to run and control their own lives. People want more than just a say, they want to make the decisions that affect their lives themselves. The cold evil monster, the State, cannot do this.

Our task is to work for a position where there are enough anarchists to make a situation as in France into a social revolution. There is a great deal of ignorance about anarchism; our ideas are not widely known. This is especially true in industry and it is up to us to rectify this and to create a much larger and widespread anarchist movement. With the further discredit of the Communist Party, many party militants could be attracted to our movement. It is up to us to reach them and all sections of the community with our ideas.
15th June 1968   P.T.

Czechoslovakia 1968

Czechoslovakia 1968 will be remembered as yet one more betrayal of socialism by the Russian Communist Party during the half-century it has held power. It joins a long line which goes from Ukraine 1918 and Kronstadt 1921 down to East Germany 1953 and Hungary 1956. Eventually there will be books about it (there already are in France, Germany and Italy), and then it will be possible to put together and understand all the details of an extraordinary story. In the meantime there are articles in the Press, trying to put what has happened into some sort of perspective; the present article is an attempt to put into focus the events of a whole year.

When Novotny lost power in January, the Communists had ruled Czechoslovakia for twenty years since the 1948 coup d'état, when they overthrew the bourgeois liberal coalition which had been set up at the end of the war. Under the Communist regime, power was held by a single dictator, a Stalinist puppet, who combined the honorific post of President with the effective post of General Secretary of the Czechoslovak Communist Party. The puppet-dictator was Klement Gottwald from 1948 until his death in 1953, and Antonin Novotny from 1953 until his fall in 1968. During the twenty years of Stalinist dictatorship, Czechoslovakia got the reputation of being one of the most docile of Russia's satellites. In fact this reputation was not entirely deserved, for the regime had trouble with both the people and the Party.

A forgotten rising
In June 1953 — just before the East German rising — there was a little-known rising in Czechoslovakia. Workers from the Skoda factory led successful attacks on the Plzen town hall and law court, fought the police for two days, and were crushed only by soldiers sent from Prague. And there were attempts to oust Novotny in 1962 and again in 1963, which failed but did force the regime to make concessions — such as the emergence of Alexander Dubcek as First Secretary of the Slovak Communist Party.

More important than either open insurrection or Party splits, there was a sort of underground thaw after 1963. Literary magazines began to discuss unorthodox ideas such as freedom of speech, which is predictable enough, and workers' control of factories, which is not. Not only did 'liberals' come out into the open against 'conservatives', but they gradually took over important posts in intellectual and administrative life, especially in such apparently irrelevant but actually crucial areas as education and economics. As in Hungary — and in Russia itself — it was the intellectuals who took the lead in undermining Communist orthodoxy, but it would be wrong to ignore the vital point that they were supported by the mass of the people. They had taken the lead before in the struggle with the Austrian and Hungarian regime until 1918, and the relative freedom of the independent State which lasted from 1918 to 1938 was not forgotten. Under the frozen surface of the regime its support had melted away.

The ice begins to crack

But the ice didn't begin to crack until — of all things — the Arab-Israeli war in summer 1967. The Czechoslovak Government dutifully followed the Russian line by breaking off diplomatic relations with Israel, but the Writers' Union deliberately passed a resolution of sympathy with Israel, and there was a hell of a row. Support for Israel became a symbol of opposition to antisemitism (most of the victims of the Gottwald purge were Jewish) and at a further remove a symbol of opposition to Stalinism (which always tended towards antisemitism). In autumn 1967 a peaceful student demonstration was violently attacked by police, and the young intellectuals were publicly ranged alongside their seniors against the regime.

Another element was Slovak nationalism, as in the widespread resentment Novotny caused by his offensive behaviour during a tour of Slovakia, also in autumn 1967. Dubcek is a Slovak and, although he is not a nationalist, his nationality is certainly a symbol of opposition to 'Great Power chauvinism' as it was applied in Czechoslovakia — the oppression of Slovaks by Czechs being seen as a reflection of the oppression of both Czechs and Slovaks by Russia.

In winter 1967 it was obvious even to Novotny that his power was crumbling away, and he asked Brezhnev for help against the new attempt to oust him. But when Brezhnev visited Czechoslovakia he told the Party leaders that it was none of his business. When the Central Committee met in December 1967, Novotny expressed self-criticism, but this was no longer enough and he adjourned the meeting. But when the Central Committee met again in January 1968, he was forced to resign as General Secretary, and Dubcek was appointed in his place (as a compromise candidate between an extreme 'conservative', the prime minister Lenart, and an extreme 'liberal', Cernik).

Twenty Years into Twenty Weeks

What happened after this was more or less that Czechoslovakia compressed twenty years' experience in Yugoslavia into twenty weeks, and even went beyond Yugoslavia, without actually destroying the Communist regime; and what was new and extraordinary was that the lead in this process was taken by the Communist Party itself. But Czechoslovakia is part of the Russian bloc, and the events in Czechoslovakia threatened the Communist regimes throughout Eastern Europe. Four things were particularly dangerous to the Communist system:

1. The Czechoslovak Communist Party went from Stalinism back to democratic centralism and then on to party democracy. In March Ludvik Svoboda replaced Novotny as President, and in April Cernik replaced Lenart as Prime Minister. Long discussions within the Party led to the publication of an Action Programme in April; this went further in the direction of libertarian socialism than any Communist Party in power since 1917. No wonder the Communist leaders of Poland, East Germany, Hungary, Bulgaria and — above all — Russia were frightened, and those of Rumania and Yugoslavia could hardly have welcomed these developments.

2. The Czechoslovak Government allowed freedom of speech. Foreign papers were on sale in Prague in January, and independent papers were published there in February. In March the official censorship was abolished after twenty years, and political discussion was freed from all restraints other than that of caution. Prague Radio became more open to varying points of view than the BBC. The Communist Party paper, *Rude Pravo*, became almost unrecognisable. The writers' paper, *Literarni Listy*, became the forum of the intellectual rebellion against all the old orthodoxies. In June it published the manifesto called 'Two Thousand Words' (after its length), drafted by Ludvik Vaculik and signed by seventy intellectuals, which represented an appeal by both Communists and non-Communists to continue the process of liberalisation — an appeal which was quickly repudiated by the Government but for which no one was punished. Czechoslovak intellectuals made contact with those in Western countries, and intellectual life in Czechoslovakia became as open as in Hungary between the revolution of October 1956 and the counter-revolution of November 1956. Again, no wonder the Communist leaders of neighbouring countries were frightened, for even in Yugoslavia non-Communists were still imprisoned for questioning Communism.

3. Along with freedom of speech, the Czechoslovak Government began to introduce economic freedom. By its very nature, this takes longer to establish and is harder to document, so little is yet known about what happened and what was going to happen; but it is at least clear that this was one of the most important things going on in Czechoslovakia this year. Workers' control of industry and peasants' control of agriculture would, if they had been

genuine, have destroyed the economic basis of authoritarian Communism and provided the economic basis of libertarian socialism. The Russian Communists fear nothing more, as they showed in Spain during the Civil War — and in Russia during their own Civil War — and once more no wonder the Communist leaders in neighbouring countries were frightened.

4. Above all, the Czechoslovak Government seemed to be allowing political opposition — something which is unique in a Communist country. In June a law was passed to rehabilitate political prisoners, and an organisation was set up to represent their interests; the political prisoners of a Communist regime are not likely to support the Communist Party, even if it is as liberal as it was in Czechoslovakia. There are plenty of social democrats in Czechoslovakia, and liberals, and probably even conservatives; and there are certainly many non-Communist communists — that is, people who believe in complete socialism without the Communist Party. The Czechoslovak Communist Party maintained support because it was doing what the people wanted, and because it was letting the people do what they wanted; one of the things they wanted was political freedom; political freedom includes the freedom to oppose and to change the system; once they had real freedom, the people might not want the Communist Party. Yet again, no wonder the Communist leaders in neighbouring countries — and even perhaps in Czechoslovakia — were frightened.

Any Resistance Better than None

There doesn't seem to have been any hint that Czechoslovakia would leave the Warsaw Pact, break the Russian bloc, and join the West. But on the other hand there doesn't seem to have been any reason why such things shouldn't eventually happen. And this was no doubt the factor which made up the minds of the Russian leaders to threaten the Czechoslovaks in the Press and in person, to hold fake military manoeuvres inside Czechoslovakia in May and outside Czechoslovakia in July, and finally to invade in August.

At the time of the invasion, the extraordinary resistance of the Czechoslovak people made it seem that the Russians had made an enormous mistake. But the surrender of the Czechoslovak Government made it certain that the Russians would eventually get what they wanted. The people, rightly admiring their rulers for standing up to Russian pressure for so long, wrongly trusted them to go on doing so for ever. During the last two months, all the gains of the last year have been lost. The Party congress fixed for September, which was prevented by the Russian invasion and was partly held underground during the occupation, has been put off, and Party democracy is held in suspense. Freedom of speech is also held in abeyance, and the brilliantly organised underground press and broadcasting of the occupation has come to nothing. The possibility of opposition has ended, and potentially dissenting organisations are quietly dismantled. And the economic reforms, which would have put the seal on all the other reforms, have been put into reverse. Jan Hus has promised not to talk heresy; the Good Soldier Schweik has been promoted; K. has admitted his guilt.

The tragedy of Czechoslovakia 1968 is not that the Russians destroyed the Czechoslovak experiment but that the Czechoslovaks stopped it themselves. For a week they had shown the world how to resist Communist oppression, and had suggested that all the previous attempts, from Kronstadt to Hungary, had been wrong. Now it seems that the sailors of Kronstadt and the students of Hungary may not have been wrong after all. Peaceful resistance is better than violent resistance, but resistance of any kind is better than no resistance at all. In the end the best thing that has come out of Czechoslovakia in 1968 is the tiny protest of a few Russians in Red Square on 25th August; on 11th October they were sent to prison or exile, but their demonstration shows that the message of Czechoslovakia 1968 was heard in the East as well as the West: the message of free communism, of libertarian socialism, even — dare we say it? — of anarchism.

As a postscript, it should be emphasised again and again that two of the very few Communist Parties which approved of the invasion of Czechoslovakia were those of North Vietnam and Cuba — that Ho Chi Minh and Fidel Castro, those glorious bearded heroes of the Marxist Left, of the armchair guerrilleros in the university common rooms, of the screaming street-fighters in Grosvenor Square, have publicly supported the destruction of free socialism by the Russian Communist regime. If this doesn't teach them, nothing can.

26th October 1968   NICOLAS WALTER

Revolution on the Agenda

Not more than most years, but certainly no less, 1968 has been a year of governmental deception covering the mailed fist; the usual practice which conceals the Great Lie of government itself. By deceit and bribery, by mis-education, conditioning and propaganda, by economic exploitation, taxation and legal robbery, by bullying, coercion and violence — by gentle and not-so-gentle 'persuasion', Governments have continued the great lie that people need Governments.

In this great con game around the world, all the world's authorities share in the shabby conspiracy — and so, for that matter, do the world's peoples. Who should we blame for this state of affairs? The minority in whose interests the great lie is perpetuated — or the majority who give of their blood, toil, tears and sweat in the interests of that minority?

The one glimmer of hope that has been raised in 1968 has come from the astonishing way in which revolution has been put back on the agenda. The word 'revolution' can be — and is — meaninglessly and easily bandied about by many with no real understanding and no real caring for its reality. Discussions by respectable churchmen on the telly end with a majority of them nodding sagely and agreeing '. . . the only way is revolution . . .' Superficial, tendentious, romantic and snide reports have abounded in surprising quarters.

Fighting for Control

But what has made the bourgeoisie sit up and take notice has been real enough. In a year of student ferment around the world, the events of May and June in France were outstanding, but by no means unique, except perhaps in the scale in which workers participated in action sparked off by students. Until this spreads in all cases, we cannot pretend really to have moved from a protest situation to a revolutionary situation — but it will come.

There have been two truly heartening aspects of the students' protests. Firstly, they have been acting for *control* of their places of work. While it would be foolish to pretend that the students are the only ones who work in universities, their situation at the bottom of the ladder, without any say in the way their immediate world is run, subject to pettifogging victorian restrictions and academically dissatisfied to boot, has proved intolerable. In places where the most inspired protests have occurred — like Hornsey — the constructive aspect of their demands has been recognisable, their responsible behaviour has been exemplary, and a large proportion of junior staff — not yet bought off with senior posts and pensions — have joined with them. The distinction has been quite clearly made between the administration, whose function is strictly authoritarian and financial, and teaching staff, whose function is educational. The parallel we draw here with workers' control in industry is surely in the distinction we make between productive technicians and unproductive profit-mongers.

The other aspect of student protest which seems to us of supreme importance lies in its international character. Not only in democratic, fascist and communist Europe, but in America (North and South), Africa and Asia, too, militant actions have been mounted. Although many of these have had connections with outside 'political' themes like Vietnam, behind all has been the demand for more control right there at home. The international aspect has been important because it has drawn attention to the identity of interests in different countries under different regimes — which are all fundamentally the same. The unifying call has been revolutionary.

The End of Authority
Here, we as anarchists should not be too starry-eyed. We have a long and sad history of going along with 'revolutionaries' who turn out to be just as reactionary as the last lot once they are in power. We are the heirs of popular revolutions in many countries where the fatal mistake has been made of allowing a central authority to be re-established, and up-against-the-wall for the anarchists.

For us, revolution means the end of central authority or it is no revolution at all. For us, revolution means, not the beginning of a 'Workers' State', but the destruction of all States; it means devolution down to the student at the desk, the worker at the bench, the peasant in the field. If the 'revolutionaries' in the International Socialists and Solidarity, if the 'Maoists' and the glorifiers of Che Guevara and the Black Power seekers still think in terms of leading a revolution through a 'Workers' State' or some similar pattern of power, then we challenge their whole concept of revolution.
28th December 1968   JUSTIN

BIAFRA

Black Gold

In January 1966 General Ironsi took over power in Nigeria and in the process dispersed some of the tribal chiefs. The Nigerians really thought that this was a step toward some form of emancipation, but as with all military coups it's the survival of the fittest, *at the time*.

Politics and politicians in Nigeria have always operated under a cloud of suspicion of corruption in some form or other, and when the chiefs Akintola and the Sardauna of Sokoto were killed there was no sense of a deep loss.

The military authority was greeted with enthusiasm, urban class rents were cut by 10%, with the promise of a cheap housing programme. Corruption was to be investigated and dealt with, regionalism was to end and commissions were to probe into the legacies left by the politicians.

After the period of the 'new broom', the military realised they had to govern, and the only people who knew anything about civilian administration were the Civil Servants, therefore the people who really governed the country were the Permanent Secretaries.

Many outside observers expected tribal friction to follow the military takeover, but in fact this did not happen (or was not apparent). The Muslim Northerners did not seek revenge for the death of their premier, Sardauna of Sokoto, their attitude was 'good riddance to bad rubbish'. It appears that the rule of the politicians was so corrupt and incompetent, that anything or anybody that took their place could not be worse. Under the federal system, duplication of industrial projects was common, investment brought in by contractor finance left a legacy of £35 million in short term debts. The allocation of contracts is one of the easiest ways to make quick money.

Ironsi's military regime, whilst popular, was precarious; many of his best officers were killed in the coup, the four young officers in charge of the four regions had ambitions. By August 1966 the struggle for power began within the military set-up. Troops mutinied in Abeokuta and Ibadan and their leader, Army Chief-of-Staff Lieut. Colonel Yakubu Gowon, announced in a broadcast that he had assumed power. Tribal loyalties now became apparent — although Gowon is a Northerner, he is not a Muslim but a Christian from a small tribe. Ironsi is an Ibo officer, and was accused of Ibo bias and incompetence.

Gowon is now head of a Central Government which is 'shaky' to say the least, with the various regions watching each other like hawks. The biggest rebel is the Eastern Region under Colonel Ojukwu who wanted to and has seceded from the Federation. Attempts were made to prevent the secession through a National Conciliation Committee but its proposals were rejected by the Eastern Region, who claimed that the four members nominated to represent the Eastern Region were not acceptable because they were Eastern residents in Lagos who had not visited their region for some time.

The Central Government's present policy is to split the four Nigerian regions into 12 States and to divide the Eastern Region into three separate States, hoping to weaken Ojukwu support.

At the end of May the Eastern Region proclaimed its independence as the Republic of Biafra.

Since 30th May, Biafra has been subjected to blockade by the Federal Government. The land and sea blockade has been recognised by the shipping conference which is responsible for most of the trade between Britain and Nigeria. The Federal Government is defending economic sanctions to bring Biafra 'into line' but blockades work both ways, nothing going in *but* also nothing coming out; the Eastern Region is Nigeria's main supply of coal and the rest of Nigeria faces a critical shortage. From a war of attrition could develop a military war.

Whilst it can be said that tribal differences do not assist the situation in Nigeria, the comparatively new and overriding factor is *oil*. Proceeds from oil exports in 1965 totalled nearly £70m, of which £20m was paid to the Government. Two-thirds of Nigeria's oil is produced in the Eastern Region and of this two-thirds, another two-thirds comes from the Ibo districts which formed one of the States of Gowon's plan to split the East into three. Britain looks on with anxious eyes. Nigerian oil could be the alternative to the Middle East supply. Once that is established, we will see how much sympathy any Government has for Arab problems.

24th June 1967   BILL CHRISTOPHER

Biafra — The Sordid Truth

After ten months of bitter and cruel fighting, the war in Biafra is beginning to attract attention. Fantastic estimates of the casualties begin to be publicised, some observers saying that there have been more deaths in Biafra in ten months than there have been in Vietnam since the Americans started their escalation of hostilities! The word 'Genocide' is bandied about as the Federal Government's forces massacre women and children, inexorably moving forward against the weaker Biafran fighters, who do not get taken prisoner, but are slaughtered where they stand.

Slowly, slowly, the sluggish British conscience is stirring, as the extent of British aid to the Federal Government is seen to be the main contributory factor to its success.

The British role has been to supply arms to the Federal Government in considerable quantities — and Britain has not been alone in this. The Soviet Union has also sold arms to Lagos, and now that the extent of the massacre is getting out of hand — or rather, knowledge of it is getting out — Britain finds herself in a very tricky situation precisely because of Russia's contributions.

If it is possible for the British Government to squirm, that is what it is now doing, for public opinion is building up — even Members of Parliament are beginning to ask questions about arms to Nigeria — but Britain dare not cut off its supplies of guns and bombs to Lagos because the Nigerian Government has made it perfectly clear that if she does so, then the trade with Russia will be stepped up to make good the difference.

At the moment the cash value of the trade with Russia is quite considerable because the goods that Nigeria is buying is high-priced merchandise like Mig fighters, while from Britain they are buying smaller arms like machine-guns and bombs. If this supply ceases, then Russia will be only too happy to step in.

But this is not all. The Nigerian Government has also made it plain that trade in general goes with the arms deal. If Britain cuts down on the sales of arms, then the Federal Government will cut down on its purchases of 'peaceful' goods as well. Trade in general will suffer. And who will step in to supply the consumer goods and the generating plant as well as the military hardware? You've guessed it — the Socialist Fatherland, of course.

Such is the barrel that Britain is over in Nigeria. Such are the ethics of the situation. But whereas the Wilson Government has declared its horror at the idea of using force against the 'illegal' regime in Rhodesia, it has no compunction in giving massive assistance to the use of force in Nigeria — because, there, trade follows the guns.

This is the sordid truth of the matter. For this, it is genocide in Biafra.

29th June 1968   P.S.

Biafra — Triumph of the Politicians

Nobody seems to know quite what to say about Biafra. All the usual supporters of good causes flounder in a welter of holier than thou criticisms: pacifists criticise Friends; 'Left' intellectuals criticise 'The Left'; progressives support either Biafra or the Federal Nigerians — or both; Governments criticise Governments — as usual — while, as usual military leaders strut and boast.

The only unusual feature of the Biafran tragedy is the scale of the starvation. Not since the opening up of the concentration camps in conquered Germany in 1945 have we been confronted with man-made starvation in such numbers, have we seen so many thousands of skeletal children with hopeless, helpless, empty-breasted mothers watching them die, before they die themselves.

It is easy to say 'Stop the war' — but all the good, well-meaning people who are now (presumably genuinely) horrified by what is happening in Biafra are, by and large, the very same good, well-meaning people who have supported the good, well-meaning, pro-gressive causes that have led the African continent into its present sorry state.

And today nobody knows what to say or do about Biafra (beyond shouting 'Stop') precisely because none of the progressives can really believe that 'Independence' could lead to this kind of horror. What has gone wrong, they are asking themselves, and coming up with all the good old anti-imperialist clichés masquerading as answers.

Sure the old imperialist influences are still at work in 'indepen-dent' Africa — but although violent outbreaks provide splendid opportunities for selling arms, making friends and influencing people, this is really not the way that imperialists want to go to work in the 1970s.

What the progressives have always refused to see is that in the creation of African States under African politicians, the old venal power seekers were not eliminated — they were added to by the new venal power seekers, with black faces. In the great African stewpot now, the old greedy white capitalists have been joined by the new greedy black bourgeoisie who, economically, are nowhere, but who hold political and military office and want the world to know about it.

The African leaders who have risen like scum to the top in the last twenty years are all either London-trained or Moscow-trained. They are products of English public schools and universities or the London School of Economics or of the special type of education that the Kremlin is delighted to offer potential leaders of the black masses.

It is for this reason, among others, that anarchists have refused to get excited about 'national liberation' and 'independence' and the 'anti-colonial struggle' when it is carried on under nationalist parties whose sole aim is to get power and carry on the same kind of government as before with different personnel. Since we see no point in preferring bosses who speak English to bosses who speak German or Russian or Chinese or Welsh or Gaelic, neither is there any point in preferring bosses with black faces to bosses with white faces or vice versa.

And certainly there is no point in preferring African generals to American or British or Greek.

It is astonishing to us that there are still elements among the so-called 'NEW' Left that still go along with the idea that nationalist politicians engage in anti-colonial struggles for revolutionary purposes — and that they should be supported in their struggle for power. If we had gone along with this we should, in the fairly recent past, have supported Nkrumah and Kenyatta, Banda and Nyerere, Nasser *and* the Israeli Zionists, the Congress Party of India, Ben Bella and Makarios — and the present ruling party in Nigeria.

Perhaps it is understandable that in the past well-meaning socialists, who have never understood the power struggle as anarchists have done, should have supported bourgeois nationalist parties. But to go on doing this when experience shows what the reality is, is pathetic. One can understand the Wilsons of the world doing it, but for the Revolutionary Socialist Students' Federation, for example, to make support for 'national liberation' movements one of their main principles is ludicrous. Even more ludicrous is it for individuals calling themselves anarchists to limp along behind this line.

This is not the digression it may appear to be, for what we are saying is that the fearful tragedy that is murdering Ibo children in Biafra today is an inescapable part of the emergence of modern States in Africa, just as the tragedy that is going to overwhelm the Middle East will be the inevitable outcome of the power politics inseparable from Israeli and Egyptian nationhood.

You cannot have nations without a State structure. Nations must have politicians; State structures must have armed forces. Those so-called progressives who think it is in any way an improvement to create nation States should go and have a bloody good look at Biafra today. What makes one despair is that 'intellectuals' can do just that and still come up with the same old political rubbish.

On 12th December last, *Peace News* published (with an introduction criticising the rest of us for ignoring it — though *Peace News* must have missed it also when it was originally released 'earlier this year') an open letter on Biafra from 22 distinguished French intellectuals. In a tone of confused surprise, the writers try to rouse the conscience of the Left — primarily the British Left, but the only positive statement they make is this:

The Left must thus undertake, with all the means at its disposal, a *political* campaign to bring about the end of the war in Biafra, and to bring about a solution, whatever the constitutional and economic ties which could bring Biafra back into Nigeria, *which will guarantee the Biafrans their own instruments of defence*, in other words an autonomous army.

Pathetic, isn't it? Still thinking in terms of constitutional arrange ments at government level, a call for this kind of settlement, leaving all the apparatus ready for another go in a few years' time, is supposed to stir the British Left!

Well, it won't, for the good reason that there are approximately three sections of the British Left, and this won't appeal to any of them.

First, the Official Left — Labour and Communist Parties, etc. These actually support Federal Nigeria, because the Governments they support — the British and Russian respectively — are both selling arms to the Federal Forces.

Second, the Pacifist Left, are not going to warm to a solution guaranteeing the Biafrans 'their own instruments of defence'.

Third, the Revolutionary Left — the 'New Left', RSSF, etc. These are precisely the politicos who favour nationalist Governments, new nations, centralised economies — *progress*. Disruptive, breakaway tribalism, like the Ibos, must be suppressed, like Czechoslovakia, the suppression of which was supported by Ho Chi Minh and Castro. This is good Leninism.

Of these, only the pacifists have any conscience, and to its credit, *Peace News* has been hammering away with plenty of information and varying views.

So what of the anarchists? Well, we haven't done very much have we? It is time we did. Demonstrations in 1970 should be on Biafra, on the following lines:

Condemn the British and Russian Governments for selling arms to the Federal Government, and the French Government for selling to Biafra. We are not concerned with the economic arguments why Britain has to sell, and we despise the 'Communists' for doing the same.

Condemn General Ojukwu and the Biafran leaders for being prepared to see millions of people die for their ambitions. Biafra is the richest part of Nigeria and the fight for secession may have more to do with greed and power lust than desire for freedom!

Condemn the Federal Government of Nigeria for being prepared to wage a genocidal war to maintain its federal power.

Call for direct action here in Britain and throughout Africa against the war.

Dockers in Middlesbrough have already walked off an arms ship. This must be repeated wherever arms are being loaded for Lagos.

Every opportunity must be taken to hamper the supply of arms, and at the same time, ways and means be found to send medical supplies and food. Demonstrations must be mounted to embarrass the Government (this may be election year!).

The children of Biafra must be saved!

It is not their fault if they are the victims of political dogmas and power-seeking leaders — any more than the children of Vietnam.

As it stands, Biafra is a triumph for the disgusting politicians.

We say: **Make the end of the Biafra war the anarchist aim for 1970!**

10th January 1970   JUSTIN

Biafra — Agony of the People

We hardly imagined, as we went to press last week, that by the time we started to write this week's paper the war in Biafra would be practically over.

Thus we ended our leading article with the call for the movement to 'Make the end of the Biafra war the anarchist aim for 1970'. If we felt like being funny about it, we would say that never before has an anarchist call to action met with such remarkable and immediate success! But the Biafran situation is just about the least likely subject to raise a laugh on anarchist lips.

The violent death and the starvation that have been the lot of the Biafrans for the last three years is, perhaps, about to come to an end — at least the violent death is. The starvation is still capable of providing a Tom Tiddler's Ground for politicians to play in for some time to come.

Yet undoubtedly what we are now about to witness is just what the world is capable of doing in the matter of sending aid to Biafra. Mr Wilson, that well-known humanitarian, has immediately leapt nto action. He actually held a meeting of the Cabinet on a Sunday evening and after an hour's deliberation, our leaders came out with two tremendous decisions:

1. one airplane has been sent off to Nigeria loaded, not with beef and two veg, but with an observer from the British Government to find out what the Red Cross needs there; and

2. an appeal has been made to America to supply it.

Well, we are used to politicians being ignorant of what the whole world already knows. The number of 'diplomats' who did not know what was going on in Nazi Germany; the millions of good Communists who did not know what Stalin was up to in Russia; these astute chaps fell over with surprise when their noses were eventually rubbed unwillingly in the truth. Mr Wilson's myopia about what the Red Cross needs in Biafra is equally unbelievable. He is providing us yet again with an example of the slimy politician who just doesn't want to know — yet he, of all people in Britain, should have sources of information far-reaching and complete.

Leaders pulling out

For the rest of us, we have to rely on what the television and press tell us, and depend upon our own judgement in analysing it. Suddenly we learn that General Ojukwu had removed his own family

from beleaguered Biafra 'some time ago' to Libreville, capital of pro-French Gabon, whence he is now thought to have removed himself, too, making no public statement to his troops to surrender. (Compare Churchill's intention in 1940: 'If the worst comes to the worst, I will take the Fleet to Canada and carry on the war from there!')

But there is little possibility that General Ojukwu will be able to do anything from Gabon. One main reason for the sudden collapse of the Biafran resistance is the war-weariness of the Biafran people — and now we hear another side to it as well, a side implicit in what we were saying last week about the bourgeois nature of the national States of Africa.

An article in Monday's *Times* (12th January) by Antony Terry of *The Sunday Times*, gives us some telling examples of the class-divisions in Biafra. We quote:

A contributing factor to the decline in civilian morale was the contrast between the comfortable living conditions of the well-to-do Biafran upper class and the dreadful sufferings of the average civilian and peasant, not to mention the refugees.

Right to the end there were private cars circulating in the streets of Owerri, one of them a red British sports car driven by a young man who was known as 'Biafra's chief playboy'. With petrol at Biafran £10 a gallon and motor oil £60 a gallon on the flourishing black market, it is no wonder that a friend called the driver 'the richest man in Biafra' . . .

Some days earlier little things like the sudden disappearance of an expensive record player from the living room of a senior Biafran officer — which, together with his attractive girlfriend, had been there only the night before — had been the first indication to me that things were beginning to go seriously wrong for the first time in Biafra's war strategy and that the high command was secretly making plans to pull out . . .

For Biafra's highly intelligent and educated Ibo ruling class of soldiers, civil servants and businessmen there is scant hope of survival unless they can brave 100 miles of federal-held territory to the north and east and reach the friendly territory of the Republic of Cameroun. It is no doubt in the hope of stopping this massacre of his country's intellectual aristocracy that General Ojukwu has decided to fly out and try to arrange a peace settlement.

A bitter lesson

Well, well. Isn't it the same old story? And isn't it sad that the African people have got to go through just the same appalling suffering as the working classes of more 'advanced' countries, in order to experience what it means to 'have your own Government'. It means *more* suffering, *more* exploitation, because under 'your own Government' you are supposed to be more gullible and more patriotic. This bitter lesson is now being learned a most hard, hard way by the poor people of Biafra. Ironically, 'national independence' has brought them to a worse pass than your actual old fashioned imperialism!

Not that these sort of comparisons have much point. Or any anarchist theorising, for that matter, when you are faced with 1,500,000 refugees and twice that number starving in their own villages or camps or in the bush. The solution is a simple technical one of getting in what is needed.

There is no anarchist solution to this here and now. The people of the world have shown their lack of concern for Biafra in the three years it has been suffering. The world is no doubt heaving a great sigh of relief that the fighting is coming to an end; it can now turn over and go to sleep again, leaving it to the world's Governments to clean up once again the filthy mess the world's Governments have made. Until the next time. And the next time, gentle reader, it may be *you* getting it in the neck.

17th January 1970   JUSTIN

Footnote
As we go to press, an official plea for an armistice has been made by a Biafran spokesman — still in Ojukwu's absence — and British planes *are* flying in with medical supplies and food. The speed with which this is now being done shows clearly that plans must have been made long ago. We don't believe our Royal Air Force could not have got through — but it just wasn't politic until now.

J.

'Aid' to Nigeria

'Why send aid to Nigeria? They're an independent country now, aren't they?' commented a colleague in my office a few days ago.

Why, indeed?

Well, Michael Lake ('Biafra — the morals of investment', the *Guardian*, 15th January 1970), answered that question — and spilt the beans on the business of 'aid' to Nigeria, and all so-called under-developed countries for that matter. 'British policy on Nigeria', says Lake, 'has been dominated all along by the balance of payments'. Not starving Biafrans!

'This remains the Government's preoccupation, in spite of the plight of the last three million dying Biafrans, the anguish and frustration of hundreds of relief workers, and the provision of £5 millions from aid funds.' But future financial stakes are much higher. That is why the British Government is crawling to General Gowon. Moreover, the 'socialist' Soviet Union, with its 'socialist' Mig fighters, is becoming increasingly influential in Nigerian high places.

Remarks Lake:

The Cabinet has no intention of jeopardising the £350 millions-odd British investment in oil in Nigeria; the oil could yet be nationalised and the product sold to keener buyers, such as the Russians who are short of oil for their build-up against the Chinese threat. Neither has Mr Wilson any inclination to undermine the private investment British firms have made in Nigeria, £75 millions on paper, much more in current values, which represents substantial potential income for the balance of payments.

King Harold and 'schoolmaster' Stewart may have 'Soul', but Royal Dutch Shell-BP take precedence over starving Biafrans. That is why the British Government has been 100% behind (and at times in front of) the Federal Government of Nigeria. Indeed, 'The routine of providing traditional supplies to a traditional customer turned into a greatly increased, permanent pipeline of armoured cars, small arms and ammunition'.

Not only that, but British big business, backed by Wilson and Stewart, expects to reap a £1,200 millions rehabilitation order — against strong French, Italian, Polish, Russian, and even Chinese, competition.

Simple, isn't it? First you help someone to devastate and smash up a country: then, at a price, you offer to help them build it up again. Good old capitalist morality and ethics! That's what 'schoolmaster' Stewart calls 'an honourable settlement'! Bloody (literally) hypocrite!

24th January 1970   PETER E. NEWELL

Oh the Popular War Leader!

Arising out of our two recent articles on Biafra: 'Triumph of the Politicians' and 'Agony of the People', we have received two letters which we feel need answering.

The first letter was written immediately after our first article and we did not publish it because by the time we were going to press the following week the Biafran resistance had collapsed and history seemed to have caught up with Nigel Wright's arguments. Nevertheless, we think it only fair to present his central argument, even though we have cut his letter slightly.

The second letter came after our second article, and we reproduce it in full out of respect for its writer, Roger Moody, who is

Nigeria/Biafra Editor of *Peace News* and who has worked tremendously hard on this subject, doing perhaps more than anyone else in any minority paper to keep the Left alert to the Biafran tragedy.

Make Up Your Mind, Justin!
Dear Comrades,
   When a group of people are threatened with decimation, as the Ibos, Ibibios, Ijaws, Efiks and others of the Eastern Region of Nigeria were in 1966/7, they are quite justified in taking up arms to defend themselves. These conditions of extreme emergency, it seems to me, demand strict organisation and responsible leaders: a time when you are surrounded by an invading army is not the time to indulge in libertarian experiments. Justin seems to use much the same argument as Harold Wilson, that the Biafran people should have surrendered, should have put themselves at the mercy of a murderous army (remember the 1966 massacres?), and allowed themselves to be kept in the corrupt, unworkable Federation under the control of the old 'venal power seekers' whom Justin rightly condemns.
   Under the circumstances (and comrades should know these by now) the only feasible course of action was secession by the 14 million people of the Eastern Region. What kind of structure these 14 million people might have adopted was predecided by Gowon's invasion. At this perilous moment (according to Ojukwu, the Biafran army possessed a total of 150 rifles), it was reasonable that Ojukwu should assume command. That he should do so was a universally popular step; if at any time in the past three years Justin had been to Biafra for a bloody good look and a bloody good talk with any man in the street, he would have discovered this to his utter conviction. This fact must not be misunderstood. When Justin condemns Ojukwu, with what amounts to a new variation of the old Foreign Office handout that Ojukwu is a power-hungry lunatic driving his people to destruction, he is ignoring this extraordinary, almost unanimous, and continuing popular desire for Ojukwu to control affairs so long as the war lasts.
   Under the paragraph in which Justin accuses Ojukwu of being 'prepared to see millions of people die for (*his*) ambition', he accuses the Federal Government of waging a genocidal war. Make up your mind, Justin!

Fraternally yours,
NIGEL WRIGHT

PS For comrades who wish to find out what exactly Ojukwu's views
are, I recommend *The Ahiara Declaration: (Principles of the Biafran Revolution)*, which is obtainable from the Save Biafra Campaign, 13 Goodwin Street, London, N4, price 5/-.

Biafra On Our Conscience?

Dear Editors,

I'm afraid that the anarchist conscience will remain ineffectual
so long as the leading anarchist weekly generalises like it did last
week on Biafra.

I am prepared to believe that a Biafran elite, complete with
record players, cars, wine on the table and women in bed, survived
until the bitter end. But this was in no sense *the* upper class as we
understand one — but an assortment of individuals rightly or
wrongly striving for normality. Too many discriminating and left-
wing observers have been to Biafra in the past two years for us to
discount their evidence, with pat analyses. The facts as I understand
them are these: basic decisions about the war were taken through
a consultative assembly of chiefs, and elected representatives of
the people, from the districts. The decision to abandon the war
came from this body, and (from three different sources which I
trust) the evidence is that Ojukwu was asked to hand over command
by this assembly. He did so after making it clear that he believed
surrender was the most effective way of stopping the suffering.
There is still no real evidence that Ojukwu is out of Biafra, and
to suggest that he hotfooted it simply for his own safety is not at
all in keeping with anything he has yet done.

The conduct of the war was in the hands of a military council
which comprised active leaders of the armed forces, and was not
an armchair brigade. The Cabinet functioned in a remarkably
British manner — with its own Foreign Affairs Minister, Home
Affairs Minister, economics adviser and so on. Biafra was even
involved in helping rehabilitation of Ibos in the mid-West (the so-
called Republic of Benin, declared by Ibos there after eastern
secession).

In addition, there was an advisory council consisting of men like
Chinua Achebe, whose task it was to report to the Government
on the feelings of the people. These men formed a National Guidance College whose eventual aim was to educate Biafrans in university subjects according to the 'principles of the revolution' — principles which, as laid down by Ojukwu in his green book, *The Ahiara*

Declaration, seem a strange combination of exhortation, home economics, and Old Testament moralities — but as expressed by some of the College's founders seem to owe more to Marx and Lenin.

By and large, however, what happened in Biafra was in the hands of local administrators, village chiefs, and farmers, living close to the people — indeed who were the people — in a society that has traditionally been noted for its village democracy. Whatever one feels about the State structure imposed in 1967 in order to carry on the war effort, the fact is that the common people of Biafra had a greater part in decision-making both for themselves and for the future 'Biafra' than do their counterparts in almost every other part of Africa.

If there was anything approaching an upper class it remained largely pre-empted by the village administrative-town Civil Service class. These people came up from 'the people' by a shorter route than in most Western and certainly most African societies.

By the end of 1969 — if this is a useful guideline against which to measure class gaps in Biafra — independent estimates state that about 60% of the entire people — *including* the administrative groups — suffered from severe malnutrition, and were either refugees or dispossessed of their property.

It is strange that so many commentators who should know better, assess the merits of both sides in this war against an academic and false measuring-stick. Given that the Biafrans seceded in order, as they believed, to protect their own lives and livelihood, that of their families, and that of generations to come, the only question we had to ask over the last two and a half years was whether or not 'Biafra' gave greater immediate guarantees to the easterners and better prospects for freedom, and a non-violent, non-exploitative community, than any of the arrangements proposed by the Federal Government. I would have thought it overwhelmingly met that test.

In saying this, I do not subscribe to the values of statehood any more than I would elsewhere in the world; nor do I dismiss the possibility that a different form of resistance at the time of secession may have averted the present disaster. I only claim that, in human terms, the Federal war, British intervention on Nigeria's behalf, and the Soviet shop-front in Lagos backed by its murderous Mig fighters, caused infinitely more suffering, damned many more people, and laid the ground for more hell to come, than a settlement with the State of Biafra, on the terms offered from 1968 onwards, ever would have done.

ROGER MOODY

The Great Myth
Both our critics are obviously well informed on the internal politics of Nigeria. With respect, we should like to point out that we are concerned with something a bit more fundamental than that: the freedom of the African people.

For Mr Moody this may be a generalisation which makes our conscience ineffectual — whatever that means. The sad fact is that African politics, like politics everywhere, makes all our consciences ineffectual. Whose conscience has been effectual in this ghastly business?

The suffering of the Ibo people over the last thirty months has been completely in vain. The decision to declare UDI and then fight for it on the part of the Biafrans was a piece of political misjudgement worthy of Che Guevara himself. Nigel Wright tells us that when General Gowon invaded — after secession — the Biafran Army possessed 150 rifles! To say that they were justified in taking up arms, then, is mere rhetoric.

Nor am I impressed with the fact that General Ojukwu was a popular war leader for the Ibos. Compare Churchill in 1940 — or even Hitler for the Germans! The fact that the people are stupid enough to follow leaders in a suicidal war does not make us irresponsible enough to suggest that therefore the leaders are right — or that leadership is right.

My mind boggles at Roger Moody's apologia for the Biafran ruling class. ''The Cabinet functioned in a remarkably British manner' forsooth! '. . . the State structure imposed in 1967 in order to carry on the war effort . . .' how are ye? The way to the top was '. . . a shorter route than in most Western and certainly most African societies' if you don't mind!

And what do we make of this pathetic faith in General Ojukwu? Remember Roger is writing in a pacifist paper and presumably from a pacifist point of view — but has faith in a *general*! '. . . to suggest that (General Ojukwu) hotfooted it simply for his own safety is not at all in keeping with anything he has yet done', Roger writes, while that very week, on another page of *Peace News* cartoonist Donald Rooum has a drawing of the General with his running shoes on hotfooting it like hell.

Right to the end, while well-fed Biafrans in London were weeping 'How could he behave like this?', Roger Moody could not believe that a General had salted away a fortune in some other country, got his own family out to safety, and flown away after them.

Really, you know, these two contributions from our readers, far from refuting anything we said in our two articles, prove up to the hilt one aspect of them at least; that progressive, well-meaning left wingers *want*, in the face of all the evidence, to cling to the idea that nationalist Governments are an improvement on the old colonial administration. This is a great myth which in fact vitiates the anti-imperialist struggle, like the myth of democracy vitiates the class struggle.

When Nigel Wright asks me to make up my mind, I would like to point out that my mind on taking sides in war was made up the moment I tumbled to the power game. I am on the side of the people against whatever authority is destroying them. And if the people are gullible enough to support the authority which is destroying them, I try to make them see reason. This is the anti-war position for anarchists — and it used to be that for pacifists, too, which is why I am so surprised to see Roger Moody, by implication, approving of the Biafrans fighting on for 'the terms offered from 1968 onwards' instead of cutting their losses, swallowing their pride, and finding other methods of defending their village democracy.

In the event, two years of destruction and a million starving children later, Ojukwu leaves his understudy to surrender and hotfoots it out of it.

Absolutely nobody comes out of this stinking business well. Not Ojukwu nor Gowon, nor their gullible, loyal, tribal-minded or nationalistic peoples, certainly not the bloodstained British, Russian, Spanish and French Governments which provided the arms for the slaughter, not any of us who could not stop 'our' Government's knavish tricks.

But at least some of us have never supported any of the contributory factors!

31st January 1970   JUSTIN

Anarchism and Nationalism

Superficially, anarchism is a movement of the Left, but this is not strictly so, since it implies being part of the political spectrum. Anarchists reject this, asserting that there is more in common between Right and Left political parties (like the struggle for power) than between even extreme Left political groups and the anarchists. History has shown us that no matter how 'Left' a Party is when it starts off, the achievement of power brings it round to the Right, for every Government wants to maintain the status quo; wants to extend the control it has over the people, and isn't this what the Right really means?

Certain right-wing attitudes are specifically rejected by left-wing Parties — until they become useful in the power game. 'Divide and Rule', for example, can be played with many variations, from wage differentials to religious and colour prejudice, and although nationalism is intellectually rejected by the political Left, they quite shamelessly use what are quaintly called 'National Liberation Movements' when it suits their political ambitions — and a 'Left' Party in power knows very well the usefulness of nationalism and indeed patriotism as a weapon of government. Even if this were not deliberate cunning on the part of a so-called 'revolutionary Government', the logic of authoritarianism leads to it.

Even allowing for soviets or workers' councils, the actual operation of State power cannot be carried out by the entire population. This demands the workers' own revolutionary Party sitting at the top doing the actual governing, like suppressing all opposition in the name of the revolution and ensuring internal security by the perpetual policing of the population in its own interests to effect the immediate spotting of any deviationary elements. At the same time as this defence of the revolution is strenuously maintained, the population also has to be kept safe from external aggression, so an efficient army, navy and air force is kept at the ready, and since a workers' State is the most democratic State, a form of conscription becomes desirable to ensure that everyone does his bit.

This is really no sacrifice since the State belongs to everyone and everyone belongs to the State, but to keep the people enthusiastic for service to the State, a leader comes forward to give every citizen someone to identify with on a personal level. In order to provide the cozy feeling of collective security, of belonging to the corporate body around him, the idea of the nation is encouraged and patriotism becomes a virtue once again — if, indeed, it ever fell out of favour.

Thus, the service of the revolution achieved through authoritarian means brings the wheel full circle. The ideologies and justifications for lack of freedom — indeed for ruthless totalitarian control of the entire country — will differ from those of the old regime, but *in fact* the institutions and the realities of life are exactly the same, if not worse.

For this reason anarchists do not enthuse about revolutions which are mounted in order to bring to power another set of governors. Our interpretation above has been of a so-called revolutionary change in society; how much less, then, can we enthuse about changes which do not even pretend to be revolutionary from the start?

Into this category fall the movements for national liberation which are frankly nationalistic and call for opposition against a ruling or occupying power purely on xenophobic grounds. Although revolutionary means may be used in such a struggle, it has no more to do with social revolution as the anarchist sees it than the xenophobia of a Hitler or an Enoch Powell. Pathetic examples of this are to be found in Wales and Scotland. In fact — and here is where the situation seems to get confused — 'movements for national liberation' in the trouble-spots of the world today tend to give a social revolutionary veneer to their claims, in order to get support from the Communist States. The classic example of this is Egypt, where a successful anti-colonial struggle established a nationalistic, military regime (much like the Greek colonels!) with the aid of Russian arms and technology. By using devices like nationalisation and land reform, the veneer of socialism was applied — but, in spite of Russian 'friendship', the Communist Party is banned and Egyptian Communists are in prison. Meanwhile rabid nationalism is whipped up, patriotism by the imperial pint is kept on the boil, but nothing prospers like the State and the international arms merchants. But your authoritarian Left — the Trotskyists and the CP — support the new Egyptian State!

Anarchists do not play this political game. We are not jockeying for position and trying to further one or other of the power blocs that divide the world and its workers. We are truly international and oppose all those forces which divide people. Hence it is quite logical for anarchists to oppose an Imperial Power *and* the indigenous politicians who lead national resistance. For example, in condemning the Russian military occupation of Czechoslovakia, we did not thereby support the Dubcek Communist State which was in conflict with the Kosygin Communist State, in the sense that we wanted to see Dubcek remain in power. We supported the Czech *people* and their right to choose — even though choosing Dubcek (as the lesser evil!) — because this is a right that all people must have, and also because they were using revolutionary means (if only because there were no others) and so were learning how to do things for themselves. In the event, what opposition there was came from the people and not from Dubcek. Our attitude is the same on Vietnam (against US imperialism, but not *for* the Vietcong); Cuba (against Batista, not *for* Castro); Black Power (the answer to white racism is *not* black racism!); the American Revolution of 1776 (to hell with George III *and* the American State that followed him!); and all Arab, Jewish, Indian, African nationalisms.

The answer to imperialism is not nationalism and reactionary regimes — it is international social revolution, destroying all national, religious, racial barriers. We have learnt from history!

21st February 1970   THE EDITORS

THE MIDDLE EAST

Inevitable War in the Middle East

The demands of modern war require that the individual not only commit himself on one side or the other, but insist on the general perfection of his side. The argument that runs 'if you were a Vietnamese, you would have to choose to be involved' applies equally in Israel and also in the neighbouring Arab States. It is the more likely to appeal to people with revolutionary social consciousness. The Jewish bourgeoisie could fit in as a trading community in the Levant, to the complete satisfaction of the Arabs generally; no Zionist would object to the oil sheikhs, desert kings and Arab military leaders, provided they afforded no threat to the growth of the Jewish State. Since however Israel has evolved into a nation with a working class as well as a trading bourgeoisie; and since the Arab leaders have to reckon with a vast mass of pushed-under workers and peasants who have no chance of life at all but revolution at home or war abroad (and in the case of some, war on their own territory), there is no alternative to war in some degree or another. Ultimately — such is power politics — such a war could involve the world.

International considerations may limit the Middle East war or cause it to observe an uneasy armistice from time to time while both sides watch for the inevitable incident which can say that the other side is 'aggressing' — as if anyone really cares which side 'starts it' — so that hostilities may commence; in fact, all realists know that hostilities will commence the moment it is in the military interest of either the Jewish State or the Arab States. To judge from the standpoint of the schoolyard argument ('he hit me first') may suit innumerable paid and unpaid propagandists for either side, but it is only in default of an alternative case. No plea that 'the other side started it' is needed in order to oppose tyranny. But all who espouse from a partisan point of view either pan-Arabism or Zionism must feel uneasy at the company they keep.

The followers of 'Communism' (Moscow, Peking, Havana or

Mexico-Mausoleum brands) are almost all committed to the notion of a current Arab revolution, unless they happen to be in an Egyptian desert prison (and including many of the latter, too). Nasser's officer clique, the oil-rich sheikhs, the Nazi advisers in Cairo, the 'Socialist' officers of Baghdad and the wily entrepreneurs of Beirut who even manage to stay neutral in their own war, are all 'objectively' part of the socialist revolution because they are deemed to be anti-imperialist.

Unfortunately, the Israeli Socialists who have picked at the same texts, use the same anti-imperialist arguments and the same quotations from oil statistics, to prove that *theirs* is an anti-imperialist struggle too; it is unfortunate from this point of view that power politics aligns them now with the French Right Wing, now with the Americans (on whom domestic political pressures can also be applied). Advanced cooperation on the industrial and consumer level, with liberal injections of private enterprise from capitalists and bankers elsewhere, have produced a mixed economy in Israel that is perhaps a foretaste of the 'alternative to 1984' — the liberal-socialist-capitalist solution of involvement and integration within the present economic framework. Martin Buber held, of course, that the alternative to 'Moscow' (and to 1984) was 'Jerusalem'. This mixed economy of liberal capitalism is indeed the antithesis to feudal communism on the Egyptian plan (public works plus hereditary class control).

But the difference in economies has nothing to do with the clash which was inherent from the very beginning. One can blame 'the Jews' by saying that obviously from the start it was clear that the only way what was then Palestine could become a Jewish State would be by genocide (in those days the Zionists argued they did not want a Jewish State but merely a National Home). On the other hand, the majority of Jews did not go to Palestine voluntarily. They went as a direct result of European anti-semitism and because genocide in Russia and Germany made no other place possible. The world was prepared to accept small numbers of Jews, particularly as traders; nowhere in the world was prepared to accept millions of 'pauper' (in other words potential working class) Jews, least of all those countries which claimed to have attained socialism and solved the unemployment problem which was claimed to be the barrier.

It is for this reason that the recurrence of hostilities are inevitable, because it is the Jewish working class which has the stake in Israel, while the capitalist can (and frequently does) go anywhere in the world he chooses. And conversely the displaced Palestinian Arabs in particular, but also anyone in the neighbouring Arab countries with nothing to lose, has everything to gain from war, which — so long as it is successful — will be popular.

Has the revolutionary, therefore, nothing whatever to say in the matter? He has certainly no method of influencing the situation, because no single group emerged in any of the Arab countries without being instantly suppressed, nor in Israel at all, that was prepared even to consider the possibility of revolutionary internationalism. So far as the anarchist movement is concerned, to the best of my knowledge the Husseini brothers were the only propagandists to be directly influenced by anarchism. Within a few weeks of forming a labour movement amongst Egyptian and Sudanese workers and open to Jews, they were murdered (one by the police in open fire; one by nationalists). In Israel, despite occasional allegations that an anarchist movement is about to be created, there has certainly been no vestiges of one. (I cannot regard seriously the not unknown reformist-anarchist who retires to Israel to write an occasional broadsheet in Yiddish on the wonders of Judaism from Moses to Ben-Gurion.)

The most, therefore, that the revolutionary can ever do in the matter is to look somewhat pityingly on the people around him who, on some issues, appear to be moving in his direction, and then, at the sound of battle in Sinai, either rush to Marks & Spencer's London office to volunteer for Israel; or mutter about the sinister influences at work on the London editors publishing news of Arab defeats.

A revolutionary movement within either Israel or the Arab countries can only come from the bottom upwards; and ultimately it will. It will not do so while the working class have, or feel they have, the major interest in warfare that perpetuates the nation State. One cannot in revolutionary terms think of 'Jews' and 'Arabs'; it is only by the abandonment of nationalism and the State that we can end both exploitation and war. It is equally true, of course, that there is no solution, in those terms, to the problems of 'whites' and 'coloureds'; or 'Northern' and 'Southern' Irishmen. Such 'solutions' only solve the problems of the present exploitative society. Solutions in terms of a free society mean scrapping such abstracts as nationalism — that is why these solutions have to be revolutionary.

16th November 1968   A. MELTZER

The Name of the Game is Consequences

British European Airways will not accept mail or freight for Tel
Aviv until further notice. British Overseas Airways Corporation
will not accept any Israel-bound freight from anywhere for the next
48 hours, as we write on 23rd February.

This embargo is a direct consequence of the crash of a Swissair
Coronado airliner which crashed following an explosion which took
place within 15 minutes of take-off from Zurich for Tel Aviv on
Saturday night. 47 people were killed, but Mr Shinwell, ever-so-
veteran Labour MP, declares the BEA-BOAC decision is 'stupid
and cowardly'. He wasn't thinking of flying to Tel Aviv himself
just now.

On the same evening, an Austrian plane flying from Frankfurt
to Israel had to turn back because of a bomb explosion in its mail
compartment.

It looks as if Arab guerrilla attacks on Israel-bound aircraft are
stepping up and it may be taken that this is a direct consequence
of the attack by the Israeli Air Force on a steel works near Cairo
last week, when 74 civilians were killed by napalm and explosive
bombs. Because this attack had been made in error, Israel's military
bossman, Moshe Dayan, notified the Egyptian authorities of some
time-bombs that had also been dropped, giving Egyptian sappers
the time to defuse them. But the attack had been mounted against
Egyptian military installations along the (present) Egyptian-Israeli
border, which is virtually the Suez Canal, as a consequence of
continued Egyptian artillery bombardments of Israeli positions.

The Deal With Russia
These Israeli positions are of course not on Israeli territory proper,
but are where they are as a consequence of the famous six-day
war of June 1967, when the Israelis attacked and overwhelmingly
defeated the Egyptian Army and destroyed the Egyptian Air Force
on the ground. This action was taken by the Israelis as a consequence of the threats and hate-propaganda continually put out
by the Arabs in general and General Nasser in particular, in which
he threatened personally to push all the Israelis into the sea.

In June 1967, Nasser raised the ante by cutting off access for
Israeli ships to the port of Eilat on the Red Sea, and as a consequence of their provocative action and all the sabre-rattling and
all that, the Israelis took the Egyptian Army apart. Nasser had

been able to make so much noise and to get himself taken seriously
as a consequence of having done a deal with the Workers' Fatherland, or Imperial Russia, as it should properly be known. This deal
started off by Nasser's accepting aid in the building of the Aswan
Dam — a big barrier across the Nile which was going to provide
water and electric power to transform large parts of the Nile Valley
from an arid desert into an industrial desert just like the developed
nations, while other areas would have some irrigation for the first
time. The Russians were able to move in on this as a consequence
of the British being bloody stupid and refusing to help the Egyptians, because the British wanted them to remain a backward nation
and thus be for ever a market for British goods and dependent on
the British economy, and on British protection against their enemies. But the Egyptians had come to think of the British as their
biggest enemy, and thinking that 'my enemy's enemy is my friend',
they embraced the Russians.

As a consequence of getting in on the economic aid, with the
Aswan Dam for instance, the Russians were able to get in on the
military aid as well, for they would dearly love to get a good military
foothold in the oily and strategically important Middle East. So
they sold lots and lots of guns and tanks and airplanes to the
Egyptian Army which had never seen such sophisticated things
before, and thinking they must automatically be world-beaters with
such stuff they began beating their chests and doing the war dance.
But their chests turned out to be the only things they could beat,
because, after all, the poor bloody Egyptians had been educated
by the British for a hundred years and didn't know their arses from
their elbows, let alone how to get a Mig off the ground.

Into the Refugee Camps
The Israelis, on the other hand, were smart guys. They are not
really a Middle-Eastern, desert peasant people at all; they are
Europeans and Americans who have gone to live there and that
means they know how to use the weapons of mass murder and all
the sophisticated ironmongery that the Americans and the British
and the French had sold to *them* to balance the crap the Russians
were selling to the Arabs. Not only that, but they have a story in
their holy book about David and Goliath, and they have been
waiting two thousand years to re-enact it, and as a consequence
of having been dispersed over the face of the known world and
being a minority which insisted on being God's chosen people
everywhere they went, thus making themselves thoroughly un-

popular and so getting kicked around — as a consequence of all this, they had in the first place pushed their way into Palestine and changed its name to Israel (oh, all right then, *back* to Israel) and were bloody determined to stay there. As a consequence of the way they had pushed their way in, however, and of setting up a State of Israel to give themselves power, domination and gaffer's rights over all the land, they had pushed hundreds of thousands of Arabs out of their only known homes into refugee camps.

Now you would have thought that if any people in the world would not want to have anything to do with refugee camps — it would be the Jews. But it is one thing to be pushed into a refugee camp and another to push someone else into one. And if there is one thing that the wandering Jews had learned from their long sojourn among the Christians, it is that turning the other cheek does not pay, that you have to hate your enemies, that before you can turn your swords into ploughshares, you have to use them to get hold of the land you want to plough, that thou shalt kill and covet. As a direct consequence of how they have been treated in the past, the Jews have become bloody-minded Israelis. As a direct consequence of *that*, poor, simple, deprived peasants who made the mistake of being born Arabs have been turned into nationalistic lunatics, baying for the wrong peoples' blood.

From Empire to Curtains
And the whole mess in the Middle East is a consequence of British double-dealing in the days of Empire, when the Suez Canal was our life-line to India, when the earlier, gentler, Zionists and the simpler, more patient Arabs were all promised Palestine as a national home, when Aircraftsman Shaw, better known as Lawrence of Arabia, used the Arabs and their horses for British Imperial Preference, and when the wogs could all be brought to heel with a gunboat up their canal.

As a consequence of those happy days the Israelis and the Arabs are looking down their gun-sights into each other's homes tonight; civilian workers die as a result of an error of calculation, and airliner passengers in a far-off land die as a result of a calculation being only too bloody accurate.

As a consequence of how they have all been used in the past — they are allowing themselves to be used in a mad and suicidal way in the present. The consequences could be curtains for the rest of us.
28th February 1970   JUSTIN

Can Sanity Prevail?

QUESTION: Who wants peace in the Middle East?

ANSWER: Nobody.

Why? Because peace can come only from the ending of the situation which makes for conflict, and the end of that situation can come only from the destruction of the power groups and institutions which thrive on conflict and hatred and division. Who wants that? Nobody!

Nobody, that is, except a few cranky, idealistic anarchists and pacifists for whom people are more important than nations, States, oilfields, homelands, God or Allah.

The whole larger lunacy of our world is crystallised in the Middle East. Absolutely everything is there. All the crazy stupidities which make our planet a pustulating mess instead of utopia — the olive grove surrounded by barbed wire and defended by tanks; the blue skies scarred by smoke from the burning village; the schools teaching history and hate; the black-clad rabbis and the muezzins casting their sinister shadows on the sunlit walls; the children with grenades in their belts and their parents with bitterness in their bellies; the riches of the earth plundered for profit; the complete perversion of necessity; the headlong flight to disaster; living for death.

The Influence of the Super States

Against the background of madness in the Middle East, it is difficult to come up with a solution which seems to make sense.

Perhaps it would be most honest to say that there is no solution which is even remotely likely to be accepted which could bring peace and well-being to the peoples of Egypt, Israel, Jordan, Iraq, and Syria.

A cessation of hostilities on the national scale *could* come about through the total victory of one side over the other and the permanent subjection of the victims — but we already have Arab guerrilla organisations prepared to fight when their nation States are not and these would undoubtedly continue were Israel to overrun the Arab world. We may be equally sure that the Israelis already have in existence an equivalent underground army which would carry on the struggle against Arab conquerors were Israel to be defeated and 'pushed into the sea'.

Such an outcome as this, however, does not take into account the amount of involvement which the rest of the world has in the Middle East — the support given to one side by Russia and the other by America.

The presence of the two super-states behind the snarling contestants ensures in fact that complete victory in an all-out fight will not happen. If one side really looks like winning to that extent, the big boy supporting the other might come to its aid and a long-drawn-out shooting war could follow. (Both America and Russia, after all, have their own supplies of oil!)

This is not because the rulers of America or Russia care in the least for the people of Israel or Egypt. It is simply because the enormous oil-producing wealth of this area and its strategic importance make it essential that it shall not fall exclusively into the hands of one side or the other, thereby upsetting the balance of power which the world has come to live with.

Thus the 'Great' Powers will exert a restraining influence on the hotheads in both Cairo and Tel Aviv. The USA persuades the Knesset to consider a 'peace plan' and all the talk from Cairo of 'pushing Israel into the sea' should be seen for what it is — strictly for internal consumption. As for the 'revolutionary' content on the Arab side, the first thing that the pro-Arab Left seems to forget is that all Marxist-Leninist organisations in Egypt are banned and their members in jail — so the Russian support for Nasser is not based on any ideological brotherhood. It is pure, naked, political opportunism and the fact is that any revolutionary movement in the Arab countries is faced with the opposition of Nasser and his Russian masters as well as the traditional rulers — King Hussein and the oil Sheikhs.

Where the guerrilla movements are useful to the Arab Governments is in their ability to keep up the tension with terrorist tactics against Israel, while 'Diplomacy' continues at top level to carry on business as usual. As for example, the oil deal whereby the Israelis produce crude oil from Egyptian/Italian fields in the Sinai peninsula and have agreed in return not to bomb Egyptian oilfields, installations and pipelines in the Gulf of Suez.

If Peace Should Break Out . . .
At the same time as exerting a restraining influence, however, the super-states do not want to see real peace break out.

Institutions of power demand continuous crises and tensions ('War is the health of the State') and while divisions exist, there is always some gain to be wrung out of the situation. A genuine coming-together of Israel and the Arab States, therefore, would be unacceptable for both Russia and America on several counts. The most important being that opportunities for gaining influence through the supply of arms, being a friend in need, and all that, would disappear, but, even more important, perhaps, is the fact that a merger of Israeli know-how with the immense resources of the whole Arab world would produce in a very short time yet another super-state in a very important area of the world. An Arab-Jewish complex reaching along the southern shore of the Mediterranean, with outlets to the Indian Ocean and down into Africa, with resources set free from war preparation — this would present the trading nations of the world with a frightening competitor, to say the least!

So at 'Top' level, peace which could lead to real friendship between Jew and Arab is to be avoided; instead a phoney 'peace' which is nothing more than an armed truce is the proper formula. Something that will allow the pot to be kept boiling without boiling over.

It Is Up To The People
No, the real hope for a lasting peace is the same here as everywhere else: the coming together of the people concerned, who have after all, real interests in common, and the destruction of the squabbling States which keep them at each other's throats.

The bitter pill that must be swallowed by Jews the world over is that the establishment of the State of Israel has not brought the security which they were looking for after the horrors of wartime Europe. Had they gone into Palestine to work and live and integrate with the Arabs on a basis of equality instead of muscling in with a State apparatus and creating a legacy of hatred, then their technical skills and social abilities could have created an environment which would have been the envy of the world. As it is they laid the foundations of precisely what is happening today. Having gone the way of the authoritarian State, even to the extent of creating thousands of refugees just like they had been, they set the pace for the Arab States to 'get with it' too.

The Israeli Government will not go into reverse; States never do. Nor will the Arab leaders.

The situation is, as everywhere, up to the people. To pull out support from the warring States, extend the hand of friendship across the frontiers — *forget* the bloody frontiers! —

and build an *economic* reality in place of the political lunacy of the authoritarians.

Difficult? I'll say it's difficult! We can't get the Protestants and Catholics (fellow Christians!) in Northern Ireland to do it, let alone Arabs and Jews in the overheated cauldron of Palestine! Yet there are glimmers of hope. From both inside Israel among thinking Jews, and outside, among certain Arab groups, there are expressions of understanding that for the ordinary people of both sides to get together represents the only true hope. It may be a pious hope, but it is motivated by concern both for the threatened Jews in Israel *and* for the exploited Arabs surrounding them.

The State is the enemy. Everywhere and in every time. If peace and well-being are our yardsticks for sanity, then we must recognise the madness of statism, the sado-masochistic, murderous-suicidal nature of it. Reject it!

To the peoples of Israel and of the Arab States, we say 'Don't go along with this madness — it will do for you all!' Let sanity prevail!

26th September 1970   JUSTIN

The Only Good Leader is a Dead One

It is a truism that for an ambitious politician in a colonial country a spell in jail under the occupying imperialist Power is practically a *must* if he wants to become head of State after 'independence'. Gamal Abdel Nasser was an exception to this rule, and the British never forgave him for it. His coming to power as President of Egypt, four years after the military uprising of 1952 which deposed King Farouk, without ever having gone inside a British jail, was rather like getting into Eton without having his name put down at birth and going to the proper prep school. Unforgivable.

What was even more appalling was that the man showed himself to be a cad from the word 'go'. He did not play fair with the old imperial grand-daddies who had built railways and that lovely Canal through his country. He had the damn cheek to nationalise them, and the take-over of the Canal in 1956 provided him — through no fault or virtue of his own — with his greatest political victory over the old imperialists.

Oddly enough, both of what are regarded as Nasser's lasting

achievements are something to do with water. In a land of parched desert sand, relieved only by the uncontrolled fertility of the Nile, giving alternately flooding and drought, the building of the Aswan Dam has undoubtedly brought hope to many thousands of hungry peasants (although even Nasser never claimed to have built it himself!), while the seizing of the Suez Canal in 1956 was at once a claiming for the new Egyptian State of a great economic asset and a slap in the face for the hated British. Not since Moses parted the Red Sea has any aquatic exercise in the Middle East had such symbolic importance.

It is, however, entirely upon these two watery achievements that Nasser seems to have been able to build a fanatical following among the Egyptian people. And even these apparent triumphs had to be paid for in very hard currency indeed by just those same Egyptians. The hamfisted and provocative manner in which their President nationalised the Canal provided the impetus for the extraordinary conspiracy between Israel, France and Britain to launch war against Egypt. It was not Nasser's doing that this failed; it was the opposition, not of the anti-imperialist East, but of America (!), together with a threat by international financiers against the pound sterling, that led to the British withdrawal and weeping collapse of Anthony Eden. But not before Cairo and Alexandria had been bombed and thousands of Egyptians had been killed and the Israelis had yet another military feather in their caps. The Aswan Dam brought no such immediate bill to pay. But in the long term the price which the Egyptians will have to pay will be much, much more. For the Aswan Dam has been built with the economic and technical help of the Russians, which is why the British Press practically ignored its opening last year, but with the Russians, as with all good capitalists, nothing is for nothing.

Nasser had to accept military aid as well as economic aid from the Russians. *Had* to, for the Kremlin is not really concerned to provide water for the peasants of the Upper Nile, nor hydro-electricity for Egypt's new factories. Russia's leaders wanted to get a big foot into the Middle East — and Nasser opened the door very wide indeed.

The Bear's Kiss of Death

So much military 'aid' flooded into Egypt from the Russians that Nasser himself did his militaristic nut and began to believe his own belligerent propaganda. He even convinced the Israelis that he might be about to attack — so they attacked first, and the third military defeat of the Egyptians by the Israelis was meted out. This, the famous 'Six Day War' of 1967, enabled the Israelis to reach the Suez Canal, inflicting fantastic casualties on Egyptian personnel and Russian prestige at the same time as destroying enormous quantities of Russian hardware, and once again closing the Canal. Between 1956 and 1967, Nasser had also expended tremendous resources which his people could ill afford through his ill-timed intervention in the civil war in the Yemen, where gas-bombing of more or less open villages by his Air Force hardly enhanced his reputation, and where 70,000 of his troops wasted their lives, to no avail. One result of this was that the Americans were persuaded to do an arms deal with the Israelis!

When he died last week, Nasser had been President of Egypt for fourteen years and Prime Minister as well for three. (He was called back from threatened resignation in the middle of the Six Day War by popular acclaim and promptly gave himself another job as well!)

The size and strength of popular grief at his funeral last week could not have been stage-managed. It was undoubtedly genuine, although his factual achievements on behalf of his people have been minimal, to put it kindly. Nasser was a militaristic dictator, who ruthlessly wiped out all opposition. At the last 'election' he clocked up 99.999% of the votes, mainly because any opposition which could have challenged his 'revolutionary' image was in prison or concentration camps.

As a military man, he was given to military adventures — and all and every one of them has been disastrous. Not a single victory stands to his name but several ignominious defeats.

On the political side, his costly intervention in the Yemen actually strengthened Israel, his alliance with Syria in the 'United Arab Republic' came to nothing when the Syrians saw they were getting nothing but trouble out of it, and called it off, and his victory over Anthony Eden in 1956 was due entirely to the latter's own stupidity. It was also Britain's refusal to finance or build the High Dam at Aswan which threw Nasser into the Russians' arms. If we may be allowed to mix our zoological and biological metaphors, we may say that the bear's hug turned into a ride on the back of a tiger which became the kiss of death.

Egypt's man of destiny met his fate, not on a glorious field of battle but like any screwed-up Western business man. The tensions and stresses of the power game were too much for him. Coronary thrombosis is the great leveller of our time.

Nasser's fourteen years have in fact been disastrous for Egypt. If a quarter of what he spent on armaments (and this little country is now £1,000 million in debt!) had actually gone on the social revolution he talked about, the Middle East would not be the dangerous mess it is today and more Egyptians would be alive to enjoy, for a change, being Egyptian.

So on what did his personal popularity rest? Like all dictators, Nasser relied on the frustrations, fears, prejudices and hates of the people he exploited. He may have been sincere, but his sincerity was limited by the patriotic and nationalistic boundaries of his militaristic vision, which tied him to the power game and which has in its turn tied his country just as surely to subservience in the imperialist hierarchy as it was under the British — only now with a great deal more danger. Nasser was a failure — and his people loved him. Why? Because they, too, are failures — but he, at least, put up a fight and said it was for them. Nobody had done that for the Egyptian poor before, and they fell for it. Nasser made a big noise, beat his breast, slapped the imperialists' faces and breathed fire and vengeance and national greatness and hatred for another little nation that they all thought they stood a chance of — some day — actually defeating.

On such bullshit is a great leader built. And because all leaders are built on bullshit, now that he is gone, all the Western leaders are ready to say what a great guy he was — while the Eastern leaders make damn sure that *they* choose his successor.

For us, we look forward to the day when the Egyptians can grow out of the need for leaders, when nationalism and patriotism are miserable memories for them, as they are for us, when they refuse to be tools for anybody's power game, when they can say, as we do: 'The only good leader is a dead one'.

10th October 1970 JUSTIN

PLO: The Final Solution?

The comparisons that some people have made between the actions of the Israeli Army in Lebanon and the recent British action in the Falklands are really too tenuous to be worth pursuing very deeply, although it could be said that the fact that the world's attention was riveted on the British action — or over-reaction —

might have encouraged the Israeli militarists to start something they had wanted to do for a long time.

If this is so, the analogy with the events of 1956 do hold water — for there can be no doubt that it was Anthony Eden's crazy adventure into Suez (in collusion, ironically, you might think, with the Israelis and the French) that made it that much easier for the Russians to invade Hungary to quell a popular uprising. At the present time, the French Government is keeping very quiet, because it was their marvellous products, the Exocet missiles and the Etendard planes from which they were fired that played so much havoc with the British Navy, EEC and NATO notwithstanding.

Any sensible analysis of these events, as distinct from merely taking sides, as our superficial opportunists on the Left tend to do, leads one inevitably to the anarchist conclusion as far as the State is concerned. In the demonstrations against the Falkland fracas, the SWP and the Militant manoeuvrers in general were crying that the Falklands 'belong' to Argentina, and in their declamations on the 'Palestine' problem they have consistently called for the establishment of a 'Palestine National State' under the PLO, presumably thinking that this is the right revolutionary demand to make, statists that they are.

Sadly, it is this very concept of 'statehood' which is the disease which has fouled up the original concept of the Jewish National Home in the minds of many, many Jews before the establishment of the Zionist State. A place of their own is everybody's concept of security and even freedom — a State of 'their own' is everybody's guarantee of servitude.[1]

And this is what went sour in Israel. In the Kibbutzim movement of the twenties and thirties, libertarian ideas were widespread. Egalitarian socialist and anarchistic principles were actually established in many of the collectives, where all property was held in common, work was shared and decisions taken communally. Inasmuch as all the participants — mostly ideologically motivated people from Europe — saw the movement spreading all over what was then called Palestine (just as the collectives were called *Palestinian* collectives), they conceived it as establishing a rich society of self-governing communities from which Arabs were not excluded and among which the two Semitic peoples, Arabs and Jews, would live in peace and plenty side by side.

---

1. See *British Imperialism and the Palestine Crisis: selections from Freedom 1937-1949* (Freedom Press, 1989).

It could be that the very success of the settlements, 'making the desert bloom', also made the Arabs uneasy and jealous, but the factor which above all changed the whole course of events in Palestine was the emergence of the Nazis in Germany and the subsequent holocaust, after which no European Jew felt safe in Europe. The ideas of Zionism were naturally fuelled and the concept of the 'National Home' was embraced by millions of Jews who had no socialist or anarchist ideas but who — rightly — wanted to get out of this Europe stinking of Auschwitz and Belsen.

It was the British State which, having made much good anti-Nazi propaganda out of the Jewish plight during the war was opposed to the exodus from Europe after it. Britain still held the 'mandate' for Palestine, which it had won after the First World War and over the years had promised to both Jews and Arabs at different times. Or even at the same time.

Having bitterly to fight Britain to get to Palestine meant the setting up of paramilitary organisations of 'terrorists' motivated by Zionism. The 'Stern Gang' and the Irgun Zvai Leumi, of which we now know Menachem Begin was a member, spearheaded the struggle which was eventually abandoned by Britain in 1948, following which — naturally — the terrorists became the Government and respectable and legalised their terrorism by setting up a State themselves and by driving 200,000 Palestinian Arabs off their land and into the wilderness.

The justification for this is that the Hebrews lived there 5,000 years ago and thus this particular patch of land was the Hebrew homeland, to which any Hebrew was entitled to 'return' — even though he and his immediate forebears for rather less than 5,000 years had never been there before, much less been born there — and any upstart Arab, whose forebears had cultivated the ground for only 2,000 years, had no rights of tenure, or even occupation.

You would really have thought, would you not, that of all peoples, the twentieth century Jews would have understood about being a refugee and would not have wished to award that status to anyone. But no, statism is ruthless; statism is the sacrifice of people for principles and statism has cost the Israeli people themselves very dear — to say nothing of all the Arabs who have died for *their* States.

In all the wars since 1948, the issue of the displaced Palestinians has loomed large — for apart from their plight itself being a running sore, they have been used by ambitious Arab leaders as a 'cause' to excuse attacks upon the Zionist State. Most of these have now

grown tired of fighting wars they never win, and one of them —
Sadat — paid with his life for his efforts to establish 'peace' between
Egypt and Israel. Only Yasser Arafat, leader of the Palestinian
Liberation Organisation, remains still adamant that Israel must be
destroyed, and he is now an embarrassment to all the other Arab
States, who are tired of the whole Palestinian problem. They wish
it would go away — and none more so than Lebanon, which is
now suffering because it has been unable to refuse living space to
the PLO.

So Israel will do Lebanon a favour. It will blow the PLO away.
It is as though at the back of Begin's mind there is a continuous
echo of that phrase which once struck terror into the Jews of
Europe: 'The Final Solution'. It was the Nazis' phrase for the
annihilation of the Jews in gas chambers, solving forever the 'Jewish
problem' by eliminating them totally.

It is recorded that Israel's first president Ben-Gurion, once
described the ex-terrorist Begin as 'Nazi', rather as Lenin is said
to have warned his comrades on his deathbed about Stalin — having
appointed him successor! Today, it is held to be in the poorest
possible taste to link either Begin himself or the statism of Zionism
with that of the Nazis. But statism has its own logic, just as does
war, and the two together — and they so frequently go together
— lead inexorably to the corruption inescapable in total power,
impatient of any opposition, and ruthless in wiping it out.

There is one glimmer of hope: that an opposition is appearing
in Israel itself to Begin's ruthless expansionism. Civilians, soldiers
— and even high-ranking officers — are now coming into the open
with criticism of the use of the Israeli army far from the borders
of Israel proper — and coming out with the criticism while the
fighting is still going on, when, as we were all recently told, a
nation is supposed to close ranks and button up.

It would be nice to think that our opposition here to the Falkland
fracas has helped people elsewhere to break the mould of national
dumbness — but the Israelis have surely so much more reason than
we now have to be fed up to the back teeth with continual blood-
shed. Sooner or later a *modus vivendi* must be found between Jew
and Arab. If Zionism is seen to be an insoluble barrier to that —
will the Israelis have the courage to try something else?

Along the lines of the original pioneers perhaps?

10th July 1982   JUSTIN

POLAND

No Gods Nor Masters

'Après Jean-Paul — Jean Polak!' was the naughty headline in our French contemporary *Le Canard Enchaîné* when the Cardinals elected a non-Italian Pope for the first time for yonks last year.

What were the Cardinals thinking of? Having kept the Vatican safely in Italian hands for so long (455 years in fact), what was it made them decide to break the Italian connection now? And to install a new one from a Communist country, too.

In considering the motivations of the Catholic Church, one should never forget that it is an institution that is interested in power — and interested in it for eternity. Linking its interests to that of a supposed eternal God, it has no need to dangle any baits for temporary support like political parties at election time.

In this, it is like any one-party Government in a dictatorship. Like a Communist Government, in fact. As for any governing élite, what the masses really believe doesn't really matter — as long as they do as they are told.

Because Mother Church thinks she's there for eternity, she is in no hurry. She can bend before the wind; she can lose a few leaves here and there — in fact martyrs fertilise her soil better than anything else. The waiting game, with eyes on eternity, is always delayed as long as possible by a bitter rearguard action.

Generations of Catholic women can suffer grinding poverty aggravated by continuous child-bearing long after the means are available to ease their lot, while popes dish out their Papal Bullshit to justify the reproduction of more Catholics.

But when the time comes and pressure from below, expressed in the disobedience (especially disobedience by women!) which is anathema to the Church, betrays the fact that the masses are *not* prepared to go on doing as they are told — then changes have to be made, with as much grace as can be mustered.

Similarly on the political scene, the Church will heave a great

251

big sigh, wriggle its great fat bottom on its great gold throne, and
try to make the best of a bad job. It came to terms with Mussolini,
with Hitler and even, once he was on the side of the Allies and
Mussolini was out of the war, with Stalin. Though Stalin's caustic
question to Churchill, on being told that the Vatican was coming
out of its neutral corner, gave the game away. 'How many divisions
does the Pope have?' was what Stalin wanted to know.

Came the end of the war and Stalin showed the Pope just how
many divisions *he* had when he overran Eastern Europe. Communism
and Godless materialism came out of the barrels of five million
guns and the Pope just didn't know where to look.

Some vocal resistance was mounted in the early years in Hungary,
where Cardinal Mindszenty was finally forced to take refuge in the
American Consulate, but the exhausted Polish people — to defend
whom the British and French had declared war in 1939 — had no
alternative but to knuckle down to the new tyranny. The Church
slumbered with them, biding its time. You've got plenty of time
when your eyes are on eternity.

The Poles too, placed by a malevolent fate between Germany
and Russia, have no doubt learned to bide their time, the hard way.

Mind you, they've had their moments of impatience, like the
Poznan, and later the Radom and Ursus food riots, but the Church
looks for something more than that before it will make any kind
of move in the eternal chess game it plays so well. It was waiting,
as predators will, for signs of weakness.

Not weakness in the sense expressed in Stalin's question about
divisions — which showed little more than the crudity of his concept
of power — but weakness in morale, in conviction.

The signs came and are still coming, slowly but surely. Stalin's
death in 1953 was a great relief to everyone — even though they
daren't admit it, the Communists themselves. Three years later
Khruschev did admit it and his denunciation of the old dictator
led inexorably to the explosions of Hungary and Czechoslovakia
— put down, of course, by Stalinist methods — and defection of
Communists in their thousands throughout the world.

Ironically, the very thing which has exposed the weakness of the
European Communist Parties is the very thing which they have
hoped would bring back their strength — Eurocommunism.

By announcing their independence from Moscow, by denouncing
the path of revolution in favour of social democratic gradualism
and cooperation (however uneasy on both sides!) with socialist
parties, the Communists have told the world that they have gone

soft. Their materialism is wilting, from the dialectic materialism of Marx to the consumer materialism of the capitalists.

At a time like this, for the Vatican to choose a Pope from the only Communist country with a large Catholic population was a brilliant move — and to send him on a splendidly stage-managed travelling circus round that country an inspired gamble. And everybody hoped to get something out of it.

The Polish Government, for being so broadminded; the Western Governments, overjoyed at the Pope's reception; the Euro-communist Parties elsewhere, seeking the working class Catholic vote; even the Kremlin, for turning a benevolent blind eye to strange happenings just over the border — and most of all, the Vatican, laughing up its cassock and rolling in the aisles, as you might say.

For freedom lovers everywhere, however, isn't it all just a bit too sick? In 'The Struggle for the Soul of Mankind' (humankind as we would now say) those who lose are those whose souls are claimed by one side or the other, as part of the spoils of victory. For the Poles — for whom we have the deepest sympathy in their plight — to welcome a spiritual dictator as a relief from a temporal one is as absurd as it was for the Ukrainians in 1941 to welcome the Nazis as a relief from Stalin.

John Paul II is no dissident, even. He is an arch-orthodox leader of an institution with a history of repression from which the Communists still have a lot to learn.

We are not impressed, Papa, with your jolly jokes and your peasant songs. We know what you are after and that is why we still cry: NO GODS NOR MASTERS!

16th June 1979 EDITORS

The Betrayal Begins

*'We don't want to replace the old rubbish with new rubbish.' —
Striker at Gdansk*

The heady Polish summer moves slowly towards autumn; the nights draw in; the brilliant sun of the world's media begins to sink and the hot news of last month cools down on inside pages. Hot as it was, it did not quite set the world alight. The great, expected climax was not reached and the Russian tanks did not roll.

A few heads did, though, near the top. What can only be described as cosmetic changes, the sort that any Party can make without altering its own strength in any way, were publicised as culling men who had lost touch with the working class roots of the Communist Party, had mishandled their responsibilities, fallen down on the job.

On top of all this, suddenly came stories of moral corruption, financial back-handers (as distinct from the perfectly moral and justifiable privileges like fine apartments, country houses and large cars for party officials) which made the Warsaw hierarchy look just as human as any in the West.

Through the earlier reshuffle, Gierek himself sat tight, no doubt privately telling himself that he really should have carried out some at least of the promises with which he bought off the strikers in 1970, getting himself the top job. He brought people with 'moderate' reputations into positions where they could be seen to be listening sympathetically to the determined workers. After the workers had been striking for a fortnight, he granted them the right to strike — an amazing act of generosity in the circumstances since they had already taken that right by their own direct action!

He also granted them the right to form their own 'free' trade unions — the basic structure for which they had already created in their works strike committees. And then, as if all this had made him remember something about the emancipation of the workers being the task of the workers themselves — he had a heart attack.

Or so we are told. Whether Gierek's coronary will prove to be as cosmetic as the changes at the top table, we shall not know yet awhile, but the occasion was convenient to change still further the faces at the top — which is, after all, what the cosmetic art is all about.

Into Gierek's job steps a man who is hailed as a 'moderate' and has, until now, maintained a low profile. One reason for this is that he has been busy working his way up the party ladder, occupying the party posts which have given him close relationships with the police, the militia and the armed forces.

Stanislaw Kania's 'unanimous' election to the top job by the central committee was reputedly greeted with enthusiasm by Moscow. Having experienced the wonderful stability that can be maintained in a State by the greatest apparatchik of all time — Josef Stalin — Brezhnev and his boys must have heaved a sigh of relief when a similar climber crept into the saddle in Poland.

And what is the real party task facing Kania now? It was summed up in an anonymous quote from a 'party journalist' in Warsaw,

'HANG IN THERE, PAPA, WE ALL KNOW THAT MIRACLES TAKE A LITTLE LONGER...

...BESIDES, THERE'S A CRISIS OF AUTHORITY EVERYWHERE NOWADAYS—HAVEN'T YOU NOTICED? PS: HOW MANY DIVISIONS DO YOU HAVE?

the day Gierek collapsed. He said, 'First of all, we resisted the grass roots movement for change. Then we accepted it. *But now we have to take the third step and lead it*, and that is the real difficulty' (our emphasis).

That is what Kania's job is now: to lead the workers back into the Party's own backyard. To contain their demands within bounds the Party can manage. It is the oldest trick in the book — to yield in the heat of battle and then gradually to take it all back in the fullness of time.

It is said that Kania was opposed to the use of force against the strikers when a faction in the Politburo was arguing for it at the time (29th August) that Gierek was settling with the workers in

Gdansk. At that point Kania was responsible for 'security' (secret police?) and he was backed up by General Jaruzelski, commander of the Polish Armed Forces, while Admiral Janczyszyn told the local Party in Gdansk that he was not prepared to put his men in direct confrontation with the strikers.

In other words, as we suspected all along, the Party had no confidence that the Armed Forces would back them in a fight against the people — just as, quite obviously, the Russians also felt that they could not rely upon the Polish Army's support should the Soviets invade. In fact, quite the opposite, they might well have had a fight *with* the Polish Forces on their hands.

So it was a case of softly, softly, catchee monkey. On paper the Party has graciously yielded to the undeniably just demands of the Gdansk strikers — subject of course to the necessity to recognise what they call the *raison d'Etat* — the objects of the State. And it is interesting to notice how this phrase has replaced the better known *raison d'être* — a rather more objective object — the object of being.

Another State that we should not forget, of course, in all this, is that tiny State in the middle of Rome, the Vatican. It might be complete coincidence that this upheaval in Poland happened so soon after the Pope's visit, but the fact is that the other great totalitarian power fighting for the soul of Poland is the Roman Catholic Church — with more than 1,000 years of experience in wheeling and dealing to draw upon.

One of the more disturbing factors in the Polish struggle has been the role of Lech Walesa — the most publicised of the strikers' leaders — who was calling for 'caution' at about the same time as the Polish Pope was saying the same thing in the course of leading masses of Italian Catholics in prayers for what he called 'My Poland'.

Walesa has been recognised by the Communist Party as the workers' leader entrusted with the task of setting up the organisation for the new 'independent' unions. Having appointed Jacek Kuron (the dissident 'intellectual' who produced the influential underground paper *Robotnik*) as head of his advisory staff, Walesa went off to say mass with Cardinal Wyszynski, following a private audience.

'Stability' is in the interests of both the State and the Church. Both authoritarian, for each power-hungry outfit stability means the suppression of the people to their separate dogma. Discipline and obedience are key words in both of these religions — Catholicism and Communism. If the Polish people have been fighting for freedom this summer, they are well warned to beware of both these organisations — even to look, if they will, to what is happening in Iran, where the situation is not dissimilar.

The Marxists may have forgotten their most essential text of all — but we do well constantly to remind the working class that the task of emancipation is the task of the working class alone. And by Christ, as the Pope may say, are they alone!

13th September 1980

'To Avert Anarchy'

Despite one quote from the City to the effect that it was standing on the edge of the financial equivalent of thermonuclear war because of General Jaruzelski's declaration of martial law in Poland, it is more than likely that the Western banks are as pleased at what has happened as the Governments of the East.

There's a strong feeling around the place that the Poles got what was coming to them. To be an independent trade union in an Eastern European country, that's good, that's OK (in a way it isn't, incidentally, here); but to acquire ambitions, to blossom, in other words, into a whole social and political movement of radical reform, much of it laying a stress on principles of self-management and an end to hierarchy both in industry and in the Communist Party — if not in the Church — (and even, it is said, demanding the abolition of the CP itself!) — well, it doesn't take the truest and bluest of Conservatives to find such a thing unpalatable and impertinent. Not only this, but decidedly unbusinesslike.

There has always been far more to unite the Governments of East and West than there has been to divide them, and that is the lesson of *Vodka Cola*. No Western Government, no banker, no industrialist, wishes to see Poland become a hive of social-revolutionary experimentation; in short, none of them wishes to see an end to the Polish Communist Party. Solidarity was all right so long as it knew its place.

But as time went on it became increasingly apparent that Solidarity did not. A terrible thing, people began to realise that it was not a single and indivisible body, a monolith with whom business could be done on a rational basis. Poland had become 'unstable', 'anarchic' and as such anathema. The Polish authorities were due, to boot, to pay around 500m dollars in interest and principal by the end of 1981 as part of an agreement rescheduling debts of 2,400m dollars this year. And in recent months the West German Government, which has been Poland's largest creditor in the West, and from 1980 its second most important trading partner after the Soviet Union, has begun to feel its federal budget threatened and so to refuse to guarantee further loans, complaining of Polish inefficiency (as if this were something post-August 1980, rather than very much a cause of subsequent events).

According to a *Times* report, by the spring of this year

some Western bankers estimated that Poland would need 10,000m dollars of new money in 1981 alone while the country's gross financing requirement up to 1980 was estimated at 85,000m dollars.

The state of emergency must put this prospect in doubt as banks and Governments will be only too happy to use the turn of events as a pretext for not supplying more funds while still pressing for an orderly rescheduling of debts falling due in 1982 and beyond.

The *Times* account more than hints at the relief that Western moneylenders must be feeling now that martial law has been declared. For some reason there's a sense that now the General is in power 'economic reform' and stability (oh stability!) will be guaranteed or, if it is not, that the Soviet Union and its partners must, and will, take responsibility for these Polish debts. And this, after all, is what ultimately matters.

All in all, Jaruzelski's move is one that the Western Powers can afford to accept with equanimity,

19th December 1981   G.F.

THE ANARCHIST ALTERNATIVE

Corruption — A Game of Billiards

That it was to autocritical China that so many of the Western Left turned for inspiration and leadership in recent years may strike one as odd and ungrateful considering the periods of self-mortification to which the West has been prone, long before even the sado-masochistic excesses of the Christian Church!

'So farewell Rome' said the sour and sulky satirist. 'I leave you to sanitary engineers and municipal architects, men who by swearing black is white land all the juicy contracts just like that — a new temple, swamp-drainage, harbour-works, river-clearance, undertaking, the lot — then pocket the cash and fraudulently file their petition in bankruptcy . . .'

Juvenal would have felt no less satirically at home in the Rome (or London or Washington) of today, among the fraudulent bankrupts and legacy-hunters, the scheming priests and politicians of Sciascia's brilliant novels and a very definite reality; in a Rome whose time-honoured techniques of occasional public confession by the ruling class via a superficially critical Press has brought it smoothly through successive crises of oil-money, United Brands-money, CIA-money, Lockheed-money, etc, etc, and will no doubt continue to do so for some time to come . . . For both Fascist and Communist Parties, only governing alternatives to centre-this and centre-that, have been as well and truly bribed as those old corruptibles the Christian Democrats and the Vatican, the occupants of which establishment Dante had long since confined to infernal flames.

Meanwhile, in the USA autocriticism has become highly fashionable and is indulged in with zest and zeal. The evidently addictive excitements of Vietnam and Watergate have been followed by the purges of the secret services (both FBI and CIA), which are still there, and still secret, and the multinational corporations like Lockheed. No Presidential candidate can now escape charges of bribery and corruption, or even of straightforward tax evasion, considered until recently to be the duty of every superior citizen and self-respecting

State Governor. But the Presidential *office* is as heavily supported as ever by the millions who read *Burr* and *1876*. And Gore Vidal waxes rich on the fruits of his cynicism, scouring the past for unsavoury characters in high places, questioning the true motives of the founding fathers, posing as a new Gibbon to suggest that the American Empire, unlike the Roman, will collapse through its *internal* barbarism. ('Supposing *we* are the barbaric hordes?' he asks with indulgent self-deprecation.) But his 'People's Party' was a non-starter.

Britain lacks the American sense of drama, the Italian sophistication. Recent fusses over the lucrative interests of MPs (Honest Jim Callaghan, for instance, who was recently spotted haunting the City banks, found himself up before the Committee of Privileges where he 'gave a swift and complete retraction, after he had told his constituency dinner that he did not think a Member spoke for such and such a constituency, but rather for such and such a business interest'.) — fusses, I say, over the interests of MPs and the flesh-pots of Local Government, though important, cannot really be said to have caught the media's attention; and with the arrest on Saturday of several police chiefs on charges of corruption, this word continues obstinately, where Britain is concerned, to preserve its predominantly sexual, apolitical, connotations.

However, it will not escape us that the police's latest exercise in autocriticism is mainly designed to improve its image, and that the raking up and ritual persecution of those three peacefully retired gentlemen — Virgo, former head of Scotland Yard's murder squad; Drury, former commander of the flying squad; and Moody, former head of the obscene publications squad (himself once in charge of an inquiry into police bribery) is being done with the primary purpose of impressing people with the integrity of the British police force at a time when, under Mark, it is actively engaged in increasing its powers.

In the same way the Watergate sackings and jailings and the perusal by the Church Committee of the uncensored worksheets, mistakenly sent to Washington by Lockheed's auditors' lawyers, have led many impressionable Americans not to call for the sacking of the multinationals, the secret service or the Presidency, but on the contrary to boast of the basic openness and honesty of a political system which permits of such public criticism. Revelation of corruption, in other words, may harm the individuals at its centre — the hapless Nixons, Agnews, Virgos, et al, who are offered up upon the altar of public relations for a time — but it does wonders for the system as a whole! And this is because accusations of corruption have always been limited to certain aspects of a system, studied in isolation, and never involve the questioning of the system itself. Despite all the enthusiasm, what cultural purge, parliamentary committee or Government inquiry will ever sit in cross-examination and in judgement upon, not just the honesty of its personnel, but the necessity for its existence?

'Power corrupts' says the anarchist, 'because man is corruptible'. Others have often agreed. Yet none but anarchists can bring themselves to accept the logic of this statement, and none therefore but anarchists will see that the real corruption lies in the institutions themselves.

In railing against the corruption of his day, Juvenal denounced with equal bitterness all who opposed the Establishment. Catullus before him had come closer to describing what we mean by corruption when he identified 'loot, lechery and the political game' with imperialism and war. But he still ended by misjudging his target.

'First his inheritance, second the Pontic loot, third your own war with Spain (the Tagus where you washed for gold has a story of that), and now Gaul, and now Britain shake in their shoes. Why keep him? What is he good for — beyond treating the fattest endowment as a comestible? Is this the reason Rome's topmost tycoons, father and son-in-law, have been playing billiards with the world?'

Why keep him? the poet asked and to this day the question has been the same — Why keep him? What is he good for?

But the billiard table remains intact.

6th March 1976   G.F.

Government by Stealth

Every Government governs by a combination of deceit and coercion. The crude ones more by coercion, the clever ones more by deceit – it's cheaper and gives the appearance of stability to the outside world, which is better for foreign investment.

That's the difference between dictatorship and democracy. It is by no means the only one but it is certainly the most important, because by deceit you can create the impression that you are governing by the will of the people, by the agreement of the people, and for the people.

British democracy is long in the tooth. It has built up, over the years, probably the most comprehensive system of laws for the containment and deceit of the electorate than any other State in the world. The newer, brasher, democracies like the American system, have enormous loopholes — hence Watergate — which have long been plugged in Britain, but the real brilliance of the system lies in the apparent latitude which is allowed to its critics, and the myth that, within the system, you can use the system to change the system.

This is the biggest lie of all, and the one for which the trade unions and the social democrats have consistently fallen. The rank and file, that is. The Labour Government and the trade union bureaucracy are under no such illusion. They know that you can steal democracy easier than you can steamroller over it. That's why we have government by stealth, not by rubber truncheon. Much more efficient!

13th May 1978

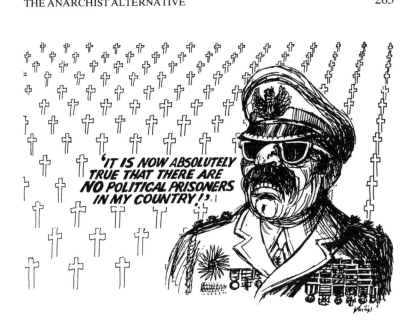

Don't Cry For . . . ?

In Northern Ireland the men 'on the blanket' fight for the right to be regarded as 'political prisoners'. In half a hundred countries around the world that is hardly a category that would seem even remotely desirable.

There are today — thirty-three years after a war for freedom or something — more military dictatorships in the world than ever before, nearly all ruled by colonels or generals who never fought any but their own people, nearly all established with the help of democracies (through international conspiracies like the CIA and the equally international arms trade) and maintained by the torture and execution of 'political prisoners'.

Especially true of South America, there the tradition of the Spanish conquistadores and the Inquisition dies hard. The original search for gold has changed to more mundane cash crops, as greedy traders in the commodity markets of the First World seek to corner the coffee and tin, the rubber and wheat, beef, oil, uranium, or whatever will make them rich — and keep the people poor and humble and subject to an élite which knows better.

The CIA and dollar imperialism have successfully kept the Russians out of South America — which is why Soviet 'diplomacy' and militarism is now making such determined efforts to get into Africa — cynically using Cuban ground-troops to provide for Africans an on-going frying pan / fire situation. It was no coincidence that in the same week that General Videla, President of Argentina, was welcoming World Cup visitors to his 'land of peace and liberty', a Kremlin spokesman was describing Russia as 'a just democracy' as Orlov was led off to begin twelve years of prison and exile.

The anarchist analysis of power, as distinct from phoney scientific jargon about dialectical materialism and historic processes, carries more weight as time goes by. The struggle is, quite simply, the people against every kind of State.

10th June 1978

Pawns in their Game

The Russian trials against 'dissidents', coming more than forty years after the infamous Moscow Trials of the '30s, when the megalomaniac Stalin crucified in court and then murdered the old guard of the Bolshevik Party still remaining from 1917, shows only too well how little the Russian dictatorship has changed its character over the years.

It is now twenty-two years since Kruschev made his 'astounding' denunciation of Stalin's tyranny and cut down to size the man who had been regarded almost as a god by millions of faithful and servile communists all over the world — who denounced as fascists, counter-revolutionaries and agents of imperialism all those who had drawn the obvious conclusions — that the dictatorship begun by Lenin, aided by Trotsky, had led in a straight line to the lunacy of Stalin.

To this day, Marxists will not accept the built-in fallacy of their creed — the concept of using the State as an engine of revolution.

Exactly the same fallacy corrupted the earlier, non-Marxist democratic revolutions. The French Revolution and the American

Revolution have equally fallen into the authoritarian trap. 'Liberty, Equality, Fraternity', no less than the principles of the Gettysburg Address, have been corrupted by power in the hands of a minority.

This is what makes a total hypocrisy of the West's moral indignation about the dissidents' trial in the Soviet Union. The American Constitution provided no defence for Sacco and Vanzetti any more than for the victims of the McCarthy witch-hunts. The USSR's 1936 Constitution, dreamed up by Stalin himself (no joke!) has, predictably, provided no more than the framework for punishing those who oppose the Soviet State.

All those who blindly support a State become pawns in the power game. The Soviet dissidents — mostly no revolutionaries — refuse to play that game any longer.

We don't have to agree with their motives to admire their courage. We, too, are proud to be — dissidents!
22nd July 1978

States Need Secrets

Since knowledge is power, it follows quite logically that any group seeking to maintain power over another will try to withhold information, which is what makes such phrases as 'Open Government' such a load of nonsense. No Government can be open with its people since the purpose of government is to govern. The excuse for secrecy will perhaps be that 'national security' demands it, because of that other State beyond the frontier, which will take away our freedoms if we don't voluntarily surrender them, but fundamentally the struggle that matters to any Government is the struggle with its own people — the permanent struggle that goes on all the time and is in fact at its weakest when there is an overt struggle going on with an external enemy. ('War is the health of the State'.)

We can conveniently call the internal struggle 'the class struggle' if we like — but we should be careful to dissociate our analysis from that of those who base a political theory upon the stages of the class struggle leading to the dictatorship of the proletariat through a leadership seizing or being elected to power — for that leadership, having read its Marx itself, will know precisely what to do to prevent itself withering away — it will withhold knowledge, the better to govern.

This is what makes faintly ridiculous complaints against State secrecy from any who think in terms of any kind of government bringing about a better world.

The only kind of open society possible is one where there are no organs of power, economic or political — a society without government. An anarchist society.
2nd September 1978

The Relevance of Anarchism

Anarchism is a philosophy of freedom. It is a body of revolutionary ideas which reconciles, as no other revolutionary concept does, the necessity for individual freedom with the demands of society. It is a commune-ist philosophy which starts from the individual and works upwards, instead of starting from the State and working downwards. Social structure in an anarchist society would be carefully and consciously kept to a minimum and would be strictly functional; where organisation is necessary, it would be maintained, but there would be no organisation for its own sake. This would help to prevent the hardening of organisations into institutions — the hard core of government.

The heart of anarchism is its opposition to government. Not just a particular Government, but government as an institution. This is explicitly expressed in the word 'anarchism', meaning the philosophy or ideology which aims at 'anarchy': the absence of government. This aim is shared by other ideologies — socialist and communist — who see the 'withering away of the State' as a desirable goal, but conceive the way towards that goal as lying through the use of the very institutions they want to abolish. Anarchists maintain that the use of these repressive institutions in the name of the revolution, or of progress, or of freedom, corrupts the revolution, inhibits progress and crushes freedom.

For anarchists, the end determines the means. If your end is a society without government, then you do not do anything to support

the idea or fact of government or to encourage the idea that government can in any way be desirable. If your aim is the abolition of
the State — which is the concentration of the institutions of government — then you do nothing to encourage the life of the State by
pretending it can be used for liberation. All the means by which
people are governed are anathema to anarchism.

This adds up to a coherent and logical ideology and within itself
anarchism is a perfect set of ideas. In its application to the existing
'real' world, however, it is being applied to very imperfect situations.
And furthermore, anarchists themselves differ in their interpreta-
tions of anarchism, both in relation to current events and in the
emphasis they put upon the various aspects of the overall philosophy.

This can lead to apparent contradictions. Anarcho-syndicalists
who advocate the abolition of the wage system support workers
on strike for higher wages; individualists who are opposed to the
State see no reason why they should not avail themselves of the
social services when they are unemployed; anti-parliamentarians
support the abolition of a law (hanging, abortion, homosexuality)
which can only be done through Parliament; anti-imperialists
condemn 'national liberation' 'movements which are fighting an
imperialist oppressor; anti-war militants who have gone to prison
rather than take up arms support a violent revolution . . . and so on.

This is not quite as absurd as it may appear. We have to live in
the world as it is — but as anarchists we are going to do our
damnedest to make it as we would like it to be. We know how
beautiful life could be, but we have to start from the ugly reality.

Now each anarchist will make his own moves and if we respect
each other we will respect our comrade's own scale of priorities.
Thus, for example, the anarcho-syndicalist will be concerned
primarily with achieving workers' control of industry, and this
necessitates building up workers' confidence in their own powers.
Every victory in even a minor struggle encourages this confidence;
every defeat diminishes it. So the anarchist in an industrial context
will throw in his effort to help win a dispute which perhaps in itself
is irrelevant as far as a money-less society is concerned, but which
will teach the workers more about tactics, about the value of direct
action, about their importance in society, the strength they gain
through solidarity, the creativity of their work, their dignity as
human beings — perhaps a hundred lessons.

For we should not forget that there are two aspects of anarchism:
the end and the means. We have implied the end: anarchy, the
society without government or any of the means of government,

without money and the wage system and the exploitation they bring; without the State which defends that exploitation through the law, the police, the prisons, the constitutional murder of the gallows or the gas chamber, all backed up by the army, navy and air force; the inculcation which passes for education, the subtle pressures of the bureaucracy and the Church. Anarchy means the replacement of these anti-social forces by free association and mutual aid, by free access to the means of life, by the joy of making and sharing and living. A delightful ideal!

Anarchism also means the struggle to achieve all this. A bitter struggle against ruthless forces which will apparently stop at nothing to maintain the power set-up as it is. The great advantage anarchism has is that it is not side-tracked into diversions like the parliamentary struggle, like 'workers' government' or the 'dictatorship of the proletariat', trying to achieve power in order to abolish it or the historical process or any other mythology. Anarchism teaches the governed to use their strength where it matters — at the point of production; and to use it in the way it matters — by direct action.

The means of freedom for the end of freedom: that is the relevance and strength of anarchism.

14th February 1970   BILL CHRISTOPHER
                                                        JACK ROBINSON
                                                        PHILIP SANSOM
                                                        P. TURNER

It's OUR world!

CAPITALISM was always a system based on waste and savage exploitation of both raw materials and labour for private gain. It has been joined in the 20th century by Communism - a cynical perversion of the ideals of socialism producing grotesque misuse of power and natural wealth in the service of the state.

Anarchists, opposing both 'free enterprise' and state communism assert the time is overdue for ordinary people to claim back the raw materials of the earth to use them for the benefit of all, without national or racial distinction.

Then we could use technology to avoid pollution, to husband our resources and make the best use of what we have.

The snag is, WE don't have it - our rulers claim it for themselves.

Time to take it back! Time to say loud and clear: This is OUR world!

29th April 1978

A DECADE OF ANARCHY: 1961-1970
Selections from the Monthly Journal
Anarchy

Anarchy was published by the Freedom Press for the first ten years of its existence, and during that period it became known as the leading voice of reflective anarchism in the English-speaking world. No fewer than 118 32-page issues were published under the editorship of Colin Ward, and the present volume contains a representative selection of less than 10 per cent of all that material, chosen, arranged and introduced by him.

The thirty items included are classified under seven headings — **Restatements**, in which a number of anarchists seek to link anarchist thought to the contemporary scene; **Experiences**, which are descriptions of the human condition in different parts of the world as witnessed by the writers; **Work**, consisting of four detailed essays ranging from the practical experience of the Gang System in Coventry to the theoretical future of work; **Education**, the ever-topical subject with contributions among others by Paul Goodman and Harold Drasdo; **Deviance**, yet another burning topic of the day, with contributions from Tony Gibson and Stan Cohen; **Environments**, a topic which has assumed increasing urgency ever since; and **Retrospects**, which gives Colin Ward's contemporary discussion of *Anarchy* in *Freedom* and Rufus Segar's account of doing his famous covers.

Colin Ward's introduction describes the conception and creation of the paper and reflects on its relevance two decades later.

283pp   0 900384 37 9   £5.00

FREEDOM PRESS

ABOUT FREEDOM PRESS

● FREEDOM PRESS are the publishers of the fortnightly journal *Freedom* and of the anarchist quarterly *The Raven*.

● FREEDOM PRESS are the publishers of books and pamphlets on anarchism and allied subjects. Our current list comprises some 50 titles.

● FREEDOM PRESS BOOKSHOP (open Monday to Saturday) carries a comprehensive stock of anarchist literature from this country, the USA and Canada. We also issue lists for the benefit of our mail order customers.

● FREEDOM PRESS DISTRIBUTORS are European Sales Representatives for Black Rose Books (Canada) and a number of other publishers including Charles Kerr Publications (Chicago) and See Sharp Press (San Francisco).

● This book has been typeset and printed on the premises by ALDGATE PRESS, a successful co-operative venture which also undertakes commercial printing work.

All particulars from FREEDOM PRESS
(in Angel Alley) 84b Whitechapel High Street,
London E1 7QX